THE GUIDE
TO PRACTICAL
PASTORING

THE GUIDE TO PRACTICAL PASTORING

C. Sumner Wemp

Thomas Nelson Publishers
Nashville • Camden • New York

All Scripture quotations are from the King James Version of the Bible.

Copyright © 1982 by C. Sumner Wemp

Published in Nashville, Tennessee, by Thomas
Nelson, Inc., Publishers and distributed in Canada
by Lawson Falle, Ltd., Cambridge, Ontario.

Printed in the United States of America.

Library of Congress Cataloging in Publication Data

Wemp, C. Sumner.
 The guide to practical pastoring.

 1. Clergy—Office. 2. Pastoral theology.
I. Title.
BV660.2.W4 1982   253   82–12562
ISBN 0-8407-5271-7

Contents

Part 4/Preaching and Teaching

Part 5/Conclusion

Dedication

To Celeste—"Angel"

As my wife—a godly helper.
As a pastor's wife—an elegant first lady.
As a housewife—a queen on her throne.
As a mother—her children call her blessed.
As a teacher—an excellent example.
As a Christian—the same yesterday, today, and forever.
As my sweetheart—I love you.

Foreword

Dr. Sumner Wemp is a man who knows God. In the ten years I have known Sumner Wemp and worked closely with him, I have found him to be a man who consistently walks in the Spirit and continually manifests the joy of a Spirit-controlled life. As Vice-President of Spiritual Affairs for Liberty Baptist College, Dr. Wemp is deeply loved by administration and students alike. He is an ardent soul-winner whose counsel is widely sought by both regenerated and unregenerated men and women.

It is no wonder then that Sumner Wemp's previous three books have enjoyed widespread success and have ministered to thousands regarding soul-winning and living a consistent, Spirit-filled Christian life.

The Guide to Practical Pastoring is a much-needed and indeed extremely important book for pastors. It is a bountiful storehouse containing scores of valuable practical insights. Sumner Wemp has written from many years of personal experience as a pastor, evangelist, teacher, and counselor, and his wise insight is an outgrowth of those years of serving God and living in His perfect will.

This book could literally transform the ministries of hundreds of pastors nationwide. It is a book with an impact that cannot be ignored by any pastor desiring to be used by God in the ministry the Lord has entrusted to him.

DR. JERRY FALWELL
Chancellor and Founder
Liberty Baptist College
Lynchburg, Virginia

Foreword

Sumner Wemp is dynamite! He is consistently the same, whether in the pulpit, classroom, or on the telephone. He lives an excited, vigorous, enthusiastic life.

Dr. Wemp writes as he talks—energetically, vitally, and personally. This book, *The Guide to Practical Pastoring,* has been written to help others. It comes from the heart and hand of a man who has had wide experience as a pastor and years of service as a teacher and administrator.

Each chapter gives full information on an important phase of church work. Remember: "Everything rises or falls on leadership."

LEE ROBERSON
Pastor and Chancellor
Highland Park Baptist Church
Tennessee Temple University
Chattanooga, Tennessee

1/THE PASTOR

1

Characteristics of a Successful Pastor

"Preacher, you can't leave us. Why, you led me to Christ, and you led half of my family to Christ. You married me and my husband, and you dedicated our baby and our home to the Lord. In fact, you were in on every wonderful thing that has happened to me." So said Delo the day I resigned as her pastor. Nothing humbles a pastor more, but, bless God, this is the joy of pastoring.

Little Sandra lived only eight months. No one could have been more attached to their baby than were Hugh and Olive. I saw Sandra take her last breath. I had nothing to say. All I could do was squeeze Hugh's arm. He understood, because I had prayed with him and his wife many times. No one could have been dearer friends than these two were to my wife and me. This is the challenge of ministering.

I had been in a couple's home witnessing to them. Neither had received Christ. While preaching the following Sunday, I became greatly burdened for them. When I gave the invitation, Leonard and Grace stepped out to receive Christ, along with Joe and Mildred for whom the church also had been praying. Heaven came down that day. For twenty years these four have gone on with the Lord to become spiritual pillars in the church. There are no finer people in the world. This is the reward of preaching.

What a thrill to be a preacher! What a privilege to be a pastor. What an honor to be a servant of God. Don't let discouraged, defeated Christians deter you. God lives! The church is alive and well. All the church needs is a few Elishas who will take up the mantle and cry out for a double portion of Elijah's spirit.

Like a radiant diamond, the pastor has many facets, many sides. When each facet has been cut and ground and polished, the result will be a beautiful reflection of Him who is the true light. If you want a ministry that is powerful, glorious, and fruitful, be sure you work on all sides. Consider these seven essentials of a successful pastor.

1. *Personal knowledge of God.* Paul said, " . . . I count all things but loss for the excellency of the knowledge of Christ Jesus my Lord. . . . That I may know him . . ." (Phil. 3:8,10). You had better know Him, too. You may not know sports heroes or society personalities, but you must know the bright and morning star. Know Him for yourself. Know *Him,* not just *about* Him. Oh, dear brother, if you are going to minister, know Jesus. Know Him, till He is altogether lovely. Know Him till you cry out, "My Lord and my God!" (John 20:28). Know Him till you "taste and see that the LORD is good . . ." (Ps. 34:8). You get to know someone as the two of you spend time alone together.

Know "the power of his resurrection" (Phil. 3:10). You'll need it. Satan is powerful. Hearts are hard. People can be cruel. You need nothing short of the power of His resurrection. The ministry is impossible in your own strength. Winning souls is hard. Building up Christians is a struggle. It takes the power of God, nothing less, nothing more. Determine now to settle for nothing less in your ministry.

Know "the fellowship of his sufferings" (Phil. 3:10). Nothing is more precious. This is the pressure that produces that fragrant perfume in your ministry that all want but most are not willing to pay the price for. Oh, to suffer with Him. "For unto you it is given in the behalf of Christ, not only to believe on him, but also to suffer for his sake" (Phil. 1:29). "All that will live godly in Christ Jesus shall suffer persecution" (2 Tim. 3:12). This preparation for the ministry only comes as you pass through deep, dark waters, often all alone. Sometimes the reason is unknown. Many times it brings a deep groan, but the results are priceless for "If we suffer, we shall also reign with him . . ." (2 Tim. 2:12). Hallelujah!

Be made ". . . conformable unto his death" (Phil. 3:10). The reason many are not greatly used by and blessed by God is that they are still very much alive to the pleasures of this world. "Except a corn of wheat fall into the ground and die, it abideth alone: but if it die, it bringeth forth much fruit" (John 12:24). This is the deepest verse in the Word of God on Christian living. Are you dead? Have you fallen into the ground and been buried? Do the pleasures of this world and praises of men affect you? If so, then you are not dead. What difference does it make whether you are appreciated? Who cares whether you are known or not? So what if you never own a home? Live, my dear brother, in the light of eternity. Conform to His death. Die and you will bring forth much fruit.

2. *Humility.* Solomon was humble when he said,

> And now, O LORD my God, thou hast made thy servant king instead of David my father: and I am but a little child: I know not how to go out or come in. And thy servant is in the midst of thy people which thou hast chosen, a great people . . . Give therefore thy servant an understanding heart to judge thy people . . . for who is able to judge this thy so great a people? (1 Kin. 3:7-9).

If you are going to lead God's people today, you had better feel totally inadequate and, like a little child, cry out for wisdom and help. Gideon felt that way when he said, "Oh my Lord, wherewith shall I save Israel? behold, my family is poor in Manasseh, and I am the least in my father's house" (Judg. 6:15). Paul revealed his humility when he said, "[I] am less than the least of all saints" (Eph. 3:8). Saul realized his inability in the beginning, for Samuel said of him, "When thou wast little in thine own sight . . ." (1 Sam. 15:17). "We have this treasure in earthen vessels . . ." (2 Cor. 4:7) that all the glory might be to God. Don't ever forget this. Don't forget the pit from which you were dug. "Humble yourselves therefore under the mighty hand of God, that he may exalt you in due time" (1 Pet. 5:6). "Pride"—which has ruined a host of preachers—"goeth . . . before a fall" (Prov. 16:18). D. L. Moody said, "Two things always amazed me, that my wife married me and that God uses me." No wonder God could use him.

Here are some thoughts about humility that I have gathered over the years:

> "The fastest way up is down."
> "From hero to zero is a short trip."
> "You can be too big for God to use but never too little."
> "Few people are big enough to be small enough for God to use."
> "The flower of humility grows on the grave of pride."
> "Men who deserve monuments don't need them."
> "God humbles you without deflating you
> and exalts you without inflating you."
> "Neither success nor failure is permanent."

3. *Sincere love of the people to whom one ministers.* I honestly believe most preachers do not really love their people; at least many preachers do not act as if they do. Yet, people are starved for love. One of our deacons, introducing me at a meeting where I was to speak, said, "At our church, our pastor loves us and we know it."

It broke me up. I cried out in my heart and said, "Oh, God, have there been moments when my people didn't know that I love them?" I am afraid there have been, and that is a shame. A "Dennis the Menace" cartoon, showing little Dennis on his mother's lap, comes to mind. Dennis said, "You mean you would love me no matter what I did? Boy, that takes a load off my mind!" Our people need just such confidence in God and in God's servants.

I once was asked to preach each evening for a week in a church in a distant city. One evening after the service a group of us were in the pastor's home for fellowship. The song leader for the week suddenly said, "Sumner, all week all you have done is rave about the people in your church. Not once have you said an unkind word about one of them. I have been in scores of meetings and heard preachers tell about some hypocrite or cantankerous deacon or some gossipy woman, but you haven't done it once. It is really refreshing." I was totally unaware of what I had been doing. Now, after twenty-one years of preaching in different churches almost every week, I realize how many preachers magnify the faults of their people.

The Sunday after that week away, I said, "Folks, I love you. I have missed you terribly this week. It is good to be back home." After the service, one of our deacons' wives said to me, "I have gone to church since I was born. I guess I've known my pastors loved me, but when you *said* it this morning it broke me up. I never realized how much you really love all of us. Thanks for being such a pastor to me." Folks, people are starved for love. They are looking for a pastor who will genuinely love them. This is absolutely essential.

On the first day of the pastoral theology class I teach I say, "I'm going to write one statement on the chalkboard. Learn this, internalize it, and apply it, and we could dismiss the class and you could go out and build a great church. It is really all you need to know to do so." Then I write in large letters on the board LOVE YOUR PEOPLE. If a pastor loves his people and they know it, he can preach as hard as he wishes and they will not be offended.

4. *Determination to be an example.* Paul wrote, "Be ye followers of me, even as I also am of Christ" (1 Cor. 11:1). That's the way it must be. Every church is a reflection of its pastor. This is a profound truth. If a pastor loves the Lord Jesus, the people will. If he loves and lives in the Word of God, they will. If he makes witnessing a life style, so will the people. When he regularly visits the unchurched, they will follow his example. Hosea 4:9 says, ". . . like people, like priest."

Sheep follow the shepherd. They cannot be driven; they must be led. Christians don't want their pastor to be a dominating dictator, but they need a loving leader. Someone said of a certain preacher, "The text he preached and the life he lived meshed perfectly." May it ever be so.

5. *A burden for people's souls.* Hebrews 13:17 reads, "Obey them that have the rule over you, . . . for they watch for your souls, as they that must give account. . . ." The most sobering thought is that, for every man, woman, boy, and girl who ever walks into the church, the pastor will have to give an account. The deacons aren't accountable. The choir isn't. The treasurer or any other person isn't the responsible one. But the pastor, who is called by God, is responsible. He must watch for their souls.

A surgeon may take a man's life into his hands and perform a most delicate operation on his brain. But that is nothing compared to a pastor, who has people's spiritual well-being in his hands. It is the difference, not just of a few more years of life, but of eternity.

Paul said, "I could wish that myself were accursed from Christ for . . . my kinsmen according to the flesh" (Rom. 9:3). Moses pleaded to have his name blotted out for the sake of his people. Jesus wept over Jerusalem. How essential that pastors agonize over the souls of the people God has given them.

6. *A desire to have a balanced ministry.* The great commission of Matthew 28:19,20 indicates that people are to be evangelized, baptized, and edified. This is the plan for Christian ministry, and a pastor must purpose in his heart to carry out the whole counsel of God. It is common knowledge that too many are weak in one area or the other. Sinners must be caught, and saints must be taught. The balance won't be there unless you work at it.

God wants workers and worshipers. The pastor can train his people for both. He must provide opportunity for both. This is like a row boat. If you do not pull on both oars, you will go around in circles. The boat just won't go forward. Christians must be balanced to both worship the Lord and work for the Lord. Jesus said it once, and it still holds true: "Why call ye me Lord, Lord, and do not the things which I say?" (Luke 6:46).

7. *A compulsion to preach.* Paul declared, "Woe is me if I preach not the gospel" (1 Cor. 9:16). What a privilege to preach in the power of God and see folks convicted and converted. The desire to be God's messenger must burn in the preacher's heart until, like Jeremiah, he cannot help but speak up (see Jer. 20:9).

Jesus said, "As ye go, preach . . ." (Matt. 10:7). Paul said, "Whereunto I am ordained a preacher . . ." (1 Tim. 2:7). Whatever else a pastor does, preaching has to be primary. He is ordained a "preacher." "The preaching of the cross is to . . . us . . . the power of God" (1 Cor. 1:18). What power there is in that message! In fact, "It pleased God by the foolishness of preaching to save them that believe" (1 Cor. 1:21). God is pleased to use preaching and to save people from hell through preaching. The pastor then must place a very high premium on this part of his ministry.

When Paul was on his way to Jerusalem and was told over and over how bonds of affliction were waiting for him there, he said, "None of these things move me, neither count I my life dear unto myself, so that I might finish my course with joy, and the ministry, which I have received of the Lord Jesus . . ." (Acts 20:24). What a goal. What maturity. What determination. With such a conviction, a man can live right the whole trip down here.

Then, at the conclusion of his life, Paul could joyfully say:

> For I am now ready to be offered, and the time of my departure is at hand. I have fought a good fight, I have finished my course, I have kept the faith: Henceforth there is laid up for me a crown of righteousness, which the Lord, the righteous judge, shall give me at that day . . . (2 Tim. 4:6–8).

What a glorious end. What a way to finish one's life. If this goal grips a preacher's heart, he will make it with flying colors and no regrets. God grant that it be so of everyone called to preach.

2

Hearing the Call

Men do not choose to preach; they are called to preach. This is essential, for "how shall they preach, except they be sent?" (Rom. 10:15). Paul wrote that he was "ordained a preacher, and an apostle" (1 Tim. 2:7). One who enters the ministry of preaching and lives by this means *must* be called by God.

The prophets of old were sure of their calling, and this assurance sustained them through dangers and discouragement. Jeremiah explained:

> Then the word of the LORD came unto me, saying: Before I formed thee in the belly I knew thee; and before thou camest forth out of the womb I sanctified thee, and I ordained thee a prophet unto the nations. Then said I: Ah, LORD GOD! behold, I cannot speak: for I am a child. But the LORD said unto me, Say not, I am a child: for thou shalt go to all that I shall send thee, and whatsoever I command thee thou shalt speak. Be not afraid of their faces: for I am with thee to deliver thee, saith the LORD (Jer. 1:4-8).

It was not Jeremiah's idea to be a prophet. God had decreed it to be so before Jeremiah was born. He was set apart by God and ordained as a prophet (see v. 5). This is a solemn statement. When the realization of this calling breaks upon a man, he, too, will be humbled and feel as but a child (see v. 6). The boldness to go preach for God comes with the assurance that one is sent by God. "Whatsoever I command thee thou shalt speak" (v. 7) is the sole authority of his message. With this conviction in his heart, he will not be afraid, knowing God is with him (see v. 8).

Preachers of the past have laid claim to being called by God to preach. The pastoral ministry should not be considered alongside medicine, law, or business as just another career option, but rather it must be considered in the light of the will and call of God. Usually the second question asked of a ministerial candidate has to do with his "call." A host of ministers have left the ministry, and many have written articles on "Why I left the ministry." It is no wonder they left if they were not specifically called by God in the first place.

Discerning the Call

"Preacher, how does a man know when God is calling him to preach?" Max asked me, his face white as ash. Max, in his early thirties, was a traveling salesman, married, with a fine family. He was chairman of our deacons. No finer Christian could any pastor desire to have in his church. To encourage a man at this stage in life to leave a secure job, go to school, and prepare for a whole new calling is a serious matter, and one must have some sure and right answers to the question Max posed.

The story is told of a farmer who said he had been called to preach. He knew he was called because he had seen in the sky the letters "G P C," which he interpreted to mean "Go Preach Christ." After hearing him preach, someone said he had misread the sign. It really meant "Go Plow Corn."

Next to salvation, no decision in life needs to be more definite and sure. Those describing the call to preach can run the gamut from visions or dreams or signs to the nebulous "You'll know it when you are called." "But *how* will I know it?" one might ask.

The Desire to Preach

"This is a true saying, If a man *desire* the office of a bishop, he desireth a good work" (1 Tim. 3:1, italics added). The call of God to the ministry is an inner *desire* to preach the Word of God and pastor the people of God.

God speaks of salvation as a calling (see Rom. 8:30, 1 Cor. 7:18,20). How does God call to salvation? "No man can come to me," said Jesus, "except the Father which hath sent me *draw* him" (John 6:44, italics added). Through an inward desire and drawing, God convinces us that we ought to repent and that God wants to save us. We respond by yielding and accepting God's invitation to salvation.

By a parallel procedure God calls one to His service. Basically, it is a hunger, a yearning, a longing, an urge, a *desire* born of the Holy Spirit within to enter this great business of preaching.

Knowing Where the Call Comes From

"For it is God which worketh in you both to will [desire] and to do of his good pleasure" (Phil. 2:13). The *desire* "to do of his good pleasure" comes from God. He works from within by drawing one to His service.

Better to be drawn than to be driven. The Lord is a Shepherd who leads. Where does one get a desire for the ministry? Why, it comes from God! This is His call. Satan surely would not give one a desire to preach the Word of God, for Satan can only say "Hath God said?" (Gen. 3:1). The world certainly doesn't want anyone to preach Christ to them, for they hate Him (see John 15:18). The flesh has no desire to do the will of God (see Rom. 8:7; Gal. 5:17).

The call of God is so simple that many stumble and fumble around for weeks and months looking for some spectacular, dramatic "call" from God. The call, however, is not just a desire to see people saved or a desire to be used by God—most Christians have these desires—but it is a desire for the office, the whole work of the ministry. After long struggling and wondering, preachers will look back and see that this desire was there from the beginning. Of course, right away a man will feel inadequate and humbled by the thought. No one wants to be presumptuous, and consequently much thought and prayer are given to the matter until one is sure his desire is God's call.

Testing the Call

A check list will help discern if one's desire is God's call. Let's look at some negatives.

First, be sure the desire to enter *the ministry is not for fame.* One must say with Jesus, "I seek not mine own glory" (John 8:50). Of course, ministers often are accorded a measure of fame and prestige. In days gone by, the ministry was as highly esteemed as medicine, law, or most other professions. A desire for respect must not be the motive for entering the ministry. Here lies the reason for the admonition that the preacher must not be a "novice [new Christian], lest being lifted up with pride he fall into the condemnation of the devil" (1 Tim. 3:6).

Second, *one must not enter the ministry for the family's sake.* Like father, like son, is true in many ways, but not necessarily when it comes to deciding God's call. Any man called by God to preach would not dare push or urge his son to do the same, apart from the call and will of God. To be sure, some have testified that they entered the ministry because of family pressure. A parent's wish or advice has nothing to do with a call. In fact, Jesus says, "If any man come to me, and hate not his father, and mother . . . he cannot be my disciple" (Luke 14:26; cf. Matt. 10:35–39; Luke 9:57–60).

Third, *the ministry is not the place for accumulating wealth.* Specifically, God says, one must not be "greedy of filthy lucre" (1 Tim. 3:3). As one looks around at the pastor's home, the car he drives, and the clothes he wears, these days one can come to the conclusion that it pays to preach. The heart attitude a minister must assume is "having food and raiment let us therewith be content" (1 Tim. 6:8). Because of the money motive many ministers have "pierced themselves through with many sorrows" (1 Tim. 6:10).

Another desire which surely is not from God is a fleshly desire to preach. The example of Christ who "came not to be ministered unto, but to minister, and to give his life a ransom for many" (Mark 10:45) will cull out those not called and save many from the psychiatrist. When a pastor feels he is being intruded upon when he is called at all hours of the night, or when he has no desire to "weep with those who weep," or when he resents the fact that his life is not his own and he has to live in a glass house, then it is doubtful he was called to the ministry! Never be a hireling. The ministry means giving up one's own desires "to do the will of him that sent me" (John 4:34).

It should go without saying, but *one must not enter the ministry with the idea that such a life will be easy and fun.* Pastoring is full of soul-satisfying joy, but fleshly fun—no. Running to all the luncheons, country clubs, and sports events to "get in" with people can easily sidetrack one from the ministries of visitation, witnessing, praying, and studying that are essential for an effective ministry. Remember, the Lord Jesus was a "man of sorrows" (Is. 53:3), and to desire the ministry for the sake of fun is a travesty.

Now let's turn to the positives.

The desire to preach ought first of all to be for the Lord's glory.
Anyone called by God will be able to say with Jesus, "I have glorified
thee on the earth" (John 17:4). Paul's admonition, ". . . do all to the
glory of God" (1 Cor. 10:31), is more fitting for the work of the ministry than for anything else ever done. "Let your light so shine before
men, that they may see your good works, and glorify your Father
which is in heaven" (Matt. 5:16). This must be the preacher's paramount purpose. The heart that yearns to glorify God to the fullest, to
exalt the Lord Jesus Christ before the world, and to cause men to
praise Him has received his desire for the ministry from God.

Love is another basic motivation for preaching that can come only
from God. "The love of Christ constraineth us" (2 Cor. 5:14) was the
apostle's testimony. The love of Christ burning in a man's heart, bur-
dening him to get the gospel to everyone, is a good sign the desire is
from God. "Though I speak with the tongues of men and of angels,
and have not charity [love], I am become as sounding brass, or a tinkling cymbal" (1 Cor. 13:1). No one who is not motivated and mastered by the love spoken of in this passage will ever make a successful
pastor.

*The needs of unbelievers and the desire to win them to Christ are
important concerns* of the one who would be a pastor. Dr. L. R. Scarborough, in his book *With Christ After the Lost,* said, "Whatever
else Christ calls his preachers to do, he does not call them away from
the high duty of soul winning."* This holy hunger to reach the multitude is a God-given desire and part of the call of God. A pastor may
not have the calling of an evangelist, but he is certainly to "do the
work of an evangelist" (2 Tim. 4:5), and this desire is from above.

The longing to preach is part of God's call. Preachers called by God
testify to their love of preaching. The person with this longing can
hardly wait for the next opportunity to stand and proclaim the Word
of God. Isaiah, when he had the vision of God and of those without
God, quickly responded to God's question, "Who will go for me?"
"Here am I; send me," he answered (Is. 6:8).

A final evidence of God's call is a sense of urgency to get the gospel

---

*Dr. L. R. Scarborough, *With Christ After the Lost,* (New York: Broadman, 1953), p. 79.

out. Paul said, "Woe unto me, if I preach not the gospel" (1 Cor. 9:16). Anything besides spreading the good news seems rather insignificant to the one called by God. Time isn't marching on; time is running out. This urgency must grip the preacher's heart.

Confirming the Call

A verse that greatly helps us to know if we are rightly discerning the will of God is Colossians 3:15: "Let the peace of God rule in your hearts. . . ." When one walks in the Spirit (see Gal. 5:16), he will experience "the fruit of the Spirit" (Gal. 5:22), which includes peace. When one is led by the Spirit (see Gal. 5:18), the peace of God will certainly accompany the one being led. The prerequisites are that one must walk in the Spirit and seek the will of God. If a person lacks peace or doubts whether the ministry is the will of God for him, he should seriously reconsider his call. This is borne out in the principle of Romans 14:23: "And he that doubteth is damned if he eat, because he eateth not of faith: for whatsoever is not of faith is sin." This doubt, evidenced by lack of peace, is a warning signal to the one seeking God's will that a particular decision is not the right one.

The instruction is to "let the peace of God rule." The word "rule" means "to judge, umpire, or arbitrate." That's revealing, isn't it? Peace acts as an umpire to judge or arbitrate what the will of God is. If one lacks peace, then the Holy Spirit must be leading in another direction. Of course, many commands and admonitions in the Word of God do not require questioning, only obedience. But when it comes to decisions about which the Word of God says nothing specific, then inner peace is the decisive factor.

The domain of peace is "in your heart." The word "heart" means "the seat of emotions." How important that one have his heart fixed on God (see Ps. 57:7).

Seldom does God reveal His whole will at one time. The Christian life is a walk, one step at a time. Most servants of God never dreamed they would finally be in the very place where they are now. It would scare most of us to death to know all that God has in store. Instead, then, there seems to be a progression, set forth in the Word, which characterizes the experience of most who are called by God.

When God called Samuel he had no idea God was calling him. He

24

thought Eli was calling and so ran to him (see 1 Sam. 3:1-9). As is often the case, when the desire for Christian service enters a Christian's heart, he isn't sure where the desire comes from and so runs to his pastor for guidance. The tragedy with Eli was that his eyes were dim (see v. 2), not only physically but spiritually, and his advice was not the best at first. It took a while before Eli realized that God was calling Samuel. Finally, his instructions were to answer, "Speak, LORD; for thy servant heareth" (v. 9). Samuel was to say, in effect, "Tell me what you want of me. I'm listening and ready to do what you want." Today we might call this the experience of dedication. God cannot call a person until he is yielded and ready to listen.

The next experience is more specific. It happened to the prophet Isaiah. He first saw the Lord in His majesty sitting on a throne (see Is. 6:1). If people are going to be used by God, they need to understand something of God's majesty and power through His Word. Then Isaiah saw himself as "undone" and "a man of unclean lips" (v. 5). Recognition of his sinful condition enables a minister to admit that he needs God's cleansing just as much as anyone else. Finally, Isaiah saw himself "in the midst of a people of unclean lips" (v. 5). Having experienced God's cleansing, Isaiah realized that someone needed to tell the people of Israel how they, too, could be cleansed. When God asked, "Whom shall I send, and who will go for us?" Isaiah not only answered, "Here am I" but "Here am I; send me" (v. 8). He had the vision of the need, the desire to spread the message, and finally the determination. To a man with these convictions, God says, "Go, and tell . . ." (v. 9). God will guide him to the very place of service He has for him.

An example of God's getting a person to the very place He wants him is in Acts 16. When Paul and Silas set out on their journey, they were "forbidden of the Holy Ghost to preach the word in Asia" (v. 6). Someone has pointed out that only a moving ship can be guided. They then tried to go to Bithynia, and again God closed the door (see v. 7). Finally, Paul had a vision and heard the call, "Come over into Macedonia, and help us" (v. 9). When a person sets out in faith to go where God would lead, the Lord will see to it that he arrives where God wants him. How confidently you can "Commit thy way unto the LORD . . . and he shall bring it to pass" (Ps. 37:5).

In summary, the call of God is a desire in one's heart, placed there

by God, for God's work. It is a hunger, a yearning for the glory of
God. It is a longing to become a shepherd of God's people, to preach
the Word of God, to reach the multitudes with the gospel, and to build
up the saints to love and serve the Lord Jesus Christ.

3

Qualifications and Credentials

There are no double standards with God. What *ought* to be true of every member of Christ *must* be true of the minister of Christ. The minister does live in a glass house. A Christian lady once said to a pastor, "It's nobody's business how I live." He wisely replied, "Lady, it's everybody's business how you live." Surely this is true of the pastor, for "none of us liveth to himself" (Rom. 14:7).

God has set the standards for church leaders. Make no mistake about that. The nature of a pastor's responsibility *demands* high standards. We have no more right to change the qualifications for God's servants than we do to change the conditions for salvation.

A pastor has to "endure hardness, as a good soldier of Jesus Christ. No man that warreth entangleth himself with the affairs of this life . . ." (2 Tim. 2:3,4). Men who are not qualified physically to serve our country in the military are classified 4F. They not only cannot fight and defend our country, but consequently they cannot receive the medals, rewards, and praise for valor. Some would-be soldier/ ministers of the cross are classified 4F for the following reasons.

Faithlessness. A faithless man certainly is disqualified. He must be born again. It may seem shocking, but some preachers will end up in hell. Jesus says, "Many will say to me in that day, Lord, Lord, have we not prophesied [preached] in thy name? . . . And then will I profess unto them, I never knew you: depart from me, ye that work iniquity" (Matt. 7:22). In verse 15 God calls them "false prophets, which come to you in sheep's clothing, but inwardly they are ravening wolves."

No wonder God exhorts, "Beloved, believe not every spirit, but try the spirits whether they are of God: because many false prophets are gone out into the world" (1 John 4:1). These "blind leaders of the blind" (Matt. 15:14) have nothing to offer and are disqualified for the gospel ministry. They will receive greater condemnation (see James 3:1).

Fleshliness. One who is fleshly is unfit for God's service. Samson, so strong physically, who "wist not that the LORD was departed from him" (Judg. 16:20) was absolutely powerless in the flesh and fell to the enemy. He had so much potential, but his fleshly lust destroyed him. The number of good and gifted men who have fallen to the flesh is legion, and because of them many are defiled (see Heb. 12:15). They thought they could steal one scene from God's great drama, but the curtain fell on them. The admonition, "Dearly beloved, I beseech you as strangers and pilgrims, abstain from fleshly lusts, which war against the soul" (1 Pet. 2:11), is no simple suggestion but an absolute requirement for a pastor.

Foolishness. ". . . I have played the fool . . .," Saul confessed (1 Sam. 26:21). He lost his kingdom, too. How foolish. Some pastors have played the fool in marriage and thus have disqualified themselves from the ministry. Marriage vows are valid and serious. To promise God for better or for worse, and then to go back on one's word, disqualifies one from spiritual leadership. One of the reasons marriage is so serious a matter is that it is a picture of Christ's relationship to the church. The picture is marred and becomes a lie when a man is divorced from a woman. Christ would never be divorced from His Bride, the church. A pastor cannot bear that image before people.

Fear. He must not be fearful. The fearful were not to be in Gideon's army and were told to go back (see Judg. 7:3). God told Jeremiah to speak what He commanded and "Be not afraid of their faces . . ." (Jer. 1:8). To preach the whole counsel of God without fear or favor is the demand of God and the duty of every soldier of the cross. Paul feared men so little because he feared God so much. The Jezebels are still after the servants of God, and the fearful will surely fall. Let a man not enter this sacred service if he has not experienced the power and promise of God's protection.

To be sure, some "4Fs" can serve God, but not as shepherds of the flock. There is a place for them. Many who are disqualified from the pastorate are men of God, but they dare not take upon themselves the pastoral responsibility.

Satan is tricky. The heart is deceitful. That is why we must always examine ourselves and our motives in light of Scripture. The scriptural qualifications that a potential pastor must consider are listed in 1 Timothy 3:1-7. Some are absolutes; some are relative. Lest they be glossed over, let's look at the passage and then examine the qualifications one by one.

> This is a true saying, If a man desire the office of a bishop, he desireth a good work. A bishop then must be blameless, the husband of one wife, vigilant, sober, of good behavior, given to hospitality, apt to teach; Not given to wine, no striker, not greedy of filthy lucre; but patient, not a brawler, not covetous; One that ruleth well his own house, having his children in subjection with all gravity; For if a man know not how to rule his own house, how shall he take care of the church of God?) Not a novice, lest being lifted up with pride he fall into the condemnation of the devil. Moreover he must have a good report of them which are without; lest he fall into reproach and the snare of the devil (1 Tim. 3:1-7).

The word "bishop" is sometimes synonymous with "elder" in the New Testament. The two words are used about the same people and office in Acts 20:17-28 and Titus 1:5-7. In his very fine commentary on the pastoral epistles, Dr. Homer Kent says, "It is not the office which is emphasized but the function of overseeing."

The one who would seek the awesome responsibility of pastor must be blameless. This means "without reproach." Dr. J. H. Bernard in the *Cambridge Greek New Testament,* says, "It implies not only that the man is of good report but that he deserves it." He gives no cause for blame. Many a man's ministry has been ended at one church, or permanently, because he was not above reproach.

"The husband of one wife." There are four possibilities of interpretation here: (1) Polygamy is forbidden. (2) The pastor must be married. (3) If his wife dies, the pastor must not remarry. (4) The pastor must not have more than one wife living at a time. Number 4 is the most acceptable explanation. The verse seems to say that if a Christian breaks his vow of commitment to his wife, divorces her, and remarries, he should not aspire to be a minister.

"Vigilant." This primarily refers to being temperate in the case of wine but, in a wider sense, it means temperance in all things. Gluttony is a sin many Christians—including pastors—are guilty of; an obese pastor should be as unthinkable as one who gets drunk regularly. A minister must have good judgment and not run off on tangents or go to extremes.

"Sober." Here this word means soberminded, discreet, prudent, well-balanced. This refers to inward and mental attitude. With spiritual counseling to be done and decisions to be made, a minister needs sobermindedness.

"Good behavior." Sobermindedness results in outward demonstrations of goodness. One must not only talk well but walk well. In short, a pastor must practice what he preaches.

"Given to hospitality." To pastor people, one desperately needs to be hospitable. If a minister loves people and enjoys Christian fellowship, his labors of love will be a delight, not drudgery. It is tragic to see some ministers stay so aloof that few of their people even feel they have a pastor. Having a genuine love for people and showing it will certainly cover a multitude of shortcomings any minister might have.

"Apt to teach." Henry Alford says, "able and skilled at teaching." A. T. Robertson says "qualified." Most Bible scholars believe that Ephesians 4:11 lists teaching and pastoring as one gift. If this qualification were given more attention, the frequent complaint "We are not taught the Word" would not be heard. A minister must be able to feed the flock—and not with husks either! Few pulpit committees are careful enough to ascertain this gift in the men they call.

"Not given to wine." Until recent years it was almost universally accepted that ministers totally abstain from alcohol. With the broken hearts and broken homes caused by alcohol, there should be little doubt in the mind of one called by God to avoid wine as one would avoid a serpent. Dignity cannot be preserved in alcohol.

"No striker." Not quick-tempered or given to acts of violence, not pugnacious, "either with hand or tongue," says Fausset of this phrase. This is the frequent result of one "given to wine." A minister certainly must be filled with the Holy Spirit, and the fruit of the Spirit includes temperance, or self-control. Just one outburst from a servant of God can cause a church to lose confidence in a minister, thus ending his effectiveness.

"Patient." Gentle, reasonable, or forbearing. A pastor must put up with a lot, but a Christ-like character pays off. "Vengeance is mine; I will repay, saith the Lord" (Rom. 12:9). Even as Christ,

"Who, when he was reviled, reviled not again . . ." (1 Pet. 2:23), so a minister must commit himself to God.

"Not a brawler." Not quarrelsome or contentious. It is one thing to "earnestly contend for the faith" (Jude 3) but another to be contentious about the faith. "The servant of the Lord must not strive . . ." (2 Tim. 2:24).

"Not covetous." The Greek literally says not a "lover of money." In the Greek, the best manuscripts do not have the phrase "not greedy of filthy lucre," but certainly "not covetous" covers the desire for money. The love of money has been one of the greatest downfalls of preachers.

Things that really count are things you cannot count. Being "content with such things as ye have" (Heb. 13:5) is a must for a minister. If God's servant works hard and walks with God, God will take care of all his needs—but not his greeds.

Too often when a minister worries about finances he loses his burden for souls and for building up the saints. It then shows up in his preaching. "For the love of money is the root of all evil . . ." (1 Tim. 6:10). Paul continued, "But thou, O man of God, flee these things; and follow after righteousness, godliness, faith, love, patience, meekness. Fight the good fight of faith" (1 Tim. 6:11,12). How young ministers today need this admonition. God meets the needs of the one who heeds these commands (see Matt. 6:33). Remember, the Levites had no inheritance in the land. To be rich in God is better than to be rich in goods. This world is not our home.

"One that ruleth well his own house." "Ruleth" means "to place before or in front of or in charge of—to preside over." If a man is not able to govern his own family, he can scarcely be expected to govern the household of God.

A wife can make or break a preacher and often does. Many a minister has lost his place in the church because his wife will not be the helper he needs. Nothing is more tragic. If a man will not assume his rightful place as leader in the home, he cannot be a leader in the church. Often the problem lies with the wife who refuses to submit to her husband's leadership as God commands (see Eph. 5:22). Sometimes the wife is jealous of the praise her minister-husband receives and covetous of his recognition. Such an attitude, though, only causes her to

31

receive less praise. A man should not accept a pastorate, the ordination committee should not ordain the man, and a church should not call him if he does not rule well in his own house.

"Having his children in subjection with all gravity." Here is proof he rules his own house well. Whether we know why or not, when children go astray someone did not train them in the way they should go (see Prov. 22:6). This is strong language, but better one should be offended than a whole church hurt by a pastor's family going astray. If he does not discipline his children in love, he will not discipline the children of God, and it is still true that "He that spareth his rod hateth his son . . ." (Prov. 13:24). Some disqualified by God on this point have been approved by councils and churches, much to their sorrow later.

"Not a novice." New converts should not pastor till they have been seasoned. "Lay hands suddenly on no man . . ." (1 Tim. 5:22), God says. Pride is subtle. New converts are susceptible to deceit about God and about themselves.

"A good report of them which are without." It *does* matter what neighbors think. We are accountable for our behavior in this world. "When a man's ways please the LORD, he maketh even his enemies to be at peace with him" (Prov. 16:7).

The pastor is a shepherd of the flock. A shepherd leads and feeds the flock. A pastor must be a loving leader, not a domineering dictator. You don't drive sheep, lest you drive them away. Read what the apostle Peter wrote in reference to elders:

> The elders which are among you I exhort, who am also an elder. . . . Feed the flock of God which is among you, taking the oversight thereof, not by constraint, but willingly; not for filthy lucre, but of a ready mind; Neither as being lords over God's heritage, but being ensamples to the flock. And when the chief Shepherd shall appear, ye shall receive a crown of glory that fadeth not away (1 Pet. 5:1–4).

"Feed the flock." Don't fleece them. People are hungry, spiritually. Just as restaurants that serve good food are filled, so are churches that teach the Word well.

"Take the oversight." This refers to responsibility and initiative. Watch out for the souls entrusted to you. Be accountable. Pastoring is serious business, and the one not willing to accept this responsibility is not ready for the privilege.

"Being [examples] to the flock." "Be ye followers of me" should be our battle cry. The people need a good pattern to copy. Without a willingness to be that example, no one should enter the ministry.

You say you have been called to preach? Do you have the proper qualifications? If so, and you are determined to press on to higher ground day by day, then go. There is no higher calling. There is no harder work. There is no holier service. There is no happier privilege than serving the living God.

A Word About Education

Jesus used proper grammar. Preachers won't be perfect in their preaching, but there is no excuse for sloppy speech. It is a discredit to preachers and distasteful to people. Proper preparation, sufficient schooling, and timely training are essential to a well-balanced and abiding ministry.

God calls, God ordains, and God anoints his preachers, but He still says, "Study to show thyself approved unto God, a workman that needeth not to be ashamed, rightly dividing the word of truth" (2 Tim. 2:15). We are not of this world, but we certainly are in it. We live in an educated, sophisticated society. We had better have something to say and know how to say it.

Jesus trained and taught the Twelve for three years. Pastors need training. One good reason for going to a Bible school to be taught and trained is that one is not to go out as a novice (see 1 Tim. 3:6). No matter how much education and experience one has, he is still going to make mistakes and have problems in his early days as a pastor. He had better learn all he can before he starts, in order to minimize the potential for mistakes and problems.

What shall he study? As already mentioned he must be educated in English grammar and communication skills. Good English won't drive away the less educated, but poor English will drive away the better educated.

A good general education in history, science, and literature helps one gain a broad perspective of contemporary life. Also, you will be conversant with more people. A course in writing and journalism can be beneficial to effective self-expression, especially if you desire to write articles and books. Of course, courses in Bible, theology, and biblical languages are essential. Courses in logic, philosophy, business, and economics can be extremely helpful. Every preacher wishes he had more education. Courses in speech, homiletics, and pastoral theology are essential to be effective in the ministry.

Finally, preachers don't get into nearly as much trouble for not knowing how to marry and bury as they do for not knowing how to get along with people. Any course that helps you understand people and get along with them is worth the price. For years I have taught Dale Carnegie's book, *How to Win Friends and Influence People.* There are Scriptures that fit every principle he gives. Preachers must apply these Scriptures and principles so they can "win friends and influence people" for God.

Practical training is also invaluable. Most Bible schools realize this and offer opportunities for practical Christian work, such as jail ministry, street preaching, youth work, or pulpit preaching.

Be involved in a good local church. Teaching Sunday school or working in a bus ministry is essential preparation. Go with your pastor to funerals, hospitals, and visitation. Every pastor would love to have a genuine, sincere Timothy to help train. Learn to listen and you can learn a lot from men of God who went down the road ahead of you.

4

Personal Conduct

Conduct is what you are on the outside. Character is what you are on the inside. It takes a lot of character to produce the right kind of conduct in today's society. The boundaries of right and wrong are being extended almost daily by the world, but before God the way is still narrow. Once you begin to assuage your conscience by calling something a necessary evil, it usually looks more necessary and less evil. It is better to be one-sided than two-faced. A great old gospel tract is entitled, *Others May; You Cannot.* Others *may* do a lot of things, but you as a man of God *cannot.* Here are several areas of conduct to consider.

Spiritual Conduct

You are either spiritual or you are carnal. You are either walking in the Spirit or walking in the flesh. God is either producing the fruit of the Spirit in you or you are producing the works of the flesh at every given moment. There is no middle ground. Did you get that? Let me repeat this most profound truth: *You are either Spirit-controlled or self-controlled.*

This is the Holy Spirit's day. God, the God of Abraham, Isaac, and Jacob, was the prominent One at work in the Old Testament. When the Lord Jesus came, He was the prominent One at work on earth. Revelation tells about the wrath of almighty God once again during the tribulation. During the millennium the Lord Jesus will be prominent once again. Today, in the church age, the Holy Spirit is the prominent One at work on earth.

The Lord Jesus suffered, died, rose again, went back to heaven, and sat down on the right hand of the Father. Why? He had finished what He had gone to earth to do. Then He sent the Holy Spirit to take up where He had left off. Christians now need to know who the Holy Spirit is and what He came to do, and then let Him do it. Believers are to "be filled with the Spirit" (Eph. 5:18), "walk in the Spirit" (Gal. 5:25), "grieve not the . . . Spirit" (Eph. 4:30), "Quench not the Spirit" (1 Thess. 5:19), "be led by the Spirit" (Rom. 8:14), and be "changed" by the Spirit (2 Cor. 3:18). They are to mortify the deeds of the flesh by the Spirit (see Rom. 8:13). Just as there was a conscious dependence on the Lord Jesus to save you, there must be a conscious dependence on the Holy Spirit to control you and work through you.*

Oh, to love and preach in the power of the Holy Spirit! What a thrill it is to see God take simple sermons and use them to break people's hearts until Christ be formed in them. He, the Holy Spirit, glorifies Christ (see John 16:14). No man can say that Jesus is Lord but by the Holy Spirit (see 1 Cor. 12:3). Paul said his speech was "in demonstration of the Spirit and of power" (1 Cor. 2:4). Again Paul said, "our gospel came . . . in power, and in the Holy Ghost . . ." (1 Thess. 1:5). "God anointed Jesus of Nazareth with the Holy Ghost and with power . . ." (Acts 10:38).

The fullness of the Spirit is essential to success in the ministry. You must take two steps to gain and maintain this control, this filling, this power of the Holy Spirit. One, you must always confess and forsake sin. Don't quibble with God. God knows that secret sin. It is open scandal in heaven. Confess it, and He will forgive and cleanse you (see 1 John 1:9). Next, ask for the Holy Spirit to take over. "If we ask anything according to his will," we will have it, according to 1 John 5:14,15. We are assured it is the will of God that we be filled with the Holy Spirit (see Eph. 5:17,18). Begin living by faith, not by feeling. Claim these great truths for yourself.

Family Life

At the risk of repeating myself, let me again underscore the importance of family life. If you really want to know what a man is like, ask

---

*My earlier book, *How on Earth Can I Be Spiritual,* (Thomas Nelson Publishers) may be of encouragement to you. God has unusually used it; it went into the second printing in three months and was chosen "book of the month" by Word Book Club.

his wife and children. It is absolutely inexcusable for a pastor to treat women in the church with more respect than he treats his wife. Love your wife "even as Christ also loved the church and gave himself for it" (Eph. 5:25). You will never build a great church if you don't build a great home. There need not be conflict between one's marriage and one's ministry, but don't forget, you married a wife, not a ministry. The country is strewn with great preachers who wrecked their marriages while they ran their ministries—and now both are defunct.

Magnify your wife's good points. Don't belittle her and habitually point out her weaknesses any more than you want her to do the same to you. Keep courting her after you are married. Here is where couples get off the honeymoon: They stop courting and begin to take each other for granted. Tell her—and show her—that you love her every day. Talk with your wife. She needs companionship, too. Brag on your wife in public. Let people know in little ways from the pulpit how much you love her. (This also will keep love-starved women away from your door.)

Play with your children. Life is short, and children grow up terribly fast. Keep the lines of communication open. Children will open up to someone who cares, and to them, that is someone willing to spend time alone with them, doing what they enjoy. Teen-agers appreciate individual attention too; take them out to eat once in a while, just you and one child at a time. My heart aches when I hear college kids say they don't think their dads love them. Many are preachers' kids. Regularly tell your children you love them—and prove it.

Pray with your family. Yes, "the family that prays together stays together." But your prayers must be from the heart, not by rote. Teach your family the Word of God and spiritual principles to live by. It's worth the investment. What a thrill to hear your son say one day, "I want to be like you, Dad," or to hear your daughter say, "I want to marry a man just like you, Dad." I know—bless God—I've heard it!

Take vacations. This is a must. The church won't fold up without you. If it does, you aren't much of a leader. A leader doesn't do all the work. He knows how to delegate and give authority to those around him. Don't turn every vacation into a trip to visit relatives. You need time together alone with your immediate family. Never say you can't afford a vacation. You can't afford not to take one.

Find common interests and hobbies the whole family can enjoy: picnics, boating, skiing, or whatever. Help make joyous memories for your family.

Social Conduct

Personal hygiene is essential. Take baths daily. Use deodorant whether you think you need it or not—you do. Brush your teeth. Use breath mints, especially after preaching. Keep your shoes polished, your clothes clean and pressed. Dress conservatively but be in style. Colors should blend, not clash. Buy good clothes. They last longer and look better. Learn pleasing color combinations so your suits and ties go together. Don't wear gaudy socks, ties, or shirts. They attract undue attention to yourself. You don't see successful businessmen dressed that way; you should dress as tastefully as any executive. The size of your wardrobe isn't important as long as what you have is clean and fits well.

Know proper etiquette. Good table manners are essential. Chew with your mouth closed. Don't slurp food or drinks. Break bread, then butter it, and never bite from a whole slice. Never leave a spoon in your beverage while drinking it. Seat ladies before seating yourself. Watch your posture—don't slouch. Avoid all crudities. Cut and eat one piece of meat at a time. Watch the hostess and follow her example when in doubt about what to do. A pastor should feel at ease in the most elegant home.

Be prompt for appointments. Don't overstay a visit to a person's place of employment. Be brief. Pay attention when someone is talking to you. *Remember names.* This is one of the greatest assets a minister can have. Avoid criticism, arguments, and interruptions when visiting someone—or at any time, for that matter.

Learn how to be relaxed with people of importance. They will deeply appreciate it. Don't try to impress them. They can read it a mile away. Be yourself. Everyone likes someone who is for real. Don't avoid prominent, wealthy people. They need friends, too.

Years ago in Birmingham, Alabama, I was visiting the executive vice-president of a large bank. The president and chairman of the board was a fine Christian and one of the most powerful and important people in the city and the state. Everyone respected him. He heard I was in the building and sent someone to ask me to come by and see him before I left. I did. He closed the door to his office, and we spent a solid hour visiting and fellowshiping. He was just as human as anyone and hungry for Christian fellowship. We had a great time.

I have learned that millionaires are just like everyone else, only with a little more money (which often doesn't mean that much to them). Don't gush over the rich and their possessions. God says, "Love not the things of the world"; yet some pastors go into a beautiful home and make enough remarks about the person's wealth and possessions to make one wonder about his love for God and for possessions!

Conduct in the World

You must live in this world, but you cannot live as part of it. How does a pastor react to this old world?

For starters, don't be holier than thou. I don't mean you have to tell or laugh at shady jokes. I do mean you can enjoy sports and be interested in politics, parades, and plays. Aloofness can be spotted and equated with snobbery. You can act as if you are above others until your behavior becomes obnoxious. You should know your neighbors, whether they are Christians or not. Chat with them. Be interested in them and help them when you can.

"Owe no man any thing . . ." (Rom. 13:8). Some take this to mean that we can't buy anything on credit. Others believe we don't owe anything when our bills are paid up to date. For sure it means don't get behind or leave town without paying off debts. What's wrong with starting out on the bottom rung of the ladder? When a person gets head-over-heels in debt, it's sin. Nothing hurts the testimony of Christ like a pastor's unpaid bills.

Beware of social clubs and organizations. To say you will join such crowds in order to win some to Christ sounds good. But check up on any pastor who has done so, and find out how many people he has won to Christ. It's so easy to get sidetracked. Soul-winning, church-building preachers just don't have time to be "one of the boys." Remember, you don't have to get drunk to win an alcoholic.

Pastors need to be informed about politics and public education. The local PTA and school boards need to hear the voice of God through local preachers. The man of God should not hold back from using his influence in the public arena. Don't run for office yourself, but get to know the mayor, city council, and school board members. Let them know your interest, support, and concern when decisions are being made.

Conduct Among Fellow Pastors

Our enemy is the devil, not fellow pastors. We must love the brethren (see 1 John 3:14) and "esteem them very highly in love for their work's sake" (1 Thess. 5:13). Don't judge (see Rom. 14:1-4). Don't criticize or gossip about a brother's ministry (1 Thess. 5:20). Never allow the poison of jealousy to pollute you, but rather "Rejoice with them that rejoice . . ." (Rom. 12:15). "As ye would that men should do to you, do ye also to them likewise" (Luke 6:31).

I have such a job keeping Sumner Wemp straight, I don't have time to straighten out other preachers. A pastor ought to be so busy winning the lost, helping Christians, and building a church that he doesn't have time to tear down someone else. Don't curse the dark; light a candle. Fighting preachers, people, or churches only produces a sour spirit. People are fed up with fighting and fussing. When Peter asked, "What about John?", Jesus said, "What is that to thee? follow thou me" (John 21:22). If you find fault in others, you can be sure your people will do the same to you.

Personal Conduct and Disposition

Be of good cheer. "A merry heart maketh a cheerful countenance . . ." (Prov. 15:13). Let it show. Where is the joy of the Lord? Walk by faith and say with the psalmist, "This is the day which the LORD hath made; we will rejoice and be glad in it" (Ps. 118:24). Why not live that way? Get excited about the important things in life. Jesus is alive! God is on His throne.

There are millions looking for what we have—love, joy, peace—and that's the truth. Love people. They are starved for it. People will flock to you if you genuinely love them.

Be given to hospitality. We have found a fantastic response to having at least one family from the church over to our house for a meal each week. They never forget the evening, nor do you.

Have a sense of humor. Learn to laugh at yourself and your mistakes. Don't take yourself too seriously, or you'll have ulcers for sure. A good sense of humor will save you from a breakdown. Learn to live and enjoy life. "In the world ye shall have tribulation: but be of good cheer; I have overcome the world" (John 16:33). Live on victory ground. Be for real. People are looking for reality as never before.

The Pastor and His Staff

Friction and fighting, jealousy and judging characterize many church staff relationships. These things ought not to be. They must not be.

There ought to be and can be sweet fellowship among fellow laborers in the Lord's work. What a joy to work together as a family to build the greatest church in town. Everything rises or falls with leadership. The church will be a reflection of its leaders' relationships. Here are some keys to building a great staff.

Be loyal. There must be total loyalty to one another, both the pastor to his staff and the staff to the pastor. At the very outset, a pastor must assure his staff of his loyalty. Likewise, staff members must pledge and prove their loyalty to the pastor.

Foster fellowship. Get to know each other. A pastor and his associate pastor (if there is one) ought to go visiting and soul-winning together every day the first month of ministering together. This way the associate will catch the vision, burden, and heart of the pastor. They need to spend much time together to really understand one another's total philosophy and thinking about ministry.

Go out to eat with the staff, individually or as a group. Informal fellowship is essential. If staff relationships are formal and businesslike only, you will never establish the closeness that leads to team spirit.

Share. Share the glory of all that's done. A wise pastor will exalt his associates before the congregation. Pastors must love and respect their associates if the ministry is to be effective. This means all jealousy must be removed.

Praise. Compliment and praise your associates before others. Be genuine. Jerry Falwell has built a great team of coworkers by his willingness to recognize regularly the efforts of each staff member.

41

Pray. Pray together. Your hearts will be bonded together through prayer. Nothing of eternal consequence is accomplished apart from prayer.

Love. Express love to one another. First Corinthians 13 shows that love is the key to relationships. Every staff problem is listed in this passage. Love is part of the fruit of the Holy Spirit. Don't let the flesh in for one minute. My, how people improve when we begin to love them!

Magnify your associates' good points. Don't be a fault-finder. We all have weaknesses and failures. Don't dwell on them. No one is perfect. Don't expect it. If you do, your staff will expect it of you!

Never criticize an associate before others. This is an absolute no-no.

Delegate authority and responsibility. Many pastors never learn to delegate. To get the job done, staff members need to know they have some authority. This lets them know you trust them and boosts their feelings of confidence and freedom. Loose them and let them go. They must know their responsibilities. Spell them out.

Listen. Have time for your staff. Listen to their suggestions. They must be in on planning sessions. Make them a vital part of your ministry from beginning to end.

Have a sense of humor. Learn to take a joke on yourself, but never use jokes that poke fun at a staff member's weakness.

Be human. Admit your own mistakes. If you blow it, admit it. Don't try to lay the blame on your staff for all the weaknesses of the church.

Don't play favorites. Nothing hurts more than for one staff member to have an inside track to the pastor and others be made to feel inferior.

Be discreet. To say that it is essential to be discreet at all times with staff members of the opposite sex is an understatement. Avoid being alone with them, especially outside church business situations. Never eat alone with them. The cost is too high. Avoid the appearance of evil, no matter what.

Pastor, you have one thing more precious, more essential than all else: your character. Don't blemish it. It can't be restored nor revived. Your testimony, your reputation, your character must be valued and protected at the cost of all else.

5

The Ordination Ceremony

Ordination is sacred and serious. God says, "Lay hands suddenly on no man. . . ." (1 Tim. 5:22) What was said of the priests of old certainly applies to pastors today. "And no man taketh this honour unto himself, but he that is called of God, as was Aaron" (Heb. 5:4). One must be called by God and sent forth by the Holy Spirit. This is the very first qualification.

Who should be ordained? Pastors, of course, should be ordained and associate pastors, if they have a pastoral ministry. There is a difference between a youth pastor and a youth director. A youth director directs youth programs and activities. A youth pastor has the oversight spiritually as a pastor. They should be ordained. Anyone with a pastoral ministry such as bus pastor or senior-saints pastor should be ordained. Evangelists and missionaries should be ordained as preachers of the gospel. This list will differ with different religious groups.

Why should there be ordination anyway? Because it's scriptural. Also, it is for Christian authority. It shows the public a man has been examined and is qualified. He is not self-appointed. He should be ordained for church authority. It identifies him and his basic beliefs with a denomination. He also should be ordained for civil authority. The civil laws grant him legal authority to marry.

When should one be ordained? This varies among believers. Most often it is when one has been called to a particular ministry and is now functioning in a pastoral or preaching capacity. This is usually after his schooling is finished and he begins to live by his calling.

How is one examined? The church calling the man to pastor requests his home church or a church of his preference to examine and ordain him. The candidate usually picks a church where the pastor and he are well acquainted and are of the same faith and practice.

This pastor calls a number of pastors together as a council. Usually there will be at least five. These can include pastors whom the candidate knows and has been close to. These come together usually on a Saturday morning before the Sunday he is to be ordained.

The council is formed with the group selecting a moderator and a secretary. Sometimes one other is selected as an interrogator to lead the questioning. Otherwise, the moderator leads the questioning.

All of the questioning should come under three headings. The candidate is questioned about his conversion, his call, and his creed—what he believes.

The candidate should be instructed to be brief about his answers. If the council wants additional information, they will ask for it. Then the candidate should use Scripture to support his doctrinal belief. To set the candidate at ease he should be told he will not be asked trick questions. The council should assure him they love him and are there as brother ministers. Many councils now ask the candidate to have his doctrinal position written out beforehand and a copy given to each pastor before the meeting.

The doctrines he is asked are usually comprehensive. They start with what he believes about the Bible. The questions should encompass the whole gamut of theology, such as the doctrines of God the Father, the Son, the Holy Spirit, salvation, security, sin, Satan, eschatology, the church and its ordinances.

The host pastor usually goes over, with the candidate, the questions he will probably be asked several weeks before this meeting. Every regional area will have some emphasis that it stresses about certain doctrines. Sometimes it is because of local problems or doctrinal errors faced previously in the area. The candidate should be made aware of these.

The questioning usually takes two hours or more. When the questioning is finished, the candidate leaves the room. The council discusses his answers and any problems they see. If all agree he is qualified, they vote and recommend that the church proceed with the ordination.

The candidate is called back into the room and informed of the vote. If he has been weak in any answers, he can be encouraged to study further in that area. The meeting should be closed in prayer, and each pastor should speak to the candidate and assure him of his love and prayers. A pastor's encouragement means much to a young pastor, and often these men have a great influence in the years to come on the young preacher. Their council and encouragement can mean so much, and they should offer themselves to help in any way they can.

The Importance of Ordination to the Church

The coronation of a king, the inauguration of the President, and the installation of a commanding general are child's play compared to the ordination of a gospel preacher. God's man being set apart to preach the unsearchable riches of the gospel of the grace of God is incredibly important.

Why, then, have most people never been to an ordination service? The ordination service should not be shoved to an insignificant Sunday afternoon when just a few relatives and close friends will come. If it's important, why not have it during the Sunday morning service when most people will be there?

The ordination ceremony can be one of the greatest blessings a church will ever experience. It is common for the service to become a revival meeting. At the ordination service of one young preacher recently, eight people were saved. With fewer than one hundred in attendance, the whole church was in tears and a spirit of revival prevailed that brought the church together as nothing had in eight years. I have seen this repeated in one ordination service after another when it is given its rightful place.

The place the service is held is important. If the one being ordained has just been called to pastor a church, its meeting place is the best location. The ordination ceremony will weld the new pastor and his people together as nothing else can. The church will have a part in ordaining their pastor and, in turn, will feel responsible for helping him be successful. Church members will be burdened to pray for the pastor and his ministry. The whole church will catch a new vision of the ministry and their part in it.

If the one being ordained hasn't been called to a church yet, then his home church is the best place for the service. To host such a ceremony is one of the greatest blessings and privileges a church can experience. Weeks in advance, the pastor can prepare the church for the special day by reminding them of the high honor of setting aside one of God's servants for the Christian ministry.

According to Acts 13, it was the church that ordained, laid on hands, and sent out Barnabas and Saul. It should be so today. However, there should be other ordained preachers to oversee the service and to bring the message. Sometimes it isn't easy to find preachers who can leave their pulpits on Sunday morning. Perhaps professors of the alma mater of the one being ordained can be brought in. Associate pastors, evangelists, missionaries, teachers, and Christian workers in various ministries can be called upon to lead the service. These, together with the men of the church, can adequately represent the church that has been requested to ordain the candidate.

As much as possible, the one being ordained should have the privilege of choosing the principal participants. One preacher should moderate and bring the ordination message. Usually this is someone who means a great deal to and has had much influence on the candidate. Another is chosen to bring a seven-minute charge to the preacher. Next comes a seven-minute charge to the church. A deacon of the church or a very close friend of the new pastor should give the ordination prayer. Finally, a church member should make a presentation of a Bible from the church to the preacher being ordained.

Begin the service as usual with a song and a prayer. Then the one leading the service should explain for the benefit of visitors that the Sunday Service is being given over to the ordination of one of God's servants. He should explain briefly the privilege and meaning of ordination. Announcements and the regular offering should be cared for as quickly as possible.

The candidate and his wife should sit on the front row, near the center. The wife should be included as much as possible because she is so vital to the success of her husband's ministry.

Next, the moderator should explain the service and its purpose more fully. He should tell how the candidate was examined by the ordination council about such matters as his conversion, his call, and his creed. The results and the recommendation of the council are then conveyed to the church. The moderator should explain the scriptural emphasis on the local church and how in Acts 13 the church was instructed by the Holy Spirit to separate God's servants to the ministry.

The ordination should then be described not as an impartation of spiritual gifts, but as recognition of God's calling of the candidate and the church's approving and endorsing this man for the ministry. By doing this, the church identifies with this preacher, saying they believe in him and will uphold him in their prayers. This lays a great responsibility on the church for the success of his ministry. It has a great effect when presented properly. The moderator then announces the order of service, introduces the participants, and sits down.

Usually, then, there is an appropriate special musical number. "Little Is Much When God Is in It" has been used at several services I have attended. "God Leads His Dear Children Along," "He Giveth More Grace," and similar songs are appropriate.

The one giving the charge to the preacher is next. The message should last only five or ten minutes. It should challenge the candidate to take care of himself, his family, and his flock. He can be exhorted to love the Lord, His Word, and His work. The message should be directed to the preacher and his wife.

The charge to the church follows. Hebrews 13:7,17,24 presents an excellent outline for charging the church. Such things as praying for him, following him, loving him, and respecting him should be emphasized.

Another solo may be appropriate next. The special music here should be brief. The one who sings should be ready and on the platform, and he or she need not be introduced. Also, the soloist should not give any testimony or introduction to the song. Time is of the essence.

Next comes the highlight of the service, the ordination sermon. It, too, should be brief, not longer than fifteen minutes. It could be about the high, the holy, and the heavenly calling. He could preach about the man, the ministry, and the message. This should be a stirring exhortation that the new preacher will never forget. The one preaching this should be at his best. Reference should be made to the candidate's wife so that she is included in this wonderful moment.

This message should be closed with prayer. Before praying and while heads are bowed and eyes closed, an invitation should be given, not for people to come forward but for them to make decisions in their seats. Those not saved should be challenged to pray to receive

Christ. They can be led in what to pray and asked to repeat the prayer in their hearts. Those who prayed can be asked to indicate their decision by looking up and catching the eye of the speaker. It is common to have people saved at such times if the gospel has been presented in the message, even briefly. Decisions of dedication or confession can be made and indicated by the raising of hands or by looking at the speaker.

Next comes the highest moment of all, the laying on of hands. The candidate should kneel facing the pulpit. His wife can kneel beside him, holding his hand. She, then, feels more a part of the whole ceremony.

The moderator should explain that the laying on of hands indicates identification and acceptance, the church's setting aside of this man for the ministry. All male church members should come, as representatives of their families and of the church, and lay hands on the candidate. The moderator should demonstrate from the pulpit how this is done by cupping his hands close together and slowly lowering them as though he were placing them on the head of the preacher.

As each man lays his hands on the candidate's head, he may say a brief prayer for the preacher. If the line is long, each man should be exhorted to pray briefly. Then each man may whisper a word of encouragement and exhortation in the preacher's ear. Without laying hands on the wife, each man may want to whisper a word of blessing to her also.

Each man should be asked to stay at the front, kneel around the candidate, and continue praying. When the last man has come, the candidate will be surrounded by men on their knees, praying. Next, the ordination prayer is made by a man who knows how to pray publicly. The whole church by now should be praying with and for the new pastor.

After the prayer, the men should return to their seats. The moderator then invites the one chosen to make the presentation of the Bible. This should be brief. Customarily the church presents the candidate with a good Bible, usually one selected by the candidate himself. The one making the presentation should mention that the Bible is the Word of God and should challenge the preacher to saturate himself with it and to preach it to the people.

The moderator now introduces the new pastor and congratulates him. The newly ordained preacher stands before his people and offers a few closing words. Usually his heart is full, as are the hearts of the people. He can express what this moment has meant to him and to his wife. He should then share his love for the people and his burden to be the kind of pastor who can lead his people to great heights for God. Someone else should be called on to close in prayer so the pastor and his wife can station themselves at the door to greet the people.

This time of ordination is a great moment. Bow before God and ask that this holy moment be before you always. Ask that you never tarnish the trust placed in you nor the testimony of the gospel.

6

The Pastor's Role in Church Planting

Giving birth to a new baby is easier than resurrecting a dead one. This is the rationale for starting a new church. An increasing number of men, called by God, feel the need to start a new church. However, the only valid reason for starting a new church must be the deepest conviction that one is led by God to do so. One must be extremely careful that there are no wrong motives behind such ventures.

The need for new churches in many areas can be well documented. For instance, in some places there is no church of a particular denominational and doctrinal position. Groups who hold to that doctrinal position can easily see a need for a new church.

In some places the existing churches have no vision, no burden for souls, no program of carrying out the great commission and church growth. The weaknesses of the seven churches of Revelation 2 and 3 can be identified readily in one church after another. Some churches are losing people rather than reaching the multitudes around them because they have become so steeped in tradition that they are stagnant and reject change.

Today the population is exploding in every kingdom but the kingdom of heaven. Whole subdivisions, communities, and cities are springing up with an enormous need for spiritual help. These and many other worthy reasons warrant the need for planting soul-winning, loving, life-changing churches.

The Need for Local Churches

There are Christians in every community who ask themselves, "Why join a church?" Well, that's a good question. Many do not. Many belong to the body of Christ and are true believers but see no need to belong to a local, visible church. Here are some thoughts on the matter.

50

The New Testament emphasis is on the local church. There are over one hundred references to local churches such as the church at Corinth or churches of Galatia. The New Testament letters were written to local churches of believers. God's purpose is to build His church (see Matt. 16:18,19). Jesus loved the church and gave Himself for it (see Eph. 5:25). If the Scriptures place an emphasis on the local church, so should we today.

The churches are to administer the ordinances of baptism and the Lord's Supper. God is for order. God is for authority. Not everyone who gets the urge should baptize in his back-yard swimming pool or serve the Lord's Supper at the garden club. The authority and supervision for these ordinances must be kept in order and under the direction of local churches.

To fulfill the Great Commission God gave directions to the church. We need the order and organization local churches give in order to get the gospel out and support those who go into all the world.

Sheep need a shepherd. Without one, they go astray. They need a leader. Shepherds are needed to feed the flock (see 1 Pet. 5:1-9). Many sheep are "scattered abroad" because they have never come under the leadership of a shepherd of a local church.

If a person belongs to no local church then he has no one with any spiritual authority over him. God says "Obey them that have the rule over you, and submit yourselves: for they watch for your souls..." (Heb. 13:17). Only a local pastor can be expected to do this. First Thessalonians 5:12 indicates that believers are to honor those over them in the Lord. There is definitely an authoritative chain of command spiritually in the Scriptures. Believers must submit to it.

Stronger still is the admonition in Matthew 18:15-19. If a brother gets out of line, the local church has the obligation to try to restore him. If he will not repent and be restored then the church is to treat him as a "heathen." This is strong language and certainly indicates the respect and responsibility of the local church. If believers belong to no local church, then there is no one responsible or able to keep Christian discipline in their lives. Of course, some like that and thus avoid belonging to any church.

The local church provides the opportunity for believers to share their gifts with one another for mutual blessings and benefit. First Corinthians 12 certainly stresses this. One must not hide his light under a bush. We need each other. Those with the gift of teaching are greatly needed in every church. This is God's order. Those who never join a local church feel no responsibility to a church. They never are around for visitation, helping on work nights, or running a bus route. They owe nothing to that church. Its success or failure is of no concern to them. They want no responsibiltiy and accept none.

Churches are a big business today. Many own millions of dollars worth of property and equipment. Baptist churches, for instance, are owned by the local congregation. Millions of dollars go through churches. Nonmembers have no part in what is done or how it is done. They usually contribute very little financially. Someone has to pay for the heat and lights. People should join and be a vital part in all of this.

Nonmembers surely cannot be deacons or teachers in a local church. The church would not have any authority over what they teach or how they live if they are not members. Many churches have felt the pain of having someone teach who was not a member and found division caused by false teaching or diverse directions of the teacher. This cannot be. Most who never settle down to a local church never help build a strong, life-changing family church in their community. This must be a strong priority of believers.

Christians are not perfect, just forgiven. The local church is not perfect. It is a hospital with obstetrics, nurseries, operating rooms, out-patient clinics, and feeding facilities. It's for everyone. Everyone is needed. The stray sheep need to get in the fold and help a local shepherd to build a strong church that will affect the world for Christ.

The Community

Where does one start in planting a church? Most who start a new church sense the call of God, burning in their soul, to a particular community, even as a missionary has a foreign country on his heart. To find the place, one should pray earnestly for God to lay on his heart the very city He wants him to reach. To be sure, God will answer, even as He gave Paul the Macedonia call.

God has given to His servants "a sound mind" (2 Tim. 1:7). God is reasonable (see Is. 1:18). A rational, sound mind would discern a sure need for a church before deciding on a community and a location within that community. To start a church in an area already filled with good soul-winning churches or only a few blocks from a church already doing an excellent job of evangelizing and edifying souls would be ludicrous.

The potential for success should be commensurate with the vision and desire of God's servant. Lack of potential for church growth has brought disillusionment and disappointment to some who have started churches, because they did not determine the need for a new church before starting out.

A deep desire and divine love for a community must be in the heart of a potential pastor. John Knox set the pace when he prayed, "Give me Scotland or I die." To some degree, at least, a man must have that kind of desire before he dare start a church.

"Let the peace of God rule in your hearts . . ." (Col. 3:15). That sweet peace that comes from the Holy Spirit and assures one that he is led by the Spirit is essential. If peace is not present, then one must wait upon the Lord before he moves one step, lest he walk in the flesh and fall flat on his face.

Who would have thought thirty years ago of going to one's home town to start a new church? But, more and more men are finding this ideal. The new pastor already knows the town. He knows the best area, with the greatest potential for building a church. He knows many of the people. Of course, he could not have any skeletons in the closet. He most assuredly would need to have "a good report of them which are without . . ." (1 Tim. 3:7). Dr. Jerry Falwell, Al Henson, Dr. Harold Henniger, and Marvin Wood have proved the wisdom of starting a church in one's home town.

The Location

In any community it is important to find the most strategic location for building and evangelizing. Find out in which direction the city is growing, residentially. If at all possible, secure property in that direction. The Chamber of Commerce, realtors, and developers can help you determine growth factors of a city.

The Building

The area of the most potential may not have a building or an ideal place to have your first meetings. You probably won't have the finances to purchase property or existing buildings. You may have to start in one location and move to a permanent location weeks or even years later.

An ideal place for the church's first meetings is in a church building not being used. A church now closed or one where the people have moved to a new location can be superb to rent or even to purchase. If the people who once worshiped there have been left without a church, they will often form a nucleus. Probably the now-defunct church had no vision or visitation program, and so a great harvest lies waiting to be reaped. If you really are going to go after people, if your vision is God-directed, people will come from all over the community to be in a church that is spiritually alive and well. The very first place you meet, then, is not absolutely crucial to ultimate success.

A school often has a good auditorium and can be transformed into a church. Many closed schools today can be rented or purchased.

A Seventh-Day Adventist church building, which is not used on Sunday, is a possibility. But some people might object to meeting there, and potential visitors might be put off. The new congregation should be consulted to see if meeting there is acceptable to other people in the community.

YMCAs, town or city halls, union halls, office buildings, community halls, clubs, lodges, funeral homes, motels, day schools, or any place that has an auditorium or large conference room has the potential for hosting church services. Check out every possibility. A store, place of business, or warehouse can lend itself to becoming a church. Hugh Pyle bought an airport in Panama City, turned the hanger into an auditorium, and eventually built the great Central Baptist Church there. Selling the excess property helped finance most of the buildings.

In today's mobile society, people will travel farther to go to a church where God is and where people are being saved, lives changed, and families reconciled. If God is there, love is evident, and the joy of the Lord is manifest, people will come. Do your best to find the ideal location and the best building, but above all else be sure the power of God is on your ministry. If this is so, you cannot fail.

Financing

God pays the bills. Ultimately, this is true. God is our Source and ever must be. This is essential to understand and to live by. Learn this before you finish school or seminary. Pity the person who does not have an invisible means of support.

Some new churches become self-supporting in a matter of weeks or a few months. Many men have gone to an area where there are ten to twenty families wanting a church, and all financial needs are met from the beginning. Unless one is in a small, economically depressed area, a pastor can work hard, visit like mad and, with the blessing of God on his ministry, have the work self-supporting in six months. If the potential of the area is limited, it may take a year or two to get established.

Plan on at least six months of financial help to get established. Several methods can be used. A church across town or elsewhere can be the mother church and finance you. Some pastors have saved enough money to carry them over for six months to a year. When a man knows where he is going to plant a church, he can do deputation work during his last year or two of school and raise support. Churches will support a pastor for six months, a year, or even longer as a mission project. Individuals will often pledge monthly support above their regular giving for a special project. Some pastors have raised several thousands of dollars to help them in their initial thrust. Wives have worked part time or full time out of necessity in the early days of a new church. Pastors themselves have worked part time until the church is established. Whatever you do, be sure you pray as you go.

How to Start

A mother church can help give birth to a new church in many ways. It can help with personnel, finances, materials, counsel, and most of all prayer. If you can find an established church to sponsor your efforts, you will have a ready and willing source to help your church get started.

A nucleus of people who want to start a church is a great advantage. Scores of people have contacted schools like Liberty Baptist Schools, Tennessee Temple University, and Hyles Anderson College asking, "Can you please send us a pastor to build a church like you have there?" You might want to contact a school or seminary of your own persuasion or denomination and ask for leads. Even one family can be a tremendous help. Many fellows, though, start out with no one but their own family.

Over the years many churches started with a Bible class. Some have come out of a series of evangelistic meetings in a tent or rented building. The most come about from the burning heart of a pastor who prays and visits as Paul did. You just can't beat his method. If it worked so mightily in such adverse conditions years ago, it surely will work today.

Preparation for the First Service

Now that the meeting place is settled and the Sunday of your first service is set, the key to people being there Sunday is visiting. If there is one task more important than any other, it is visitation. Sow sparingly and you will reap sparingly. With everything else ready, now give yourself to knocking on doors. Dr. Jerry Falwell started Thomas Road Baptist Church, now with seventeen thousand members, by making one hundred visits a day. That's right, one hundred a day. He started at 8:00 in the morning, grabbed a sandwich for lunch and another for supper, and went right on into the night knocking on doors. He got the names, addresses, and phone numbers of those who were unchurched and interested. On Saturday, he called all these people and reminded them of the services on the morrow. It worked well enough for him to have 890-plus in regular attendance one year later!

May I suggest what I would say upon that first contact?

"How do you do? I am Sumner Wemp. I'm the pastor of the Central Baptist Church on Twelfth and Yonge streets. I'm preaching for one reason. I want to help every person in Pensacola to know for sure they are going to heaven. Then I want to help those who are going to enjoy the trip. We want to build a church that is known for its love, where you can come to church and sense the joy of the Lord. Then we want to help build homes where fathers are spiritual leaders and children love and respect their parents. I was seventeen years old before anyone told me that God loved me and that Christ died for my sins and rose again. When I received the Lord Jesus as my personal Savior, God changed my whole life and I haven't gotten over it yet. I would like to give you and your family a special invitation to be with us next Sunday, if you are not already active in church."

Pause and most people will let you know if they are already active in a church or if they are at all interested in coming.

You should have tracts and a brochure to offer them. If the person at the door shows an interest, get the name and telephone number, and let him know how happy you are and that you will look forward to seeing him next Sunday. These names should be put on a prayer list that you pray for constantly all week.

If you describe your goals and plans for the church, you will create an interest in those people you visit. Pray like mad that they will come the first Sunday and be saved, if they aren't already. Or, after you have described what a Christian is in your presentation, graciously ask the person if he knows for sure he is going to heaven. If you are walking in the Spirit and sharing in the power of the Holy Spirit, you will find some people prepared to trust Christ and you can lead them to Him. You may only plant the seed of the gospel at this time and water it with your prayers all week, but look for the fruit at a later time when you feel more sure they are ready to receive Christ. Whatever you do, be sure you plant the gospel, the substitutional death of Christ for sins and His resurrection. Remember: ". . . the gospel . . . is the power of God unto salvation . . ." (Rom. 1:16).

If you spend too much time at each door, you won't contact many homes. For sure you don't want to get into a controversy with people who are argumentative. You are looking for prospects, not debaters.

Three things should have priority on Saturdays. First, prayer—bathe yourself and the prospects in it. Second, call all of the prospects and joyously remind them you will be looking forward to seeing them the next day. Third, visit people you feel are ready to be saved or who have asked that you come back to see them or the rest of the family.

A gospel team or group of students from a Christian college may be brought in to help with one of the earlier services. The group can visit door to door in your area on Saturday to announce your church service and the special music this group will perform. Music is an extremely important part of a church program. Many Christian schools and colleges will help by providing musicians and other workers as they are able. Teams from Liberty Baptist Schools have brought in up to one hundred new people in some churches on a given Sunday.

A clean meeting place, flowers, hymnals, offering plates, and a nursery are all essential. A nursery is a must if you are to reach young couples. They are your best prospects and represent the greatest potential for church growth. Young people still have enthusiasm and a spirit of adventure. You must provide for them.

When I began pastoring, the idea of starting a new church had not been introduced to me. But even established churches have needs. One church I pastored had no pianist for two Sundays in a row. During the week, I agonized over this situation and prayed for God to send one. When I was visiting, I met a couple who had just moved into the neighborhood. They had been reared in the Salvation Army but had left it years before; both husband and wife had music running out their ears. They came to our church. He became our music director and she the pianist. Our music was superb. "Pray in" your needs whether they be financial, physical, or manpower needs. God is able.

The First Sunday

The first service of a new church can be discouraging, if you allow it to be. Sometimes no one shows up. Or, maybe only two to ten visitors arrive. Or, God could send several dozen new people. Whatever happens, have a positive attitude. Pray for the power of God on your ministry and your message. Share the joy of the Lord and the love of God. Whatever you do, don't criticize or condemn anyone else or other churches. Preach Christ. Love the people. Pour your heart out.

Do it right. If you have no live special music and no piano, use a cassette of the music to sing by and of special music as well. Limit the singing if the music isn't the greatest and the crowd is small. Sing the easiest and most familiar songs. Don't waste words and time on why folks aren't there, and above all don't be negative and apologetic. Get into the message, and let those gathered get a taste of God's Word. If folks are saved in that very first service, you will be off and running. Use visitors cards to get the names and addresses of all who visit.

Sunday School

Depending on how many you have, you should, of course, have an adult Sunday school class. A pastor's class has proved to be very effective in scores of the fastest-growing churches across America. Such a class provides an excellent platform for the pastor to share his vision, goals, purposes, and philosophies about the church and the kind of ministry he intends to build. The next priority is a youth group for both junior and senior high school students. Then, a children's class for elementary school pupils should be established, and the nursery as already mentioned. Attendance and personnel, of course, will determine exactly what you can handle. To begin with, you may only have one class, the pastor's class, and a nursery attended by your wife. Learn to be flexible and innovative.

Publicity and Promotion

Put an ad in the newspaper. This will give visibility to you and your church. Place announcements in the church section of the paper where free space is sometimes available. Try to get your church service announced on a local TV or radio program. Have flyers printed announcing your church services and put them in windows of businesses, stores, service stations, on community bulletin boards, and any place else you can find. Of course, your regular church brochure should be first quality and given out generously wherever you go.

Organizing

The constitution, charter, and organizational structure of the church can be drawn up while you are still studying for the pastorate.

Be ready to explain and modify your plans with the new congregation. You must have legal counsel to be sure that all documents are in compliance with laws in your city and state. Records must be kept carefully. A financial secretary and treasurer is essential from the start. *Finances should not be cared for by the pastor.*

The number of families needed before formally organizing the church can vary, according to how many adults, particularly men, are in regular attendance. You build a church by reaching men. Never forget that. You reach the man and you will get the whole family, whereas very often if you get the wife you won't get the husband. Thirty men could organize a church. You don't want to organize too soon, without solid family support, nor do you want to wait too many months lest people lose confidence in your leadership. Get advice from the men who are coming.

Be sure to consult pastors of established churches. They can give you good counsel and direction. Many pastors have seen others start churches in their communities and fail because of careless or foolish steps taken in the early days.

Set a date to organize and legally charter the church. Ask a well-thought-of preacher, evangelist, or professor to come for the chartering service. You will need outside help on this day.

The church constitution should be circulated and explained to the people who are committed to being a part of the new church. The doctrinal statement must be complete and specific. People must know your doctrinal position. All legal transactions should be worked out before the day of organization. Incorporation papers, trustees, and bank accounts should be handled carefully from the day the church begins.

There is no one set way to conduct the chartering services. You may want to have a brief regular service of singing, prayer, offering, and special music. The main ingredients would be to have the articles of faith, the constitution, and the church covenant circulated and available for all who are considering becoming members of the church. State the purpose of the service and have someone read the covenant. This document should state the ministry and goals of the church.

Next, the visiting pastor or professor, acting as moderator, should ask for a motion from the floor to organize the church officially under the constitution and articles of faith as presented. After someone seconds the motion, discussion is called for. Finally, a vote is taken. When the motion is passed, the moderator can state, "I now declare the Central Baptist Church of Pensacola, Florida, officially organized under the constitution and articles of faith as presented." It is then in order to have the church officially call the pastor.

Trustees and a treasurer should be elected and any other offices or staff called to serve. Special music may be appropriate next, followed by a sermon of special challenge to the church.

The invitation should be given for any to receive Christ as Savior and for all those who want to become charter members. A beautifully printed document with space for charter members' signatures should have been prepared for the charter members to sign while at the front of the auditorium. This will be a high moment, filled with much rejoicing.

Invite all the charter members who care to, to kneel at the front for a prayer of dedication. After everyone has returned to his seat, the pastor comes forward and says what is on his heart. A brief challenge from him, expressing his love for the people and his burden to build a great church and reach multitudes for Christ can bring the service to a beautiful conclusion. Usually the charter is declared to be left open for thirty days to give time for some who were away that Sunday and for others who are still considering charter membership.

Now the work of teaching and training the people to do the work of the ministry really begins. That work must encompass all of Matthew 28:19,20. It includes evangelization, edification, exhortation, and education of people to obey and glorify the Lord God of glory. The church is an instrument with many strings, and for a harmonious melody to be heard, all strings must be played.

7

Pastoral Care and Leadership

Good leadership, whether in business, politics, or churches, is lacking in America. There is great need for good leadership. A common characteristic of the pastors of large, growing churches is their ability to lead well. Certain qualities are common in all leaders. Let us examine these carefully.

Vision

"The difference between mediocrity and greatness is vision," Dr. Jerry Falwell is often heard to say. A leader has to know where he is going. Without a goal, purpose, or vision (these words may be used interchangeably), a person is not properly motivated and people will not be challenged to follow. Leaders, whether motivated for good or bad, know what they want and are determined to head in that direction at all costs. The Hitlers and the Castros have a following because they possess a vision or goal. The church needs God's men with God's vision for the world.

What do you envision your ministry to be? What are some concrete goals and purposes of your ministry? Too many men enter the ministry simply "to pastor." They have no personal goals and no unique concepts of ministry. They are just going to pastor. Pastors come a dime a dozen. There are three hundred thousand in the United States. Why do we need any more? Why should any church want you above any one of the other three hundred thousand pastors? Don't let your church develop without direction. Decide what kind of church you want to have, and lead it in that direction. Most churches have about as much direction as a chip of wood on the raging ocean.

Enlarge your vision. Cry out for the whole city. Too many pastors set their sights too low. The whole city needs Jesus. You will never help too many Christians. You will never build too large a church. Big is not bad. Don't be threatened by the thought of a big ministry. There is nothing wrong with small churches *if* they are reaching their maximum potential.

In school ministry we often say there is nothing wrong with making C's if that's your full potential, but it is a gross sin if you can make B's or A's. One can't help but feel that most of us are far from realizing our potential. The ultimate reason is lack of vision. Estimates reveal that the first church in Jerusalem had over one hundred thousand members.

The church should be the conscience of the city. It was at one time. Abraham spoke up to Abimilech. Daniel had to be reckoned with by Nebuchadnezzar. John the Baptist had something to say about how Herod lived. The Jewish leaders of Peter's day heard about his boldness in preaching the gospel. Today, no one even considers divorce, drinking, dancing, and the death penalty as concerns of the church. We've lost our ministry of conviction to the world. Determine what the godly atmosphere of your church will be, and its people, in turn, will affect the social and moral conditions of the city. If the salt has lost its savor, it is worthless.

Church ought to be a joy to attend. Joy characterized early Christianity. They had "gladness" (Acts 2:46), "great joy" (Acts 8:8), and they "praised God" (Acts 2:47, 16:25). Where is the joy of the Lord? One goal of pastors should be to make people *want* to come to church.

Sunday ought to be the highlight of the week. The most exciting place ought not to be the football game where touchdowns are made, but the house of God where Christians are made. Don't just conduct routine church services week after week. To allow the service or sermon to be boring is sin. Do you have a vision of your church service filled with the best music, warmest fellowship, most edifying preaching, and most Christlike people in town?

Reaching whole families should be the aim of the church. What a thrill to see families reconciled. Build a family-centered church. Do you have a vision for this? Create such an atmosphere.

Good leadership demands that you have some vision of what your church is going to be like. Without a concrete vision and specific goals, your church will be just like others.

Positive Attitude

Attitude determines action. Wrong attitudes bring wrong results. Words and works begin in the mind. Your attitude makes or breaks your ministry.

Positive attitudes are characteristic of leaders. People who fail are the ones who always see the thorns. They always know why some idea won't work or why you can't do what you envision. If Romans 8:28 is true, and for sure it is, then see the good side and have a positive attitude about everything.

A negative attitude is like a short that drains power from a battery. When you've been around a person with a negative attitude, you feel the strain and drain. Being around a positive, happy person makes you feel energetic and uplifted.

Pastors must have a positive attitude if they intend to uplift their people. Being positive really boils down to faith. Faith says, "I can do all things through Christ which strengtheneth me" (Phil. 4:13). Live as if you believe that. A positive attitude will cause one to say every morning, "This is the day which the LORD hath made; we will rejoice and be glad in it" (Ps. 118:24). Work at it. Develop a positive attitude based on faith in the great promises of God.

What's your attitude toward God? A modernist preacher said, "God is a dirty bully." An unsaved lady screeched, "Why did God take my baby!" Her baby had just been killed in an automobile accident. Multitudes of Christians feel they have been cheated by God. Many are scared of God, and not with a holy fear.

Yet, God is good. Nail it down! Seal it in your heart till you can say from the depths of your soul, "God is so good." Don't preach as if you and God are mad at the whole world. Hasn't God been good to you? Preach like it, live like it, and you will be a great leader.

"For the eyes of the LORD run to and fro throughout the whole earth, to show himself strong in the behalf of them whose heart is perfect toward him" (2 Chr. 16:9). God is looking for people to whom He can demonstrate His strength and greatness. He's looking for you.

Don't hide. Don't hold back. Make up your mind to be that one God can use mightily. What's your attitude? Do you think God plays favorites, or do you believe you can see the strong arm of God as well as the next one? Get the right attitude.

"Call unto me, and I'll answer thee, and show thee great and mighty things, which thou knowest not" (Jer. 33:3). What a promise! Do you want in on it? What's your attitude toward this promise? Will you see great and mighty things in your ministry, or is your attitude "Well, that's not for everyone"? Oh, dear preacher, what's your attitude toward this great God? ". . . ye have not, because ye ask not" (James 4:3). Is that you?

"O Jerusalem, Jerusalem, . . . how often would I have gathered thy children together...and ye would not!" (Matt. 23:37). The tragedy in life is not what men suffer but what they miss. Think what Israel has missed. Not just once, not just twice, but *often* God would have gathered Israel together and they wouldn't let Him. Will God say of you one day, "How often I would have . . ." but you wouldn't let Him? Have the right attitude. Believe God when He says He is anxious to use you and do for you. Your attitude toward these and hundreds of other glorious scriptural promises will determine what kind of leader you will be.

What's your attitude toward yourself? Self-pity, false humility, and self-condemnation will all lead to defeat. What is your worth? Don't put yourself down. It shows. Self-condemnation is the opposite of confidence, which people must see in you before they will follow you.

"But God hath chosen the foolish things of the world to confound the wise; and God hath chosen the weak things of the world to confound the things which are mighty" (1 Cor. 1:27). My inferiority clobbered me until I got hold of this verse. Isn't it great? God delights to use the foolish and weak things. Can you raise your hand with me and say, "I qualify"? When this verse broke home to my heart, I began to realize that God wants to use *me*. What a promise! What a fantastic thought that I qualify to confound the wise and the mighty. Don't despise yourself. Rejoice that God is going to use you.

". . . This day will I begin to magnify thee . . ." (Josh. 3:7). If you walk with God and begin to minister to others for God, you will see how God will minister to you if you give all the glory to God. Don't try to promote yourself. Let Him do it. Don't try to impress anyone. "Humble yourselves therefore under the mighty hand of God, that he may exalt you in due time" (1 Pet. 5:6). Get the right attitude toward yourself, and God will be able to use you. ". . . for as he thinketh in his heart so is he . . ." (Prov. 23:7).

What's your attitude toward others? When you see people, do you see purple? Some preachers preach like they are mad at people. You must have the right attitude toward people.

Love your people. Yes, I said this at the very outset of this book, but it bears repeating. Love is the key to your whole ministry. People are starved for love. They have been browbeaten most of their lives. They get enough guff at work. What a transformation when they begin to find out God loves them. My, how they are drawn to a preacher who loves them!

"Rejoice with them that do rejoice . . ." (Rom. 12:15). Jealousy will kill you. It is worse than cancer. Learn to rejoice when someone else is blessed or is prospered by God. It's such a healthy attitude and wonderful feeling. God is honored, and He then can bless you, too.

" . . . weep with them that weep" (Rom. 12:15). People are hurting. ". . . no man cared for my soul" (Ps. 142:4) is not only the cry of the world but of multitudes of Christians as well. Learn to respond to people's needs. This is the mark of a great leader.

A leader looks at what people can be not just what they are. See the potential in every member of your church. God has started out with some awfully rough diamonds and made them quite brilliant. Look at each person as a diamond in the rough. Great leaders bring out the best in people.

Authority and Decision-making

Leaders must speak with authority. Effective spiritual leaders are not arrogant, but they carry an anointed authority that is heard in their message and seen in their manner. They are not demanding dictators but loving leaders. The trumpet needs a clear and sure sound. People have been hurt so much and disappointed so often with pastors and leaders that they need someone who says, "Thus saith the

Lord," as the Lord Jesus did, with love and compassion. Jesus had great compassion for the fallen and the weak, but He thundered out against the arrogant and pharisaical leaders. Pastors need to see people as Jesus did—scattered abroad as sheep not having a shepherd—and be moved to compassion. Having compassion, they will earn the respect and following of the people. Respect and confidence are earned, not demanded.

Great leaders have a common denominator: They are able to make fast, firm decisions. Studies have shown a close relationship between success and making decisions promptly. Failure is common to those who have a habit of making decisions slowly, if at all, and of changing their decisions easily. It is much better to make a decision, even if it's wrong, than to linger in indecision. You can cope with wrong decisions, but indecision will paralyze you.

Procrastination, the opposite of decision, is a common enemy that every person must conquer. Begin now. Get up when the alarm goes off. Make quick decisions about what to order in a restaurant. Train yourself by starting to make fast decisions in those hundreds of little situations you face every day. It will prepare you for the larger ones later. "How long halt ye between two opinions?" asked Elijah (1 Kin. 18:21). Good question. Make decisions and, like Daniel who purposed in his heart not to defile himself with the king's meat (see Dan. 1:8), stick by your decisions.

Time and Associations

Time is precious. You can't kill time without injuring eternity. Don't waste it. You must spend it. Spend it wisely. You would hate to be robbed of hundreds of dollars. Time is money in a hundred ways. Television and a thousand other things rob you daily. "Awake thou that sleepest. . . . Redeeming the time, because the days are evil" (Eph. 5:14,16). Keep a record and get the shock of your life at how much time you waste. Great leaders are jealous of their time.

Organize your time. There is a time for everything (see Eccl. 3:1ff.). Leaders know that. They set priorities. They plan their days and hours and minutes. Don't ever say "I just don't have time" to study or pray or visit. You do have time, but you probably don't organize your time

67

and plan the most important projects into your schedule. You have time to do what you really want to do, and you usually *do* what you really want to do.

"He that walketh with wise men shall be wise: but a companion of fools shall be destroyed" (Prov. 13:20). Everyone is influenced. Leaders learn to be influenced by successful people. They choose their associates carefully. Find those who stimulate and challenge you to higher levels and better purposes. Shun as you would a snake those with negative attitudes. Those who murmur and complain and gripe at everything and every person spew out enough poison to kill every high and holy desire you will ever have. Avoid them. Be choosy. Leaders are.

Health and Diligence

"The soul of the sluggard desireth, and hath nothing . . ." (Prov. 13:4). Successful leaders are alert and active. Shape up. Keep in shape. A great and terrible sin of pastors is their tendency to get fat and sluggish. ". . . put a knife to thy throat, if thou be a man given to appetite" (Prov. 23:2). Good health is so vital to vim and vitality. Take care of yourself. Cut out all that junk food. Sugar, sweets, cokes, and coffee can wreck you. Wise up. Take care of your body. It's the temple of the Holy Spirit.

Do more than is required. Leaders always do. Successful businessmen put in twelve to sixteen hours a day. Why not God's servants? ". . . always abounding in the work of the Lord . . ." (1 Cor. 15:58). Clock watchers and work shirkers just don't make it to the top.

Courage

"Be strong and of a good courage . . ." (Josh. 1:6) is repeated over ten times in Scripture. Not to be crude, but in plain English, the day requires pastors with guts. Pastors need courage to take a stand against the wiles of the devil and the ways of the world, not in a mean, contentious way but in a firm, loving way. Leaders of the world demonstrate courage. There would be no Congressional Medal of Honor without courage, and there will be no medals of honor in heaven without it.

Tact and Self-Control

Leaders are not bulls in a china shop. They don't rush in where angels fear to tread. They don't walk all over people. People have feelings. "A brother offended is harder to be won than a strong city . . ." (Prov. 18:19). Leaders don't purposely offend people. If the gospel is an offense, praise God, but if you are offensive, that's sin.

As a pastor, you do not have the option of blowing your stack or losing your cool. You can't indulge yourself. "He that hath no rule over his own spirit is like a city that is broken down, and without walls" (Prov. 25:28). Our country has been shaken by leaders who blew it, all because they had no self-control.

If you are going to lead babes out of the woods, if you are going to lead your people out of the wilderness into the promised land of victorious, joyous living, you must use tact and not break their spirits. ". . . a broken spirit drieth the bones" (Prov. 17:22). The tactless, thoughtless preaching of some pastors will make you shudder and ashamed of your profession. Great leaders are not like that.

Personality and Appearance

Have you ever seen an airline stewardess who didn't have a good personality? Rare indeed is a stewardess who isn't friendly. Leaders are like that. Look at politicians shaking hands and smiling with strangers by the thousands. You say, "I'm not built that way." A stewardess instructor said neither are ninety percent of the women who attend stewardess schools. They learn to be that way. They change their personalities. You can. You must.

Don't scold. Charles Schwab says this is an absolute no-no. Never scold your people. Great leaders learn that people just don't respond positively to scoldings. You don't lead people to your way with scolding, you drive them away.

"A word fitly spoken is like apples of gold in pictures of silver"
69

(Prov. 25:11). People are starved for kindness and appreciation. A leader must be lavish in his genuine and sincere praise. ". . . a word spoken in due season, how good is it!" (Prov. 15:23). "Heaviness in the heart of man maketh it stoop: but a good word maketh it glad" (Prov. 12:25). If you want to be a good leader, listen to the wisdom of these proverbs.

Appearance is important. It often tells a lot. A sloppy appearance is often indicative of a sloppy attitude about everything. Look at the successful leaders. They dress sharp and look sharp.

Self-Motivation

Motion creates emotion. This is an old proverb that contains a ton of truth. A self-starter motivates himself through motion. There is a fabulous scriptural example of this. In Haggai 1:12 we read, "Zerubbabel . . . obeyed the voice of the LORD . . ." and then we read of the emotion that followed his obedience in verse 14: "The LORD stirred up the spirit of Zerubbabel. . . ." And then he and his colaborers worked in the house of the Lord. That's it. Obey God by reading the Word or witnessing or praying, and you will find He will then stir up your heart. Leaders don't sit around waiting for an urge to do something. They get moving and emotion follows. If you want to be a leader, you must be a self-starter.

Be a leader. Know where you are going. Love your people and long for them to have heaven's best in their lives and homes. When they know you love them, and they see the joy of God in your life, they will do anything you ask them to do.

2/PASTORING

Pastoring is shepherding, and the friendship of a pastor with his congregation is the sweetest of relationships. We Christians are like sheep, and we will go astray without a shepherd. Oh, how we need pastors. Pastoring is rewarding, fulfilling, and demanding. The pastor pours himself out for the people, and he pours his life into the people. Pastoring is filled with new adventures and excitement daily. Meeting the needs of the sheep is exhilarating. The many facets of the ministry are discussed in this section.

8

Visitation

Pastoral visitation is exciting. It is high adventure. So many thrilling events occur that one can hardly wait to see what God is going to do next.

In one home a couple receives Christ, in another a deep problem is shared, in still another a pastor can help bear a burden and see God bring comfort to a broken heart. It may mean being in a home almost torn asunder by family strife, and you stand helpless as a husband and wife turn deaf ears to what God has to say.

Each visit adds muscle and sinew to the pastor, and he feels something of the thrill and the agony that Christ felt as He ministered to all types of people. Regular visitation will surely keep a pastor crying out to God for His power and wisdom. Seeing God work miracle after miracle gives real purpose and meaning to His work.

Not many sounds in life exceed in interest a knock on the door. When a pastor comes to the home of an individual, he will never honor a person more than he does at that moment. Visitation is the missing link between the pulpit and the people. No doubt it is the weakest link in the church today. No pastor can run a church from behind a desk; if he tries, he will run it into a grave. The church of Jesus Christ is made up of people, not of pillars, pews, and stained-glass windows. When the pastor loses sight of the individual, the church becomes a lifeless institution. Personal, perennial visitation is essential to a vibrant, virile church ministry. Your biggest responsibility to your people is to "watch for their souls, as they that must give account" (Heb. 13:17), and it can't be done from the pulpit on Sunday alone.

Most pastors freely admit that their churches could use a good shot in the arm. Have you ever noticed the excitement that comes to a church when they see the strange faces of new visitors? Just the expectancy that these might become new members will brighten the faces of both pastor and people. How are churches going to get visitors to come? The answer is as obvious as it is simple: Visit them first.

The philosophy and practice of most pastors today is to visit those who are members of the church, the sick, and the shut-ins. Why can't the need to visit those who have never darkened the church door be seen? Rather than swapping members or stealing sheep, why not reach the untouched millions who never go to anyone's church? Don't expect a person to visit your church until you have visited him first. Why should he? If church members aren't personally interested enough to go out of their way to invite new people, they don't deserve to see them coming to their church.

Why Visit?

Pastoral visitation is scriptural. Heeding the urgent admonition to "Go out into the highways and hedges, and compel them to come in, that my house may be filled" (Luke 14:23) would certainly cure the emptiness of many churches today. God is never satisfied with an empty or half-filled church. He commands us to go out and compel others to come in. The servant must say with his Master, ". . . wist ye not that I must be about my Father's business?" (Luke 2:49). Family, fun, or fleshly desires should not keep the pastor from this great business. The urgency of the task and the enormity of the consequences of failure demand the cry, "I must work the works of him that sent me, while it is day: the night cometh, when no man can work" (John 9:4).

For a church to have 20/20 spiritual vision, the pastor must have the Acts 20:20 vision of Paul, who said, "I kept back nothing that was profitable unto you, but have showed you, and have taught you publicly, and from house to house." Going out to the highways and visiting in the homes is as essential today as it was two thousand years ago. Perhaps what happened to the prophets of old is being repeated today and the warning of Jeremiah 23:2 is needed: "Ye have scattered my flock, and driven them away, and have not visited them: behold, I will visit upon you the evil of your doings, saith the LORD."

Pastoral visitation is sensible. "A homegoing pastor produces a churchgoing people." This is more than a cliché. It is a proven fact. If the pastor does not carry out his responsibility to visit people in their homes, he can't expect people to go to church. Churches that have visitors on Sunday have visitation during the week. People come when we go.

Most people have never had a pastor visit in their homes. The first time I heard it I was surprised, but after hearing scores say, "You are the first pastor to ever visit in our home," I am shocked and grieved. The need is not for people to come to church as much as for pastors to go to them.

Most people want and need a visit from their pastor. Wouldn't you love to have the Lord Jesus visit in your home just as He visited Mary, Martha, and Lazarus? Pastors are not the Lord, but they should realize they are looked up to and revered by most people as God's representatives. Their visits mean almost the same to people today as Jesus' visits meant to the people of His day.

A pastor who visits emphasizes by that act the importance of the individual. In a day when many feel lost in the masses of an impersonal world, the personal touch of a pastor's visit can be invaluable. The Lord Jesus often singled out and spent time with the individual: Recall Nicodemus, the woman at the well, and Zacchaeus. This interest in individuals is certainly a tie that binds people to the house of God.

About a month after I was converted as a seventeen-year-old boy, I was sick one Sunday. My Sunday school teacher, Jake Lyons, a sharp businessman who really loved young people, came by my house to see me on his way home from church. I was overwhelmed to think he actually thought enough of me to go out of his way to let me know he missed me in Sunday school. You couldn't have bribed me to miss church after that.

Visitation magnifies the home. The church and the family are the two greatest institutions in the world. Both need strengthening today. They are mutually dependent. A pastor's visit has a sanctifying effect on a home and surely brings the church and the home closer together. A pastor will often hear people comment, "We are honored to have you in our home." Often one visit in the home of new Christians or newlyweds can have long-lasting results, as a family altar is explained and becomes an established habit. What opportunities there are for ministry! No pastor will want to miss out.

Children can be greatly affected by a pastor's visit. Every pastor wants the love and confidence of the children in his church. To keep the generation gap closed, contact with children in the home is a must. The pastor needs to visit children in their homes, especially if the children in his church have their own church service and are not seen by him in Sunday school either. Meeting them on an informal basis and showing real love and interest in them at home can endear the pastor to children. Small children are especially impressed by a pastor's interest in them. By all means, a pastor should be vitally aware of and interested in children during his home visits.

Often as a pastor, through one visit in their home, I have won the confidence and affection of small children to the extent that they would come to me and give me a hug every Sunday. On a number of occasions a mother has told how her small child talked for weeks about the pastor picking him up and hugging him when I visited in their home. It pays off dividends for years to come, even through the child's high school years.

There are not many better ways to get to know your people than by visiting them. Lack of communication and not knowing one another can easily lead to misunderstandings. So much can be learned about a person or a family by visiting in their home. Often one discovers particular hobbies, interests, talents, needs, and problems as he visits. Many people have abilities that are not utilized in the church because no one knows about them. People often feel pushy or boastful if they make their talents known. A wise pastor will be observant and attentive to what he learns about people while in their home. He may want to keep a record of people's talents for future reference.

One pastor visited a man who had a complete home woodworking shop. The man was thrilled and honored when the pastor asked him if he would make pulpit stands for the Sunday school classrooms of the church. After the man made this personal contribution, he and his family became very active in church, whereas before their attendance had been irregular.

Sin can be seen for what it is and what it does during many a pastoral visit. Most pastors are sheltered from seeing sin in the raw. At church and other functions, conversations and behavior often change drastically because of a pastor's presence. A visit in the home, non-

76

Christian homes especially, often tells the real story and reveals a family's heartaches. For instance, when a pastor walks in on a family with a drunken husband, wife, or teen-ager sprawled out on a couch, he will be face to face with the shocking but real consequences of sin.

Once one of our members and I visited a woman who said she could not become a Christian because her husband made her go to bed with different men each week in return for a pint of whiskey. In another home a teen-age girl blurted out how her father had forced her to have sexual relations with him. When making what I thought was a sick call, one woman raised herself up from her bed and said, "Brother Wemp, pray for me. I'm drunk as hell." These situations, and hundreds of others as bad or worse, let a pastor know the reality and prevalence of sin and take him out of his protected and sheltered environment.

Such experiences will fire up a pastor's heart to preach. Probably the best, most convicting preaching I have ever heard came from a pastor whose youth director had been found to be involved in immorality. Though the pastor normally was not a forceful preacher, he became one overnight when this tragedy was fresh in his heart. There seems to be a close correlation between a pastor's awareness of the destructiveness of sin and his burden and fire in the pulpit.

The pastor who visits in homes regularly will preach more relevant sermons. People often complain that their pastor's messages never meet their needs or speak to "where they live." This is easy to understand if a pastor doesn't *know* how his people live. It is amazing how many pastors can name teachers in seminary who are quite bookish and dry but do not realize that they will become the same way unless they are in touch with their people. It is one thing to preach about communism in Russia and quite another to preach about the problems of the homes of your church.

People's personal spiritual questions and doubts often come to light during the privacy of a pastoral home visit. While I was visiting a couple who had attended our church the previous Sunday, the husband, a policeman, asked, "What does God have to say if I have to kill a man in the line of duty? Doesn't God say, 'Thou shalt not kill'?" This question had haunted him for years. No pastor had ever visited in his home, and he had never felt bold enough to seek out a preacher and ask him what was on his heart. What relief came to him when he heard he was the minister of God in the civil realm as I was in the spiritual realm. He found his answer from the Word of God in Romans, as I read it aloud.

Often one can see far greater results from one visit than from ten sermons. While visiting in a Christian home when I had been the family's pastor only two weeks, it came out that they didn't have a family altar. In fact, the man had never prayed out loud before. They didn't attend church at night, using their young daughter as the excuse, and neither did they tithe. As I drove back to the husband's place of business with him, I lovingly challenged him to begin all three and spoke of the joys and advantages of each.

Before we parted, I said, "Let's pray together about it." I asked him if he would pray aloud himself, if only to say, "Thank you, Lord, for saving me, and bless our home." He prayed rather haltingly but sweetly, and heaven flooded in. That evening after dinner he went to the living room, got out his Bible, called in his wife and child and announced that they were going to have devotions. He read a passage, and then they all knelt and prayed. They wept with joy at the blessings of God. The man grew spiritually by leaps and bounds from that day forward. The whole church was electrified by his transformation, all the result of one visit.

The best church advertisement in the world is a pastor who makes home visits. Neighbors will know of you and your church because of this effort. Unsaved and unchurched people will be aware of your concern, and when they do decide on a church, this knowledge can often be the cause of their going to yours. This has happened in our church over and over.

When a pastor stands in the pulpit and sees new people in the congregation whom he visited that week, he is greatly encouraged.

If he has led them to Christ and knows they are ready to confess Christ publicly at the close of the service, this knowledge certainly adds strength to his preaching. Knowing there will be a public confession of faith by at least one person encourages him to give an invitation at the close of the service.

That person publicly confessing Christ often encourages someone else on the verge of a decision for Christ to react positively also. One day my daughter, who had become cold spiritually, came forward, confessing sin to the Lord and rededicating her life to Christ. She said she held back until she saw another girl who had the nerve to come forward for Christ. It made me more determined than ever to give an invitation at all services.

You set the example. Sheep follow the shepherd. People will follow a leader. Paul said, "Be ye followers of me, even as I also am of Christ" (1 Cor. 11:1). It is hard to convince a church of the importance of visitation on Thursday night if the pastor hasn't done any visiting during the week. Our actions speak louder than words.

A growing church in Dothan, Alabama, called me to be their pastor, and I accepted. We didn't move right away because we had a two-week-old baby, but I drove up on weekends to preach.

A friend from Dothan called on a Friday night to tell me one of the men in the congregation was going to the hospital in Atlanta at 5:00 A.M. Saturday for X-ray treatment for cancer. He wanted me to pray for the man and his family. I calculated quickly and figured that, by driving all night, I could just make it before he left for the hospital. My friend begged me not to try it. He just wanted me to pray for them, where I was. "Don't you let him leave before I get there," I told him and hung up.

I bundled up my two-year-old son and dashed off. All night I drove, opening windows, doing everything I could to stay awake. At 4:45 A.M. I pulled into the driveway, went into the house, and had prayer. The man and his wife wept. A million dollars could not have meant more to this dear Christian family. It was the talk of the town that a pastor cared enough to drive all night just to pray with one family. What a ministry this was. It may have been the most important thing I could ever have done there. We had no trouble getting people to do visitation. They had seen and heard first-hand what it meant to people.

Visitation is the greatest single difference I know between success and failure. It will transform a preacher and people quicker than any other activity of the church. It pays the greatest dividends in the lives of people. Pastors must visit.

How Does One Visit?

Visitation is hard work. It is no mystery why pastors don't visit. To go into a home and hear all the gripes and gossip will wreck any preacher. One must know how to visit, or he will fail very quickly.

Visit with a purpose. This is the key. Unless you visit with a definite purpose and goal, the visit will quickly deteriorate into a useless waste of time. The pastor need not be abrupt, but he must take command of the conversation. Much more will be accomplished if this is done.

When a pastor visits with a purpose he conserves time. If the purpose is to win a husband or couple to Christ, he will gear everything toward that end. If the visit is a sick call, he can listen and give comfort or lovingly call for repentance as the situation demands. The pastor must not make calls to soothe his conscience or to give a good report to the church.

Learn to direct the conversation to the glory of God. This way you keep from talking about the weather and politics. The best defense is an offense. To keep from getting boxed into a corner, especially by an unsaved person asking needless questions (avoid foolish questions; see 2 Tim. 2:23), you must direct the conversation. Ask the questions. Bring up the subjects to be discussed. A wise counselor knows how to lead the conversation where he wants it.

When in the home of a non-Christian, especially, the pastor must remember that what he has to say is of infinite value. He must not allow trivialities to overtake the opportunity to share Christ. Directing the conversation skillfully and courteously avoids many problems and makes visitation more pleasant and profitable. Christ is honored; needs are met.

Don't wait. You may think you need a month to get settled into your new pastorate before visiting. That's selfish thinking. Visit on your first day. People will be impressed that you put them first.

Visit with intensity when you first go to a church. Doing so sets the pattern and pace for all your ministry. The people catch on to the importance of visitation. Souls saved right at the beginning will bring greater joy and credibility to your ministry than anything else.

During the first week as pastor in one church, my wife and I visited all the deacons and church officers each evening in their homes. On

Sunday, church was like a beehive. One would say to another, "Guess who came to my house Monday night? The pastor!" Another would pipe up, "He was at my house Tuesday!" Another spoke up, "He came to see us Monday, too." Soon it was obvious they had all been visited.

The impression this made could not have been bought with money. Not only that, we got to know each one in a personal way that could have taken months if we had settled for seeing them only on Sundays. It became obvious to them that their pastor kept busy. I was never once accused of doing nothing, and, most importantly, it proved that I was really interested in them.

Take your wife along on visits. At the beginning of one's ministry, taking your wife along has special advantages. She quickly becomes known as a vital part of the ministry. She also gets to know the people and can sense the pulse of the church rapidly. Her presence with you indicates your view of the importance of women in the church. Most leaders in the church will be a bit taken aback to see the pastor's wife with him, but the value of their meeting his wife and seeing his respect for her is invaluable. Also, her presence is especially helpful when no one but the wife is at home when you visit.

Don't play favorites. This will kill a ministry. I once followed a pastor who had had his favorites, which became obvious at a meeting when a man said, "Well, we *all* have a pastor now." A pastor must reserve deep fellowship or personal closeness for his family and fellow pastors, not for favorites among the congregation.

When your wife cannot go visiting with you, take a deacon instead. He can share the blessings of these visits with you. Also, this way deacons become trained in visitation and soul-winning. And this practice lets deacons know what their pastor is doing with his time and keeps down criticism.

Let the people of the church know you are available. Train the congregation to call you when they need you, just as they would call a doctor when ill. If trained properly, people won't be able to gripe about a pastor not "discovering" they were ill and not visiting them. From the very beginning a pastor must convey this during announcements and through the bulletin. It is amazing how many will respect this privilege and call only when you are really needed.

Be observant when entering a home. Noticing books authored by some of my seminary professors in one home, I discovered we had a mutual friend. Instantly, rapport was established and the family came to our church the very next Sunday. In one home I saw a bow-and-arrow rack on the wall. Knowing nothing about archery, I inquired. This man hunted deer with them, and he talked enthusiastically about his hunting. I showed genuine interest. He then showed genuine interest when I gave him the gospel. He received Christ. This same story has been repeated hundreds of times in my ministry.

Remember names. No name is as sweet as one's own. We all know this. Write down the names of family members after leaving the home. Use a person's name over and over while talking to him. Connect it with the face. Associate it with something that will bring it to your remembrance.

A couple visited our church, and I associated their name with the lady's smile. They moved away that very week. A year later they returned, and I called them by name. They were deeply impressed and spoke of it over and over. They became faithful members. To this day they have never forgotten that their name was remembered. They would not have come to our church regularly had this not happened, for the parents of both were in a church across town where they had planned to go. They were a great asset to us.

Keep records of your visits. For years I carried a small notebook solely for the purpose of keeping track of my visits. This is an excellent way to check up on how little you actually visit and it will spur you on. The record also can be used to let people know how much you actually visit. Here is how I kept the record.

DATE	PERSON	RESULTS
11/2	Mort and Susan	S.
11/2	Hugh Van Hooser baby	H.
11/2	Joe Gashaw	W.P.

The initials under results were S for "sick," H for "hospital," W for "witnessed a little." I used a W if I gave the whole gospel and a P when a profession of faith in Christ was made. N.H. was for "not home."

On a separate page in the notebook I wrote down the names of each person in a family if I did not know them beforehand. At the close of the day I reviewed their names and fixed them in my mind so I could call each person by name when the family visited our church the next Sunday. This practice proved to be most impressive and helpful in winning them to Christ. Also on this page I noted pertinent information about each person. This was a valuable resource and proved useful many times.

Always share a blessing or a victory when visiting Christians. Doing this turns your visit into a pleasant memory for the believer. It also trains people to share blessings, and, of course, people are encouraged when they hear what God is doing. One day I led a man to Christ, and when I told of this in the next home I visited, a little revival broke out. The story of the conversion had a profound effect on this family and caused them to rededicate their lives to Christ and become active for the Lord. This sort of chain reaction has happened over and over. Sharing blessings keeps the conversation positive and spiritually edifying as well.

Share a specific goal of the church ministry or news of an upcoming special occasion for Christians to pray about. Sharing your vision and burden every time you can helps people understand your philosophies and vision. After a while, they catch on to what it's all about. If they hear it in person as well as from the pulpit, they are impressed. You should challenge them to pray for the fulfillment of certain goals in the church's ministry. Most people don't know where a preacher is headed and what he wants to accomplish in his ministry.

Always have prayer. This seems obvious, but it still shocks me to hear people say I was the first pastor who has ever prayed in their home. My wife and I visited a Salvation Army captain and his wife, whose boy had been seriously hurt in a car wreck. Ten other pastors had visited them at the hospital that day. When we were about to leave, I asked if we could have prayer. The parents glanced at each other quickly, and then said, "Of course, please do." We prayed. When I looked up, the couple were weeping. They said, "You are the first ones to pray for our boy today. We are so grateful."

Unbelievable? I'm sorry to say that similar incidents have occurred many times.

Once, my wife and I were in a home for a meal with two couples we had pastored some ten years previously. At the door as we were about to leave, my children all stopped and waited as usual. I asked if we could have prayer. We prayed. When I had finished, the couples were in tears and said, "We talked about it all day, and we knew you would pray for us before you left. Thanks for keeping it up."

What a tragedy for a pastor to be in a home and not do for those people the most important thing he could ever do for them, and that is pray for them. Before leaving the office of a man I had led to Christ two weeks earlier, I prayed for him and for his business. He said, "That's the first time anyone ever prayed in my office. You have hallowed this place. I'll never forget it."

Make a game out of visiting. It's fun. It's exciting to see what you are going to run into next. The Lord is full of surprises. You never know what He will do next if you are faithful!

One night when I was pastoring in Chicago, my wife and I went on our regular visitation rounds despite the bitter, minus-five-degree temperature. I had been on the go for twelve hours that day and was terribly tired. As we headed to the first home on our list, I stopped at a service station run by a new Christian to say hello and encourage him. While there, a man's name came up to whom I had witnessed in another service station one day. Gene said, "I know him! Why, he lives just down the street, a half-block away." We got his address and went there.

He was not home, but his wife invited us in. We witnessed to her. She broke into tears under conviction as I told her how Christ suffered for her sins. Gladly, she prayed out loud with us to receive the Lord Jesus as her Savior and was gloriously converted. For an hour we discipled her, as I always try to do, to get her off to a good start.

When we were about to leave she said, "I knew you were coming tonight."

I said, "Barbara, what do you mean? We didn't know you existed. We hadn't planned to come here tonight."

She said, "I know that, but I have been miserable for weeks. I prayed all day that God would send someone tonight to tell me how to be saved!"

Glory! What if we had failed to go because of the cold or because we were tired? We would have missed one of the greatest blessings of our life. Her whole family has been saved since then, and they have been dear friends of ours for years.

Oh, what a tragedy that so many preachers miss out on these thrills. A pastor can face a multitude of problems when these experiences happen week after week. And they will happen if we visit faithfully. Each experience will be different but thrilling in its own way. Nothing fires a pastor up for preaching like proving that the example of the apostle Paul, going night and day from house to house, really works. To see God work daily in the lives of people is the reality of the ministry.

More Dos and Don'ts

Be prepared. Pastors must be like boy scouts because each visit presents a new challenge. Think through every eventuality and plan how you will handle each one. (Dr. Jack Hyles, pastor of a large Baptist church in Hammond, Indiana, wisely advocates that a pastor think through all that could conceivably happen at deacons' meetings and business meetings before they take place and plan how to handle each problem or conflict before it arises.)

Carry a pocket New Testament. If an unbeliever sees you with a large Bible under your arm, he or she will be on the defensive before you establish a friendly relationship. Most non-Christians are allergic to preachers to begin with. We must be as wise as serpents and harmless as doves (see Matt. 10:16). The children of this world are often more clever than the children of light (see Luke 16:8), and we can learn something about persuasion from them. A good salesman, for instance, doesn't give you his pitch until he has established a friendly atmosphere.

Avoid morning visits. Normally mornings are not a good time to visit, because wives are usually alone, if home at all. If they are home, many are busy with housework and are often unpresentable. Most don't want to be interrupted. One exception is when a pastor who is starting a new church goes door-to-door to take a religious survey and find new prospects. This does not require going inside and only takes a few minutes at each house. But for visiting the unsaved or Sunday visitors, an evening visit is often best.

Try to get the television turned off. What a hindrance it is to serious
85

conversation! A double-minded man just can't be won. After an appropriate greeting, you may simply ask, "Are you interested in watching it?" Almost always they will turn it off. When I did this in James's house, I had the joy of leading him to Christ. He became a very faithful Christian. I have had similar results many times.

Never look shocked at a person's appearance or behavior. Bill met me at the door with a can of beer in his hand. I never said a word about it. While there, I did all I could to make friends with him. Later he told me he could have eaten the can and all. He had felt terribly uncomfortable and guilty and was amazed that I hadn't scolded him for drinking. He said had I jumped on him about the beer, though, he doubted he would have ever come to our church. He came because he felt I genuinely loved and cared for him. Eventually I had the joy of leading him to Christ. Sometimes pastors give a holier-than-thou impression by their reaction to the world's sin. "Hate the sin but love the sinner" is a principle pastors must learn to live by. God the Holy Spirit often convicts a person of sin just by using the presence and manner of a man of God. Of course, pastors must *be* holy men of God. Had Bill offered me a beer, I would have declined politely.

Be relaxed and friendly. A relaxed attitude puts people at ease and makes visiting and witnessing much easier. People are unaccustomed to having a preacher in their house, and most feel nervous in his presence. It is a high tribute to a pastor when people say sincerely that they enjoyed his visit.

Preachers are stereotyped. Most people are either afraid or scornful of them. The average person believes preachers are prudes and live totally outside reality. Some do, of course. They don't know how to be friendly human beings. Yet, more than almost anything else, people, saved or unsaved, appreciate friendliness in a pastor.

Don't badger the unsaved. The minute a pastor walks into a home of unbelievers, they will erect a barrier. If caught doing something they think you disapprove of, they will be even less responsive. The pastor's goal is to win such people, not to antagonize them further. This takes skill and sensitivity and sometimes means having to postpone giving the gospel in full. If you plunge ahead and ask for a decision, some folks will say yes just to get you off their back.

I walked into a house one night to visit a man and his wife. I could have cut the air with a knife, the tension between them was so evident. They weren't talkative, and my visit was short. Later, after this couple had become Christians, they told me they had had the worst fight of their married lives just before my visit. They thanked me for being so understanding. The key to soul-winning is to find people the Holy Spirit has prepared and not to force people to listen to us. Being pushy results in fake professions of faith.

Be flexible. Be sure people have time for a visit. If they are preparing to go out or expecting guests, excuse yourself promptly and come back later. Once I knocked and the door immediately opened, revealing a couple with their coats on. They were confused as to what to do and hesitantly invited me in. Of course, I didn't enter but told them to go ahead on their date and that I'd come back later. When I did, they were most cordial and thanked me for sensing their dilemma. They became fine members of our church.

Don't steal sheep. If someone is already a Christian and active for the Lord, it is the unpardonable sin to try to get him to leave his church to come to yours. There are too many unbelievers to reach to waste time stealing members from other churches. Even if they are disgruntled with their church, you will be smart not to go after them. Often it won't be but a short time until they are unhappy with you as well.

Don't make appointments. Calling ahead gives people a chance to put up a front before you arrive. It also makes it easy for them to put you off. A man I had led to Christ called and asked if I'd go see his brother who had just that day gotten out of prison. Many people in our church had been praying for him. For sure, if I had called to make an appointment he wouldn't have wanted to see a preacher. So, on a very hot summer day I knocked at his door and awakened him from a nap. Humanly speaking, it was a bad time, but it was God's perfect time. He was as prepared as the Lydia of Acts had been. That day he received Christ and an entire family was transformed; the next Sunday he confessed Christ publicly. What a thrill!

Leave the way open for another visit. "The servant of the Lord must not strive . . ." (2 Tim. 2:24). It is extremely important not to argue with people. I wish I had learned this before I became a pastor.

Early in my ministry I visited a man who was very argumentative.

He antagonized me in every way and deliberately contradicted every-thing I said. I let his responses get to me, and we began to argue heat-edly. I left defeated and clearly had no further welcome in his home. I am thankful that years later someone else led the man to Christ.

One night my wife and I visited some newcomers in the neighbor-hood near our church. We hardly had seated ourselves when the man said I didn't preach the whole gospel. He said that people must be baptized to be saved, which I do not accept even though I believe bap-tism is an important act of obedience. We tried to change the subject politely, but he kept pressing the issue. I told him I wouldn't argue the point with him. Finally, I excused myself, took my wife by the arm, and we left. All the way to the door the man was jawing me. After we left I'm sure he felt he had conquered the world by running off a Bap-tist preacher. We are instructed not to cast our pearls before swine (see Matt. 7:6). Of others, God says let them be ignorant (see 1 Cor. 14:38).

Learn to plant the seed. On many visits all you can do is plant a seed. When this is true, be thankful, and plan to come back later and pick the fruit. Often, when I'm not invited in, I say, "I just want to let people know that God loves them and that Christ suffered and died for their sins and rose again." The gospel is the power of God unto salvation (see Rom. 1:16), whether people realize it or not. Leaving that little bit gives the Holy Spirit something to work on in their hearts till you return the next time.

One afternoon on my way home from visiting, I came to a corner and stopped. Suddenly God brought to my mind a man two blocks away in whom I had planted only the tiniest seed of the gospel. When I arrived, I found him under conviction of sin, and he gladly received the Lord. When I was about to leave he asked if I would wait while he called his dad to tell him he was saved. His dad wept as he told me how long he had been praying for Bill to come to Christ. A week later his dad drove several miles to see his thirty-year-old son baptized.

Don't take anyone's salvation for granted. This is one of the worst mistakes anyone can make. No pastor should ever do this.

A sixty-five-year-old man visited our church with several of his rel-atives who were members. They told me he was saved and was a Bap-tist church member. In his home that week, when I asked if he knew for sure he was going to heaven, he immediately said, "No, I've had a lot of doubts." After I presented the gospel, he realized he had not been saved and he then and there trusted the Lord Jesus. Six months later he was dead. How glad I am that I didn't take his salvation for granted. I have seen hundreds just like him come to Christ after being church members for years.

Always leave literature. The effects of your visit can go on long after you depart if you leave helpful reading material behind.

In one home I left John R. Rice's tract "What Must I Do to Be Saved?" The next morning the lady called happily at 6:00 A.M. to tell me she had awakened in the middle of the night. The Holy Spirit had so burdened her heart that she got up, read the tract through three times, and then knelt and accepted the Lord Jesus as her Savior. She almost called me at 4:00 A.M. to tell me the news, she was so excited! This is what visiting is all about.

Types of Visitation

Door-to-door visitation. One main purpose of this kind of visitation is to find new prospects among the unchurched. Here is the approach I use when trying to find out whether a person attends church:

"How do you do. My name is Sumner Wemp. I'm the pastor of the Central Baptist Church at Twelfth and Yonge streets. I'm going door to door in the community trying to meet everyone and give them a special invitation to visit our church. Are you a member of a local church? Do you attend regularly?"

If both answers are no, you can knock once more, this time at the door of the heart to see if the Holy Spirit has been working. Often I say,

"You know I'm preaching for one reason. I want to help every person in the world go to heaven. I haven't found anyone who wants to go to hell. For sure, no one is actually planning on going there. Sir, let me ask you, do you know for sure you are going to heaven? [If the answer is no, ask,] Have you thought much about it?"

89

If the answer is yes, you know God has been working and there's a good chance the person may be ready to receive Christ.

If the answer is no, you can proceed by saying,

"You know, where you're going when you die is important, isn't it? We live here fifty, seventy-five, or one hundred years, and then we spend forever and ever either in heaven or hell. God certainly doesn't want anyone in hell. God loves you and me so much He sent His own Son, the Lord Jesus, to suffer and die for our sins so we could be saved. Could I talk with you a few minutes about how to be sure you are going to heaven?"

If the answer is yes, go ahead and lead the person to Christ. If the answer is no, at least you briefly have shared the gospel, and the Holy Spirit can use this to further prepare his or her heart. You may want to return in a week to ask if the person has thought any further about the matter of heaven and hell.

Another purpose of door-to-door visitation is to introduce yourself and to tell why you are starting a new church in the community. On this call I would say,

"How do you do. I'm Sumner Wemp from Central Baptist Church at Twelfth and Yonge streets. You've probably seen our church or our ads in the paper. We're starting a new church and our desire is to have a church that is filled with love and joy. My sermons will especially emphasize the importance of a home where children love and honor their parents and where husbands and wives love and respect each other deeply. We will have lots of good music and singing and will stress old-fashioned values and character.

"Above all, we want to help every person go to heaven and help those going to heaven to enjoy the trip. I want to give you a special invitation to come visit with us and bring your friends. Here is a brochure that tells about our ministry. Sir, are you attending any church in the area? Would you be my personal guest this Sunday?"

Going door to door to win people to Christ means you are looking for people the Holy Spirit has already prepared. Much prayer needs to precede such visits so that you will be led to the right homes and so that the people you visit will be touched by God. One approach I have used on these visits is

"Hello, I'm Sumner Wemp from the Grandview Baptist Church at Fourth and Collins streets. I want to give you a special invitation to come visit the most wonderful church in the city. We are not trying to make Baptists out of people. I preach for one reason. I want to help every person go to heaven. You know, it's so wonderful to know that God loves us. The Lord Jesus suffered and died for all our sins so we can have our sins forgiven and be sure of heaven. So many people don't have the joy and peace God wants them to have. Do you know for sure that your sins are forgiven and that you are going to heaven?"

After an introduction similar to this, often people answer, "Not in the way you·seem to be talking about." It is quite easy then to present the gospel further and sometimes to lead people to Christ.

Of course, you will meet people who are satisfied the way they are. Some will not have a friendly response. Don't let it bother you. You represent Christ. They are not rejecting you but the One whom you represent. Always leave graciously so you or someone else may come back.

Hospital visitation. There are three good reasons for visiting people in the hospital:

1. Hospital patients are glad to have company unless they are hurting or nauseated. Of course, a pastor will be alert to these times and keep the visit brief.
2. They aren't going anyplace. Time passes slowly. Christians who aren't feeling too badly have much time for prayer and could be given special prayer requests.
3. During times of illness, people think seriously about life and death. God gets their attention. In 1967 I spent a week in Turkey and came home with hepatitis. I was terribly ill. Because I had been healthy before this illness, I had not thought seriously about the inevitability of my own death until then. What an awakening time that—my first and only stay in the hospital—

was for me. I realized how little I had done for the Lord and how short life on earth is. I came out with a renewed dedication to the Lord Jesus. Pastors can be a great help spiritually to people at this time.

When visiting someone in the hospital, be cheerful but not frivolous. At best, a hospital can be depressing. People need a little extra cheer at this time. If ever a pastor needs victory in his heart, it is during hospital visitation.

Be natural. If a pastor isn't himself at this time, the patient will be suspicious that something is critically wrong and will be frightened. Don't put on a phony clerical attitude of somberness.

Be brief. Usually families and friends can pass the time of day with the patient. People don't expect a pastor to stay long, especially when they are hurting. Also visits can be exhausting for the patient.

Never sit on or jiggle a hospital bed. I've seen people stand next to a bed and sway back and forth, bumping the bed each time. Someone with stitches or tender stomachs must be hollering inside. Bedside manners call for not touching the bed. One also should be careful about touching the patient. You may put your hand on an arm sore from shots. Wow! Does that hurt! Not wanting to hurt you, they say nothing.

Don't ask what is wrong. If they want you to know, they will tell you. A woman might have a problem she would rather not discuss. Most of the time a pastor will learn what the illness is before he visits.

Be empathetic, but don't express pity. People want understanding and genuine concern, not pity. Don't tell someone you know how he feels. Even if you have had a similar illness or experience, you cannot know exactly how someone else feels. In your zeal to comfort a person, you may end up saying what you want to hear, rather than giving the person the gift of a listening ear. I have learned it is best not to say too much.

Never criticize doctors or hospital personnel and procedures. Most people think doctors are overpaid, but they aren't. Imagine being called at 2:00 A.M. for an emergency operation on a man's brain. The doctor has that man's life in his hands. How much more he should be paid than entertainers and movie stars who make millions. We should have a profound respect for the dedication of doctors and nurses.

It has been my joy to know several doctors personally, and I've come to believe that most doctors are dedicated, overworked servants of humanity. Many of them are appreciative of ministers and their role in healing. When Buddy and Delia's baby was born dead, their doctor was as distraught as the parents. He asked me to view the baby's body so I could confirm his report that its appearance was perfectly normal. When Delia came to, I told her what had happened and was able to comfort her and Buddy. The doctor thanked me profusely for the help I had given them and him.

Visit right before the patient is taken to surgery. Most hospitals allow pastors to visit any time. About thirty minutes to one hour before surgery, a patient is given a shot to relax him. Find out when the shot will be given, get there about ten minutes beforehand, and pray with the patient. The person will never forget this and will love you and God dearly for it.

Find out how long the operation will last and try to arrive shortly after the person comes out of surgery. This is for the family's sake. The patient, still under anesthesia, won't remember the visit, but the relatives will. This is often the most crucial time for them.

Katie was in surgery. I came minutes after she went to the recovery room, and while I was there the doctor came out and announced to her husband that she had cancer. What a blow! Tom was alone, and my being there with him was worth a million dollars to him . . . and to me. These are precious moments. They give you a closeness to your people that nothing else will.

While visiting church members, visit other patients as well. They may become some of your best prospects. If the hospitalized member is a good witness, the door is often opened to win other patients to Christ or to help them spiritually. Joe was such a radiant Christian that when the man in the room with him was approached, he was easily won to Christ. What a place for a Christian to let his light shine.

Always have prayer. Pray for other patients. Pray for the doctors and nurses who minister. One time a nurse came in as I was about to pray with a patient. She was going to leave us alone for prayer, but I invited her to remain. As I always do, I prayed for the doctors and nurses. The nurse was soon in tears. We never won her to Christ, but she never got over hearing someone pray for her.

Priorities

Some visits are more important than others. A pastor should think through whom to visit and set up priorities that will allow him to make the most of his visitation time.

Church visitors. If someone visits your church on Sunday, you *must* be in his home that week. God brought someone to your church, and you had better go see what God wants you to do. God sent the visitor your way for a reason, and it's your task to find out what that reason is. What a responsibility!

Unsaved people someone asks you to visit. Almost every person ever saved in our church was prayed for earnestly by someone who loved him, sometimes for years prior to the person's conversion. People aren't saved by accident. When someone has become burdened for someone else, that's the time to visit.

Judy called and asked me to visit Harry, her husband. She was crying, she was so burdened. Judy had been a Christian only a couple of weeks. One night she said, "Harry, you just have to get saved. I'm not going to heaven and have you go to hell." These two really loved each other, and she could get away with talking to him that way. She even made him kneel with her and pray. When she told me all this, I feared she had alienated him further. She prayed all day before my visit that God would save him. When I arrived, he wasn't very friendly, but he had been under conviction of sin all day. That night, after hearing the gospel, Harry received the Lord as we all knelt. Judy's prayers had made the difference.

Newcomers. We live in a mobile society. People move to a new community every three years on the average. This is often a time they decide to turn over a new leaf and start going to church. Pastors ought to be one of the first people to greet them. We ought to beat the paperboy, the milkman, and Welcome Wagon.

One way to find out about newcomers is to tell church members to keep their eyes open. If they see a family moving in, they should stop and invite them to church and then call the pastor. People can be trained to do this, and most will be glad to do so.

Be on the alert yourself. I've been known to follow a moving van down the street to find out which house was being moved into. You can contact personnel in real estate offices to find out when the owners will be moving into houses that have recently sold. Ask the builder of a new subdivision to keep you informed about people moving in. Most contractors will be shocked and impressed to know a pastor is that interested in people, and they will help.

In an apartment complex, get to know the maintenance man or caretaker. I've known maintenance men, whom I called my "assistants," to flag me down and tell me about someone moving in the next day. Another good method is to get someone at the water-works, light company, or Welcome Wagon to give you a list of new "move-ins" each week.

New converts. As you know, new converts are spiritual babies. They need help. Often new believers lose friends and suffer ridicule. A few days after they are saved, doubts and questions come to their minds. Like newborn babes they require lots of attention. A pastor should visit them right after they are saved. Other staff and members should make themselves available, too.

The sick. People will forgive a pastor for almost anything except not visiting when they are ill. That visit will be long remembered. Especially today, with the constant scare of cancer, people want a pastor's visit. When people are flat on their backs with no way to look but up, they are often ready to look to God. These visits can be brief but powerful, and they must be made.

The elderly and shut-ins. No one will love a pastor more than these senior adults. My, how they appreciate a visit! Probably the greatest power of prayer is concentrated among older Christians. Make them your prayer warriors.

Members of the church. Even if they have no problems and you see them every Sunday, church members love their pastor and want a visit, too. A pastor must not take his congregation for granted. Just a drop-in visit while in the neighborhood will suffice. You can share blessings and prayer requests. They may open up and share burdens they didn't want to bother you with at church. Nothing can seal your relationship with your people better than home visits.

When to Visit

Life is like a taxi meter. It keeps going whether we are getting anywhere or not. Unless you plan how to invest it, your time will be nibbled away by trivia or second-rate activities. Plan your visitation time as wisely as your study time. Both are essential.

Plan to make visits every afternoon. Of course, you will miss some days but *unless you make plans for visitation you will never find time for it.* From two till six every afternoon is an excellent time for visiting.

From two till three visit hospitals, shut-ins, businessmen, and newcomers. These visits should be brief. Schedule longer visits for another time. Make *several kinds of visits in one area.* You may stop at the hospital and then visit a businessman whose office is near the hospital. Businessmen appreciate their pastor dropping in on them for a few minutes. Do not stay long. Most people have lots to do while at work. They are paid to work, not to visit.

From three to four, visit shift workers who get off work at 3:00 P.M. If you pastor where there are lots of factory employees, you must schedule your visits according to these shifts.

From four to six is a good time to visit the unsaved after they get home from work but before they have supper or go out again. To reach the family, you must reach the man of the house. Catching a couple at home may give you the opportunity to reach the whole family.

Visit one or two nights a week from seven till nine. To repeat, if you win the man of the house to Christ, you will reach his whole family. To reach men, you must visit at night.

What Can You Expect From Visitation?

What do you think will happen if you get out and visit as Paul and Jesus did?

Expect people to be saved. My experience has been that, when I prayed earnestly and was burdened to see someone saved, the Lord almost always led me to someone who was ready to be saved. Faith is expecting God to use His Word and His servants out in the harvest. If you expect nothing to happen, you can be sure it won't. Yet God is far more anxious to use us than we are to be used.

Don't be shocked at broken promises. People will make all kinds of promises to be in church on Sunday and then not show up. Some sincerely plan to come, but all kinds of emergencies will prevent them. Count on it.

Expect Satan to fight visitation. "We wrestle not against flesh and blood . . ." (Eph. 6:12). Satan will hinder you as often as he can. You are invading his domain and robbing him of his children when you visit for Christ's sake. Satan doesn't take that lying down.

Don't expect too much. Visitation is a lot like farming. There is a lot of plowing and planting to do. Very often it takes a lot of planting before the harvest comes. If there hasn't been much seed planted in the Lord's vineyard where you are, then you must do the planting yourself. You may be in virgin territory. Then, too, God may wait until you've proved your dedication before He lets you see the fruit. Remember Deuteronomy 8:2, where God is recorded as saying that he humbled the Israelites to prove them, whether they would keep His commandments or not? In my own ministry, God often allows a week or two to go by without my seeing anyone saved just to see if I'll keep on witnessing in obedience to Him, whether I see results or not.

Don't get discouraged. "A winner never quits and a quitter never wins," a wise man observed. "And let us not be weary in well doing: for in due season we shall reap, if we faint not" (Gal. 6:9). This may be the place many fail. A pastor must be faithful to God's commands and go into the streets and lanes (see Luke 14:21). The pastor who obeys God will reap.

In one church I pastored, the church had gone through some deep waters before I came. For weeks I visited without results. Satan had taken a firm grip, and people in the community had heard negative comments about the church. One Sunday I called for a day of prayer and fasting on the next Wednesday. Many people responded. The next Sunday three people confessed Christ as Savior. From then on we saw a harvest of souls almost every Sunday as a result of visitation. Fruit must come. God promised it.

9

Counseling

Remember, God called you to be a preacher, not a psychologist. There is a mystique about counseling that entices the natural mind. The desire to know the "inside story" lurks in most hearts. Beware that you aren't lured into counseling by an impure desire to hear the secrets of someone's soul.

"Some to be sure have seized upon counseling as a respectable escape from the study or from pastoral calling. But many shy from counseling—it is demanding, soul-wearying work which seldom ends either in quick success or in recognition for his service." So said L. I. Grandberg in *Baker's Dictionary of Practical Theology.* Limit the time you spend counseling others; don't allow it to become your entire ministry. But be assured: counseling can be most rewarding as Jesus, the "Wonderful Counselor," counsels through you.

The Dangers of Counseling

Beware the attraction of a woman's affections. The pastor is usually admired because people often see only his good side. Sunday after Sunday he is seen on his best behavior: kind, considerate, happy, and immaculately dressed. What woman with a miserable marriage and unhappy home would not be attracted to a man like that? A woman burdened with these problems may come to the pastor with no evil motives, hoping only to find a sympathetic listener. The pastor, in turn, may genuinely desire to listen and offer help. But all hearts are deceitful and sin is at work in our members. Only a foolish person will not realize the danger of this situation. Hundreds of good preachers who have fallen from their ministry attest to the reality of this danger.

Counseling can be a waste of time. Multitudes go to counselors simply to have someone to talk to. People are lonely. Often a wife doesn't have a husband who will listen to her and so she goes to the pastor for counseling because he will listen. Elderly people often want someone to talk to, and you need to be available to them. But they will consume all your time if you are not careful. Thoughtful scheduling is necessary to keep your time at a premium so that you may help the most people the most effectively.

Beware of sympathy seekers. Some people run from one pastor to another to find someone who will condone their actions. Some of them will admit they have talked to a half dozen preachers about the same problem. Usually the ones they have talked to have given the same answers or suggestions, but the person is not satisfied. He wants someone to tell him what he wants to hear. A newly called pastor will be mobbed by people who want to know if he will agree with something they have done.

The Delights of Counseling

What a thrill to see God break through someone's darkness and bring about victory in the life of a struggling soul. Many believers, saved from the penalty of sin, need deliverance from the side-effects of sin as well.

Guilt. Nothing is more paralyzing than a guilty conscience. Mental hospitals are filled with people crushed by guilt. They do not know about or have not accepted true forgiveness. They have not learned the purpose of guilt, which acts to the conscience like pain does to the physical body. It is God's warning system for the soul.

Mary had dreamed of presenting her husband with a pure body. She stumbled in college. Now the date of her wedding was near, and she was about to back out. Why? She was burdened by guilt from her failure. She had confessed her sin to God and to her fiancé, but she had not *accepted* God's forgiveness nor had she forgiven herself. What a relief when after counsel she accepted total forgiveness and forgave herself. Her radiant countenance was restored and her marriage became a thing of beauty.

Fear. A man lived in fear of God's taking one of his children as an act of judgment against him. He had heard a sermon on how God might deal with a person through his children. He was terrified! What

99

a blessed release came when he confessed the sin that caused him to fear God's judgment. He made things right with God and had the peace that they were now right with his family also.

Bondage. ". . . where the Spirit of the Lord is, there is liberty" (2 Cor. 3:17). Most Christians are bound in some way. I once counseled a girl who was bound by self-consciousness. She couldn't look a boy in the face because she thought she was ugly. She had never accepted herself as God created her. When she experienced the liberation of the Spirit and accepted herself, she was transformed. Her smile brought a beauty from within her and her whole personality changed. Such are the joys of counseling.

Counseling Methods

Basically there are two approaches to Christian counseling: direct and indirect.

Direct counseling involves listening, analyzing, and offering solutions and instructions based on Scripture that the counselee agrees to follow. The counselor then becomes the person who holds the counselee accountable and adjusts or supplements the solutions depending on their success. The counselee in this situation must accept the authority of Scripture and of the counselor and follow the instructions if the problem is to be overcome. Most Bible-believing pastors probably prefer this approach because of the direct application of Scripture to the problem.

For a thorough discussion of this approach, see Jay Adams's *Competent to Counsel* and *The Christian Counselor's Manual.*

Indirect counseling involves extensive listening, perceptive, open-ended questions, and restatement of what the counselee has said in an effort to help the counselee better understand his emotions. Emphasis here is on being nonjudgmental and helping the counselee arrive at self-understanding. Counseling of this type is preferred by most psychologists and often does not leave room for biblical instruction. However, many of the techniques of this approach are beneficial in pastoral counseling.

A pastor whose son had killed himself blamed himself for his son's rebellion and suicide. For two years he struggled with guilt and sought help for his depression, but he found no peace. He shared his story with several of us who were together one day. While he talked, I prayed and sought wisdom. When he had finished, I shared some direct counsel and Scriptures that seemed pertinent. Thirty minutes later, when the conversation had moved to other matters, he spoke up and said "That's it!" God had opened his heart and he had found the peace his heart needed through simple, direct scriptural counsel.

An excellent word concerning counseling is found in 2 Timothy 2:24–26:

> The servant of the Lord must not strive; but be gentle unto all men, apt to teach, patient, In meekness instructing those that oppose themselves; if God peradvanture will give them repentance to the acknowledging of the truth: And that they may recover themselves out of the snare of the devil, who are taken captive by him at his will.

Diagnosis

As is true for the physician, often the biggest job is diagnosing the problem. The cure may be simple. Good diagnosis is the key to counseling.

What causes problems? One of two basic assumptions may be held by the counselor: (1) Sin is the ultimate cause of man's problems and (2) environment, relationships, and circumstances cause man's emotional conflicts. Of course, physical causes of emotional problems, such as brain damage, retardation, aneurisms, and chemical imbalances, should be referred to a medical doctor.

Practical Matters

Each pastor needs to set a few guidelines to govern the nature and scope of his counseling ministry. Consider the following suggestions and fit them to your own situation.

Set appointments. When a person calls for help, don't have him come in the same day. Give the person a cooling off period. His problem can look much different to him a day or two later, and he may have resolved the matter and will no longer need your help. Many people live from crisis to crisis. If you see them at the moment of the crisis, you will find them much less rational than you will a day or two later when they have had time to think. Of course, there are major crises that require your immediate presence.

Counsel in your office, not in homes. Your presence behind the desk in your office creates an atmosphere of competence and authority. Arrange your office so that it is comfortable for counseling situations. If you go to the counselee's home, you will be interrupted by the telephone, doorbell, children—you name it. Before you know it, things are off track. In your office, you can ask the secretary to hold all calls.

Begin with prayer. Usually people are under stress and nervous when they come to see a pastor. They hardly know where to begin. Prayer is wonderfully settling and relaxing at a time like this.

Also, you need God's wisdom. Many pastors fail and are frustrated as counselors because they do not consciously and seriously depend on God to give them wisdom.

In the beginning of my ministry, I dreaded counseling. Then I began to seek wisdom and depend on God to change people's attitudes. Now counseling is a thrill and a delight. It is fantastic to sit back and see God work. Prayer makes *all* the difference in counseling.

Be relaxed. Your attitude will be reflected in the person who comes to see you. You set the tempo. It is a great compliment for people to say they feel comfortable around you. Knowing how to create this feeling is a beautiful art. A pastor doesn't have to be stiff and formal to be respected.

Be unhurried. Even if you are pressed for time, it must not show. Usually people cannot be rushed into telling what's on their hearts. They want and need to tell the story at their own pace. If you don't have time for them, they will be turned off for sure.

Be attentive. This is essential. Never let your mind wander or your attention be diverted. We have all had people look us straight in the eye and yet respond as if their mind had been a thousand miles away. People won't trust you if you don't listen. They immediately feel you don't really care or understand.

Facial expressions and gestures can indicate that you are listening and understanding what is being said. Verbal encouragement such as "Go on," "I see," or "Tell me more" helps get the whole story out.

Listen actively, occasionally stopping to sum up what you are being told. Help the person understand and clarify his problems by paraphrasing and simplifying his words and playing them back to him. *Let the people talk.* Let them get the whole story off their chest. This often is the best therapy in the world. By the time people talk it all out, they sometimes come to see the solution to the problem. To hear someone say, "I don't know why I'm telling you all of this," is to reach the ultimate in good listening. As you listen, give direction to the conversation through questions. Help the counselee get to the bottom of his problem and show him what to do to correct it. Assign "homework" projects to carry on the counseling process outside your office.

Remember: There are two sides to every story. Sometimes there are three sides: a husband's side, a wife's side, and the correct side. It is important to talk to couples together if at all possible. They are less apt to exaggerate the story or leave out pertinent facts when both are present. Be fair to all parties.

Keep everything confidential. People must know they can trust you, or they won't be completely honest. The unpardonable sin of counseling is to divulge confidentialities. Once your trustworthiness is gone, your effectiveness is gone. Don't even tell your wife! This is extremely important. First, you should not burden your wife with these problems. Also, it is easy for the person who has confided in you to read your wife's reactions and to realize she knows the story. Keep your wife free and neutral in these matters.

Don't jump to hasty conclusions. You can be too hasty and miss some of the facts. Evaluate all that you hear and ask questions in an effort to get the whole picture. Try to determine what are facts and what are frills in the story.

Ask questions. Ask questions that cannot be answered by a simple "yes" or "no" but that will help the person think through his situation. Help the person be objective.

Ask about family background. Often a man treats his wife the way he treats or would like to treat his mother. As he tells of his family background, this information often comes to the surface.

Find out about the person's educational background. Has he been to college? If not, why not? Social adjustments tell a lot. How many friends does the person have? How does he get along with people? Does he like people or is he distrustful? Does the person have hobbies? This can reveal whether a person's life is balanced. People with no hobbies, no special interests, and few social contacts may be too self-centered and unbalanced.

Find out about the person's health and his general attitude toward life itself. Is he happy and fulfilled, or is he fighting against the will of God? How is he doing spiritually? How often does he attend church, pray, and read the Word of God? Is there any unconfessed sin still plaguing him?

Beware of long interviews. Keep each session brief and specific. Thirty minutes to an hour is usually long enough for each appointment. Your secretary should tell the counselee how long the appointment is for. This helps the person get to the point more quickly. Take good notes for future reference and keep them filed confidentially.

Study the Bible for solutions to common problems. Psalms and Proverbs are particularly helpful. If need be, especially at the beginning of your ministry, make a file of Scripture references under general headings such as "marriage," "knowing God's will," and "forgiveness." Use the word of God. This is your most powerful weapon and healing element. You need to develop a theology of living, dating, marriage, divorce, and so on as the basis for your counseling.

Try to teach principles when offering advice and solutions. Biblical principles, when understood, can be applied by the counselee in the future to avoid similar problems.

Admit that you don't know all the answers. You don't. Sometimes you will be stumped totally. Don't fake it. Let people know if you don't have an immediate answer. Offer to pray with them about the matter. Maybe you don't have all the facts. Thinking about the counselee's problem for several days and searching the Word of God can often bring answers and solutions.

Above all, learn to genuinely love your counselees. Don't let what you learn affect your attitude toward them. Love covers a multitude of sins, but it doesn't condone them. You must continue to love people and lead them to truth and transformation under the power of God. Keep the lines of communication open. Often, you are the link between them and God.

10

Weddings

Choosing a life's companion is the second most important decision a person ever makes, next only in importance to choosing Christ. Choosing one's career is not nearly so important. One can change careers freely, with no guilt. But God calls switching marriage partners adultery. Yes, people can be forgiven if they break their vows, but the scars and wounds of doing so often never heal.

God says, "Marriage is honorable . . ." (Heb. 13:4). Jesus honored a wedding by His presence (see John 2) and performed His first miracle there. Marriage is so sacred God says the husband-and-wife relationship is like the relationship of Christ and the church. Man created in the image of God craves fellowship. God said, "It is not good that the man should be alone; I will make him an help meet for him" (Gen. 2:18). To make Eve, God took a bone from Adam's side, not from his head nor his heel. This has been thought to symbolize her place of companionship *beside* Adam, not under his heel nor over his head. They are ". . . heirs together of the grace of life . . ." (1 Pet. 3:7). What a glorious and fantastic relationship!

The wedding, then, should be one of the most wonderful moments of life. It should be a worship experience, not simply a civil ceremony. What a privilege for a pastor to share in this time of great joy. It will bind you to the couple for the rest of their lives.

Conditions for Marriage

Because a pastor is called by God, everything he does must be done in accordance with God's Word. He cannot decide the conditions for marriage by his own feelings or by the customs of the day.

Never marry a couple without counseling them first. If a couple asks if you will marry them, whether you know them personally or not, you should tell them you can't answer them without setting aside a time for counseling with them first. If they refuse to be counseled, there is something wrong with the relationship, you can be sure. Their refusal prevents your having to judge whether or not to marry them. If they agree to counsel, you should ask enough questions during that first session to determine if you can marry them in good conscience.

Determine whom you will and will not marry. A pastor needs to study the Word of God and establish his own convictions about whom he can marry before he is asked to marry anyone. Once people know a pastor's convictions, he will not often be asked to marry people he cannot marry.

Do not marry a saved and an unsaved person. God says plainly, "Be ye not unequally yoked together with unbelievers: for what fellowship hath righteousness with unrighteousness? and what communion hath light with darkness?" (2 Cor. 6:14). The argument that an unequally yoked couple will marry anyway and therefore it would be better for them to be married by a preacher in a church than by a godless judge or justice of the peace is sheer spiritual nonsense. A Christian marrying an unbeliever may simply want to quiet his conscience by being married by a preacher. The non-Christian may also want to feel a "little religious" when saying his vows. A pastor who complies thus condones a Christian's disobedience and adds to the unbeliever's false assurance of spirituality. God certainly cannot bless a marriage borne of disobedience.

What about two unsaved people? Nothing is stated in Scripture regarding this situation. Most pastors will marry them. Before marrying them, the pastor should counsel them and try to win them to Christ. Usually non-Christians won't ask Bible-believing, soul-winning pastors to marry them.

Should you marry divorced people? This is one of the more complicated issues a pastor faces today. Divorce is so prevalent, even among believers, that marrying divorced people is something a pastor faces again and again. Unless one takes the absolute stand of marrying no one who is divorced, there are no easy or pat answers. Today it isn't a matter of marrying someone who has been divorced only once but of marrying someone who has been divorced two and three times. What-

106

ever stand a pastor takes, he must be consistent. You must come to your own conclusions and convictions.

Premarital Counseling

Love is blind, but marriage is an eye-opener. Most young couples are not ready for marriage. There is so much misinformation about love and marriage. It is a wonder there isn't more divorce than there is. Surveys show that seventy percent of married people say they would not marry the same person again. Couples usually are in love with being in love and are so set on marriage before they come to you that one wonders how much good premarital counseling does. Yet, it can be profitable, and it is essential.

The first meeting should take place at least two months before the wedding. A pastor should train young people in the church to come even earlier than that.

Decide first of all if you can marry the couple scripturally. Their spiritual status should be determined. This gives you an excellent opportunity to help them settle the matter of their own salvation.

Discuss the date, time, place, and type of wedding the couple prefers. In a church with a lot of young people, often several weddings will occur in the same month or season. Who gets the church and facilities on which day will depend on who comes first. A record of these details must be maintained by you or your secretary.

Arrangements will need to be made to reserve the church, the reception room, and necessary custodial services. The date and time for the rehearsal must also be scheduled. Many a couple have been brokenhearted because they took for granted they could use the church when other meetings were already scheduled.

Outline what you wish to cover in your counseling sessions with the couple. Let them ask questions. Recommend or assign books for them to read. *Letters to Karen* and *Letters to Phillip* by Charles Shedd are excellent.

The second and subsequent meetings should cover a wide range of subjects: the marital relationship, children, and relationships to the Lord, to parents, and to the church and friends. First Corinthians 7 provides a good basis for discussion. Here is an outline of that chapter to consider: The Sacredness of Sex (vv. 1,9); Separation From the World (vv. 10–24); Sharing and Sacrifice (vv. 24–28); Secret of Success (vv. 29–31); Spiritual Service (vv. 32–35); Seriousness of Marriage (vv. 36–39). Following are subjects that need to be discussed as well.

Finances. Today very few couples want to start out at the bottom financially. They buy houses, fill them with furniture, and then they are strapped financially, which causes a constant strain on the relationship. Warn the couple against getting in debt and having the extra pressure of financial worries hanging over them. Talk with them about honoring God with their finances from the first day of marriage. Instruct them in the need for savings, insurance, and living within their income.

Family altar. Teach the couple the value of praying together and how to have a family altar. What a difference if they start the very first night on their knees together. What a difference if they know how to pray together when sickness or sorrow comes.

Family ties. High on the scale of marital problems is in-law relationships. The future bride needs to know *never* to make threats of going home to mother. The husband-to-be needs to put his wife ahead of his mother in his affections. Both need to cut Mom's apron strings and both need to love and respect each other's parents, as well as their own.

Friends. "Be not deceived: evil [companions] corrupt good manners" (1 Cor. 15:33). The people a couple associates with will affect their whole future and marriage. They should consider seriously whom they pal around with.

Fun. A family that plays together stays together. A husband and wife need to find common activities and recreational outlets. Just because they are married doesn't mean they shouldn't date. This is one reason they need to beware of getting in a financial bind. They need money for dates, for eating out, and for vacations.

Faithfulness to the Lord. If a couple wants God's blessings they must honor Him. Yet many couples are lost to the Lord in the first years of their marriage. They need to know how to "Delight thyself also in the LORD . . ." (Ps. 37:4). Most couples need instruction on how to find their place in the church as a married couple. Suggestions should be made concerning their being in Sunday school and church the first Sunday and Wednesday after they are married (yes, even while on their honeymoon).

Flesh. The movies, TV, and magazines provide information about sex—mostly about immoral sex. Pastors need to instruct couples about sex spiritually and scripturally. After listening to "Love, Courtship, Romance, and Sex," a record I made on marriage, a woman said, "You removed twenty years of fear from my mind." A Bible college student said, "If I'd heard these facts before this summer, I'd still be a virgin. Why didn't my pastor talk to us young people like this?"

I have found that couples are grateful when I discuss the matter of sex openly. Most couples are anxious to ask questions in an atmosphere where they won't be scolded or made to feel stupid. One young woman I recall came back from her honeymoon and said my counsel had turned what she had feared would be a nightmare into one of the sweetest experiences she had ever had.

Ten Simple Suggestions for a Happy Marriage

This list can be passed on to the couples you counsel—and it applies to your own marriage as well!

1. *Magnify each other's good points.* If you pick at each other's faults, you will destroy your marriage. Love covers a multitude of sins; that is, if you love someone, you will "cover" their sins rather than discuss them with other people. Imperfections, whether they relate to your job, house, car, or spouse, must be expected and accepted, or soon you will be totally dissatisfied.

2. *Continue courting after you are married.* Keep flirting with each other. Make yourselves attractive and appealing to each other in dress and actions.

3. *Talk things over every day.* A wife who is a good housekeeper needs her husband to talk to when he comes home. It always helps to be able to talk about problems of the day.

4. *Never go to bed mad.* Learn to be honest and open with each other. If you do this while your first love is burning in your heart, you

109

will establish a pattern that will last forever. God says, ". . . let not the sun go down upon your wrath" (Eph. 4:26). If you do, the anger will burn a hole in your heart and explode in some unexpected way. Practice saying, "I'm sorry." Learn to forgive. This is more valuable than making a million dollars and brings much more happiness.

5. *Say "I love you" every day.* There's magic in those words. Don't take your spouse's love for granted. These words from a husband are especially needed by a wife. They are the fuel she runs on every day. Keep her tank full, and she will be much more responsive to your desires.

6. *Put a sparkle in each other's eyes every day.* That phone call in the middle of the day, a surprise gift, his favorite dessert, being primped up when he comes home, telling her how pretty her dress or hair is—a thousand expressions of love and respect can cause it. Learn what puts the sparkle in each other's eyes, and do it.

7. *Show appreciation and be responsive.* Thank each other for little things. We usually don't mind doing even mundane tasks, if we're appreciated. Most people today are starved for appreciation. When your spouse expresses appreciation, respond warmly.

8. *Have a little fun together every day.* It doesn't take money to do this. Do something together you really enjoy. Lack of fun together can make the day as enjoyable as a cold cup of coffee.

9. *Learn the true value of time, treasures, and life.* Time must be spent. Spend a lot of it with each other. That's more valuable than making another buck. The saying "You only go around once in life" is true of earthly life. Learn the value of time. Don't waste it.

10. *Pray together and be thankful.* Taking everything to God in prayer solves more problems and pays more bills than a bank full of money. It will weld you together and keep your hearts warm. Be thankful to God for His goodness. "Whoso offereth praise glorifieth God . . ." (Ps. 50:23). Praise keeps the sunshine in your soul and the smile of God upon you.

Rehearsal Day Conference

On the day of the rehearsal, or sometime prior to this if necessary, a counsel and prayer time with the bride and groom and both sets of parents could be extremely helpful and healthy. What a good time to get the in-laws in for a session on their relationships to the couple and to each other. Genesis 2:24 should be stressed. In the presence of all, explain how the bride is not to be allowed to run home to Mamma and how the groom must consider his wife's needs ahead of his mother's now. Parents must cut the apron strings. Newlyweds must not criticize each other before their parents, nor should parents criticize their child's mate.

Parents need to be reminded of their own newlywed days. Ask them to recall some of their dumb decisions and mistakes, and tell them to expect their children to make a few. As much as parents want to help their kids avoid mistakes they must realize that newlyweds need to be allowed to grow up and live their own lives.

In-laws need to love each other and not cause friction by pulling either of the children away from his or her parents. The devil often tries to cause division through in-laws. The couple needs the love and support of both sets of parents. Parents can help by not being jealous and making unnecessary demands on the couple's time and love.

What a time for all to pray together! When my son and daughter-in-law were about to be married, her father (a preacher, too) and I got the couples together on the day of the rehearsal for a time of prayer. It was heavenly as we all four prayed. God came down. We will never forget it. (A big mistake was that we did not have our wives there.) That experience prompted me to add this section. A rehearsal-day conference could be one final moment before the wedding that would be extremely profitable.

Customs of the areas, church, and family all make it so there is no set way to have a wedding. The bride's personal preferences, within reason, are usually honored. The central fact is that the wedding should honor God, please the couple, and be performed with dignity. Weird or unseemly practices should not be asked of a pastor.

The Rehearsal

The rehearsal is sometimes called an "aisle trial." It is usually held the night before the wedding. All members of the wedding party are expected to be there. The person who misses the rehearsal can easily ruin the ceremony by one simple mistake.

Ask the wedding party to be seated in the front rows of the church for general instructions. Let them know you are honored and count it a privilege to be in on this most important step in a couple's life. You want to do all you can to make it a happy occasion. Also express that you want it to honor God and be a blessing to all.

Tell them that you are so glad this couple wants to put the Lord in their wedding. This is an excellent time to explain the sacredness of marriage and to give the gospel. (The plan to do this should be discussed with the couple during one of the counseling sessions.) You can say something like this:

"Marriage is wonderful and sacred. It is so sacred God compares the relationship of the husband and wife to Christ and His people. Just as Bill here has wooed and won Mary to be his wife, so Christ has done all He can to woo and win people to Himself. The Lord Jesus loves you and me so much that He suffered and died for all our sins on the cross then rose from the dead to be our Savior. Now, just as Bill asked Mary to accept him to be her husband, so Christ asks each of us to accept Him to be our Savior. Tomorrow night I'll ask this couple if they will accept each other as husband and wife. They must each answer individually, 'I do.' That's all. Then I'll pronounce them married.

"I don't know all of you here tonight. Bill and Mary, I'm sure, would be thrilled if one person here who hasn't said yes to the Lord Jesus would tonight, in his heart, say 'Yes, God, I will accept Christ as my Savior right now.' Bow your heads with me for a word of prayer. While our heads are bowed I promise I'm not going to embarrass anyone nor put you on the spot. If you haven't said yes to God, you would make this wedding most blessed and thrill Bill and Mary if tonight you simply said, 'Yes, Lord Jesus, I accept you as my Savior.' If you will, pray after me in your heart right where you are. 'Dear God, I know I've sinned, too. I'm so sorry. I believe Christ suffered for my sins. Lord Jesus, I accept you as my Savior. Come into my heart and save me right now.' (Pause just a couple seconds after each sentence to give them a chance to pray themselves.)

"Jesus said, 'Behold, I stand at the door, and knock: if any man hear my voice, and open the door, I will come in...' (Rev. 3:20). If you really prayed that and invited Him into your heart to be your Savior and trust Him that He did, as a token that you really meant it, would you look up at me and catch my eye until I nod at you. I'll not point you out nor embarrass you in any way." (As they look up, say a soft amen to each nod. Then pray for those and for the wedding that God will use it and make it a blessing.)

Many people have been won to Christ this way. It has added that special touch and blessing to many marriages. What a wonderful way to start a marriage, having people saved at the rehearsal.

Many couples hire a wedding consultant or director. A pastor should not feel hurt or threatened by one. Ask the couple during counseling if they have a consultant. If they do not have one, you should appoint someone who will make sure everything goes according to schedule. The selection of such a person should be discussed with the couple. An aunt or some other relative is usually willing to stand at the back of the church to keep everything in order and on time. This person will have the order of the service written out, as will the organist and soloist.

Usually the first part of the service is up to the bride's preference. After all are at the altar, the pastor takes over. It is good first of all to *talk* through the wedding once. Then *walk* through the wedding. Then have the actual rehearsal, music and all. As you talk through it, have the one directing to write down each step.

The Ceremony

Here is a brief order for a wedding ceremony.
1. Organist begins at least fifteen minutes before the wedding.
2. Mothers are ushered in at the exact hour given on the invitations.
3. Have the first song (usually a solo).
4. Light the candles.
5. Have the second musical number.
6. Ushers roll out the carpet, if used.
7. Wedding march begins.
8. Pastor enters with groom and best man from a side door at the front of the church, and they take their places.
9. Bridesmaids and groomsmen enter.
10. Ring-bearer and flower girl walk down the aisle.

11. Music gets louder and bride and father enter and walk down the aisle.
12. Ask, "Who gives this woman to be married to this man?"
13. The father says either "I do," or "Her mother and I do." He then returns to his seat, and the people are seated as the father and mother sit down.
14. As you did at the rehearsal, explain the sacredness of marriage and give the gospel.
15. Have prayer (optional). In one sentence before you pray let the people in the congregation know they, too, can say "I do" to Christ as you pray. Some have been saved at the wedding this way. The couple do not kneel at this time.
16. Start the vows. The traditional vows can be purchased in booklet form at most bookstores. Simply read them unless you or the bride wishes to write new ones. Usually the order is something like the following:
    (a) "Do you take this man (woman)". . . . Answer: "I do."
    (b) Have couple join right hands and repeat after you: "I, Bill Jones, take thee, Mary Smith. . . ."
    (c) Ask couple to exchange rings; some couples use a ring vow.
    (d) Have couple kneel for prayer.
    (e) The song of dedication is sung now, if one is used.
    (f) Pray and dedicate the couple to the Lord.
    (g) Pronounce the two husband and wife ("What God hath joined together. . . .").
    (h) They kiss.
    (i) Have them turn to face the guests and say, "May I introduce Mr. and Mrs. Bill Jones."
    (j) The wedding party exits.
    (k) Pastor remains until the mothers are ushered out.
    (l) Pastor motions people to stand and then departs himself.

All weddings are beautiful. People—especially the couple—expect the wedding to be a great moment that they will never forget. However, you can count on something going wrong. It may be only a little thing, but something is going to be forgotten, someone late, or something dropped. Here are a few suggestions to help avoid problems and assure that the ceremony runs smoothly.

1. As much as possible, maintain a steady pace and move from one part of the service to the next without a break. The director, closely following the order of service, should start the groomsmen down the aisle when appropriate, motion for special music, and start the attendants and the bride down the aisle in proper order.

2. The flower girl and ring-bearer often steal the show. Nothing should detract from the bride. Two- and three-year-old flower girls ought not to be used. Explain to the bride before she plans the wedding how very young children often wave to their parents, drop their baskets, sit on the floor, cry, and perform a hundred-and-one distractions. You can't refuse to let a couple use a very small child, but you can warn them of the problems.

3. Plan your part of the ceremony so that it is not rushed but flows from one part to the next without confusion.

4. Explain the vows carefully during the rehearsal so the bride and groom know what to expect. Encourage them to speak up as they repeat the vows. Lead them with short phrases. Tell them that if they forget a line to mumble anything. The guests won't be able to hear in most cases.

5. When the couple exchange rings, keep talking as they pass and place the rings. If someone drops a ring, let it stay and go on. Probably no one will notice.

6. Try to help everyone relax. Speak in a relaxed voice, not a stilted preacher tone. Make the vows warm and personal, not rigid and formal.

7. The prayer of dedication is perhaps one of the sweetest moments of the wedding. Holding hands, the couple present themselves afresh to the Lord. An appropriate solo adds much and the following prayer should be very personal. If the couple have been in your church and you have led them to Christ, this moment will be a touching one for you. Don't be afraid of your own tears at this point. Others will be in tears, you can be sure of that.

8. The reception and picture taking is up to the bride, and you need not feel responsible for this part of the celebration.

9. Sign the marriage certificate and send it in right away. Be sure to have a witness, the best man perhaps, sign it also.

10. By tradition, the pastor's wife gets the wedding honorarium.

She should use this for a personal need or something she normally would not buy for herself. She deserves every penny of it.

11. Don't be afraid of innovative wedding ideas. We tried something new at my son's wedding, and it was fabulous. Instead of the preacher facing the audience and the people seeing the backs of the bride and groom, I stood a few steps below the bride and groom with my back to the congregation. Chuck and Cheryl faced the congregation. The guests saw the smiles and glow on the couple's faces as they said their vows. I have used this arrangement several times since then, and almost everyone believes it is a great improvement. You want to do everything you can to make this an hour the couple and their families will cherish the rest of their lives.

Postnuptial Conference

Wouldn't it be wise and helpful to set up a conference with each newlywed couple one month after the marriage ceremony? Plan it ahead of time and ask the couple to be prepared to talk openly about the surprises and differences of married life. Encourage them to speak frankly so you can help them over the hump before they establish some wrong patterns and attitudes. This could be an important checkpoint that sets the tone of their whole married life. It has been a most successful and appreciated aspect of my own counseling ministry.

11

Funerals

People need a pastor when a loved one dies more than at any other time. You must not fail. A pastor will be forgiven for many mistakes but seldom for falling short at the time of death. What you do for people during their grief will be appreciated much and remembered long.

When Someone Dies

Go see the family as soon as you learn of the death. They need you now. It is usually best to go to the nearest relative. Your presence means more than you can imagine.

Expect anything. Sometimes people will be hysterical. Don't be afraid to go to them right away.

A boy hanged himself outside the bedroom window of a teen-age girl who would not run off and marry him that night. When I arrived, she was uncontrollably hysterical. I went straight to her, feeling helpless. She grabbed me, dug her fingernails into my arms as she clutched me, and cried her heart out. Everyone was speechless. It was astonishing, but in just a few moments she calmed down to a soft sob, and we were able to talk with her and pray with her. This experience humbled my heart and brought a soberness to my soul when I realized how God uses a pastor even when he does nothing but be where he ought to be.

Don't try to say too much. You won't know just what to say until you see what the situation is. Often your quiet presence, your touch, and only a brief prayer are more beneficial than anything you can say. The Lord will surprise you at how He will use you and others at these times.

Early in my ministry I was called at 4:00 A.M. to a home where a father had committed suicide. I was asked by the mother to awaken her thirteen-year-old son and tell him the bad news. My heart almost stopped.

Bless the Lord, He already had a godly woman from our church there, with her great wisdom. She taught me so much by her calmness and carefulness. She woke the boy, made sure he was wide awake, and then asked if he knew who was in the room. He did. Very kindly she told him his father had died suddenly. He loved this lady and immediately threw his arms around her and began to cry. Then as she comforted him she told him, oh, so gently, that his father had taken his own life. Even seminary can't prepare you for each and every situation, but if you walk with God He always comes through with the help you need.

If the person who died was not saved, don't give his loved ones false hope. This is dishonest and an insult to God. You may be asked directly, 'Where is my loved one right now?'' My answer has been, "It's not my business to judge where he is but to help you and try to be a blessing here and now." You cannot do anything to help or hurt the one passed away, but you are responsible for the living.

"It is not what happens to you that counts, but what you do with what happens to you." Many years ago a fellow pastor gave me this statement to share with people who are crushed by tragedies. No one statement has helped more people. This is the heart of the whole matter. Use it often. It really is the answer to many perplexing questions.

What if the person was saved? If those left behind are true believers and the deceased was also, the bereaved won't sorrow like those who have no hope (see 1 Thess. 4:13). They do have a sure hope. The obvious is to remind them that their loved one is much better off than we are, for he is with the Lord. Of course, Christians already know this, and their tears express the pain of their own loss, not some sadness over where the deceased now is. *Never scold loved ones for crying.* Let them release their emotions. It would be unnatural not to cry.

Always have prayer. Prayer at a time like this is not a ritual, but a source of comfort. Thank God for the memory of the loved one and what his life meant to the Lord, to his church, and to you personally. He may not have been producing but thirtyfold (see Matt. 13:23), but you can praise God for what he did produce. Being thankful for what the person meant to you personally always strikes a responsive chord in the bereaved ones.

Call the loved ones' Sunday school teachers. They will want to know about the death and visit their bereaved class members as soon as possible.

Have the women of the church prepare food for the family for the next few days. The whole church can have a great ministry by maintaining a standing committee for these occasions. The committee would be responsible for enlisting members to help with the housework, baby-sit, prepare meals, and make phone calls. Sometimes a family who has lost a loved one will have no immediate relatives to help and support them. The church, as the family of God, must not ignore these needs.

Visit the family again, during the day of the death or the next day, to plan the funeral.

Visit the funeral home at least once to pay respects to the family. They will appreciate this. One need only stay five minutes or so. Have prayer there as well.

One final visit prior to the funeral may be necessary. The night before or morning of the funeral, last minute details of the funeral may need to be discussed.

The Funeral Service

Make the acquaintance of local funeral directors early in your ministry. They will help you all they can.

While I was still in seminary a friend of mine died. His family did not know a preacher in town, as they were not Christians. I was asked to conduct the funeral—my first. At the funeral home, the director was extremely helpful, especially when I told him this was my first funeral. He was most kind and went through every step with me. Be thankful for directors. Local customs prevail, and they can help you understand. Cooperate with directors and they will become your friends.

The organ prelude starts about ten minutes before the service. Often funeral directors provide the organist.

Whether the service is at the church or at the funeral parlor, the order of the service is generally as follows:

The director will seat the family at the appointed time and nod for you to begin.

Begin with special music. The family usually arranges for their favorite soloists and songs.

Read Scripture and pray. If there is more than one pastor participating, divide responsibilities. The family will request one to bring the message. The one not preaching usually reads the Scripture, makes a few comments if he likes, and then leads in prayer.

Have the second special song.

The pastor brings the message. The message should be brief, usually not more than fifteen minutes. Aim the message at the living, not the dead. Eulogies are to be brief and not too flowery. Be sincere and bring honor to whom honor is due, but don't overdo.

First Thessalonians 4:13–18 is an excellent passage to read and expound on at funerals of Christians. Paul wrote the words to comfort and reassure the church at Thessalonica, and that's what you want to do for the loved ones of the deceased. These words of hope also clearly present the gospel. Probably there will be more unbelievers at a funeral than you ever have in church on Sunday. This may be the only time many of them will hear the gospel. Christians in your church should be taught to expect and want the gospel presented at this time.

Give an invitation. An invitation is always in order. The invitation, of course, is not to join a church nor to come down an aisle but to receive Christ, then and there, without leaving one's seat. This is one of the greatest places to win souls. Most people do not become offended because of it.

Have the people close their eyes and bow their heads for prayer at the close of the message. Tell them you know the deceased would be thrilled if someone at his funeral was made ready for his own death and received the Lord Jesus. Ask those who want to receive Christ to pray in their hearts as you lead them. Pray slowly, pausing after each statement so they can pray silently after you. The prayer can be something like this:

> Dear God, I know I have sinned. I'm sorry for what I've done. I believe the Lord Jesus suffered for my sins. Lord Jesus, I accept you as my Savior. Come into my heart and save me right now.

Let them know you won't embarrass them or point them out to others. Then continue:

Everyone please remain bowed in prayer, eyes closed. If you prayed that from your heart and trusted God that the Lord Jesus is now your Savior, would you let me know by looking up at me until I catch your eye and nod at you?

To have ten to twenty persons receive Christ is not uncommon. Later, you can follow up the ones you know already. Ask the ones who made a decision to call you or come see you if they have questions. Then close in prayer.

The director takes charge. Usually you will lead the pallbearers with the casket to the waiting hearse. The director helps the family into cars. You can ride with the director at the head of the line or drive your own car. (It's good to ride with the director and witness to him. I'm amazed how many have told me no one ever witnessed to them before!)

At the graveside you stand at the head of the casket. The director will show you where to stand.

Keep the graveside ceremony brief. Read a few appropriate verses, make some brief comments, and close with prayer. Sometimes pastors just read Psalm 23 and pray. Only a few use the committal of dust to dust and ashes to ashes. What you do depends on where you live and the customs that prevail there.

After you have prayed, go to the family who will be sitting in front of the casket, shake each one's hand, and give assurance of your prayers. The director then takes over and leads the family to their cars.

After the Funeral

Visit the family the evening after the funeral. Doing this will give you a chance to meet the out-of-town guests and relatives before they leave. The family will appreciate this show of respect and concern.

Visit the family a few days later. The reality of their loss will have begun to sink in, and they will need a word of encouragement and a listening ear.

After this chapter was written, my eighty-nine-year-old father passed away. He had trusted Christ when he was eighty-five. He died in his sleep. He had been in excellent health, and I was grateful he went so easily. On the way to make arrangements for his burial I had the joy of leading a sixteen-year-old boy to Christ on the plane.

My heart was full and the Lord then said, "Sumner, you preach the funeral." My dad had been very active in veterans groups, a carpenters union, and a bowling association. The family asked friends from these groups to be pallbearers and honorary pallbearers. At the funeral there were several hundred friends. I preached and gave an invitation like the one I have described above, and some thirty prayed to receive Christ as Savior. Heaven came down. I could only praise God for all His goodness.

12

The Ordinances

Two ordinances practiced by most evangelical groups are the Lord's Supper and baptism. Both are beautiful pictures of profound truths. Observance of these ordinances ought never to be taken lightly. The benefit and blessings of the ordinances come as people are taught the purpose and importance of each.

The Lord's Supper

Details are given for the Lord's Supper in 1 Corinthians 11:17-34. Study the passage carefully, and come to your own convictions regarding frequency and manner of observance.

The purpose. There are two primary purposes for observing the Lord's Supper stated in the Scriptures themselves. If these two purposes are explained from the pulpit and understood by the participants, the communion service will be holy and helpful.

Publicly, the communion service is to "show the Lord's death till he come" (1 Cor. 11:26). Christ's death is the essence of our salvation. God wants it preached and pictured. In the Old Testament the need for a perfect sacrifice for sin was pictured in the thousands of lambs that were slain. Jesus is the "Lamb of God" who takes away our sins. His once-and-for-all sacrifice is pictured in the Lord's Supper.

The broken bread pictures Christ's death for the remission of our sins. "He was wounded for our transgressions . . . ," Isaiah prophesied (Is. 53:6). "Christ also hath once suffered for sins. . .," taught Peter (1 Pet. 3:18). ". . . while we were yet sinners, Christ died for us," wrote Paul (Rom. 5:8). Christ is the bread of life broken for us (see John 6:35).

The cup pictures the blood shed for the pollution of sins, for ". . .

the blood of Jesus Christ . . . cleanseth us from all sin" (1 John 1:7). What a beautiful picture. This surely needs emphasizing. Too many believers bear guilt because they don't know the reality of the cleansing of sins. This can be a sweet time for believers to apply the blood of Christ for the daily defilement of sins.

The carrying out of the ordinance of communion is itself a powerful sermon. Never will I forget hearing Dr. H. A. Ironside tell of a person being saved in his church during the Lord's Supper. What a joy it was to have the same thing happen in a church I pastored years later. This is the height of observing the Lord's Supper.

Applied personally, the communion service is a reminder of Christ's death for believers. ". . . this do in remembrance of me" (1 Cor. 11:24). Meditation is a lost art, but its practice is essential if the blessings of the Lord's Supper are to be realized. What blasphemy it is for people to chat, laugh, or prepare to leave during communion. Believers must be taught to pray and meditate while the elements are being passed. As they do, and only as they do, will their hearts be blessed. What a difference can be seen and felt when a church learns to meditate during the Lord's Supper on the suffering of the Savior and the shedding of His blood.

Often I will weep when I think of Christ's suffering for my sins. Seeing Him on the cross in my place through the eye of faith can break my heart and evoke a flood of love. This response comes only through deep, concentrated meditation on what our blessed Savior did for me personally.

Rejoicing comes at the wonderful realization that Christ's blood cleanses us from all sin. That lift, that joy that so many desire but rarely experience during worship can be a reality at the Lord's Table. Much counseling would be unnecessary if believers personally and regularly experienced the truth set forth in the Lord's Supper. Assurance of forgiveness and cleansing is strengthened as the child of God partakes of the Lord's Supper in remembrance of, that is, as he meditates on, Him.

The practice. The time and frequency of the Lord's Supper varies from church to church. No prescribed time or frequency is mentioned in Scripture.

Once a month is probably the most accepted frequency, though in the historic church communion was observed each Sunday. However often it is observed, it should not be allowed to become a meaningless ritual that must be carried out without the time for making it meaningful. Yet, to have it "too often" seldom robs a church of a more powerful service. If some members must work a Sunday morning shift, have the Lord's Supper Sunday evening once in a while to give them the privilege of observing communion.

However, Sunday morning during the regular worship service is most often the time to observe the Lord's Supper. Do not tack it onto the end of the service, but instead make it an integral part of worship. Make the whole morning service flow from preaching to participation in communion.

Observe the ordinance within the organized, local church. The Bible says, ". . . when ye come together in the church . . ." (1 Cor. 11:18). Some pastors are quite dogmatic that the Lord's Supper is an ordinance for the local church and that therefore only members of a particular local church should participate. The point is, there is grave danger of abusing the ordinance, and to observe the ordinance apart from a scriptural, God-ordained leadership is a questionable practice. God is a God of order and authority. No one is a law unto himself. No one should observe such sacred ordinances outside the authority of the local church. God says, "Obey them that have the rule over you, and submit yourselves . . ." (Heb. 13:17). There is God-given authority and leadership in spiritual matters that should be submitted to.

The manner in which one takes communion is extremely important. To take the elements "unworthily" brings the chastening of God. (see 1 Cor. 11:27). "For this cause many are weak and sickly among you, and many sleep" (1 Cor. 11:30). Herein lies the real reason some people are in hospitals and even in cemeteries. This is a serious service. Many still mix up the Word and say they are not "worthy" to take communion. The issue is not being worthy. None are worthy apart from the grace and blood of Christ. It is a matter of the manner in which it is taken.

Many times I've looked at the actual hill of Calvary. There is nothing mystical about it. It's full of graves. There is a cemetery on top of it and a bus station at the foot. Thousands see it daily and are totally unaffected. But when looking at it and remembering His death, you cannot help but be moved to tears. The blessing comes in meditation on the suffering of Christ for our sins and the shedding of His blood for cleansing. To let one's mind wander during the service robs a person of the blessings. To think about the bread being a Nabisco cracker or the juice being Welches' grape juice kills the effect of the whole service. People must be taught and trained to concentrate and meditate on Christ's sacrifice.

The preparation. A committee should be in charge of preparing to serve the Lord's Supper. They should be sure there are more than enough cups. It is unforgivable to run out of them in a service. Be sure to notify the committee if there is any change in the day or time of the Lord's Supper. The table should be set well in advance of the service and covered with a cloth.

The order of the service. The pastor directs the service. Whatever you do, don't intone the words of this service as if chanting some ritual to an unknown god. Enter into it from the heart. Speak of each part of the service with deep conviction and meaning, or else the service will deteriorate into a meaningless addendum.

The deacons should be seated on the front row during the entire morning worship service. This prevents your having to break the flow from preaching to communion by calling the deacons to the front.

Read 1 Corinthians 11:17-34 before serving the elements. Explain the teachings and blessings of the service. Follow with prayer and an exhortation for all to examine themselves and to confess their sins. This can be the most important part of the service.

The deacons stand and two of them remove the cover from the table and fold it up.

The pastor tells in a few sentences about the bread symbolizing the broken body and suffering of Christ for each one personally.

Call on a deacon to thank God for Christ's dying for us. Be sure he faces the congregation so they can hear and enter into the prayer with him. It is not at all helpful for someone to bow his head, with face away from the people, and mumble a prayer no one hears.

The pastor passes the trays to the deacons. In a large church with dozens of trays, the pastor and chairman of deacons should both pass them out to conserve time. Handing two at a time helps also.

The deacons pass the trays to the people in an assigned manner. Be sure to have a deacon at the end of each row being served so that no one has to pass a tray over his shoulder to those in the next row. Someone should be sure to serve the pianist and organist.

Have special music. This is a good time for someone to sing a hymn like "When I Survey the Wondrous Cross." A trumpet solo of a song about Christ on the cross is very effective. Encourage participants to meditate on the crucifixion.

The trays are returned, and the pastor collects and places them on the table.

The deacons sit down and the pastor then serves them.

Some have the chairman of deacons then serve the pastor. Or the pastor can simply serve himself.

The pastor holds the bread up and reminds the people how the Lord said, "Take, eat: this is my body, which is broken for you: this do in remembrance of me" (1 Cor. 11:24). Then he puts the bread in his mouth. The congregation follows his lead, and in a few seconds the pastor thanks the Lord again for dying for sins.

Repeat the same procedure for passing the cups. Another special musical number is appropriate.

Give an invitation. Properly done this is an excellent time for people to respond. After the drinking of the cup, the pastor can ask that all heads remain bowed and then call for decisions to be made silently. At the close of the service, an invitation to make the decision public can be made.

If there are no places to put the cups in the pews, have the deacons pass the trays to collect the cups. Have another special song.

The pastor can close with words of praise and victory regarding God's work in people's lives that morning or during the past week. Send people away with their minds on the goodness of God. Remind them to tell someone else what they have heard.

Some churches take an offering for the indigent at the doors after communion. This offering is put aside for needy people who come to the attention of the pastor or deacons.

The Lord's Supper. What a fantastic observance. Don't let it become a meaningless ritual.

Baptism

Churches place either too much or too little importance on this beautiful picture. Paul said, "Christ sent me not to baptize, but to preach the gospel . . ." (1 Cor. 1:17). Peter proclaimed, "Repent, and be baptized every one of you in the name of Jesus Christ for the remission of sins, and ye shall receive the gift of the Holy Ghost" (Acts 2:38). Don't minimize baptism and don't unduly magnify the importance of it, but make it meaningful.

Those of us who believe that the Bible teaches salvation by grace alone stand vigorously opposed to any teaching that makes baptism essential to salvation. Historically Baptists, despite their name, do not believe baptism is necessary for one to know God personally. We do insist, though, that baptism is essential to obedience and discipleship.

The Great Commission given by Jesus exhorts us to "Go ye therefore, and teach all nations, baptizing them in the name of the Father, and of the Son, and of the Holy Ghost" (Matt. 28:19). To say that baptism is not important is sacrilegious. You might as well say missions are not important, witnessing is not important, or teaching is not important. They are all listed here in the same context. Most churches make baptism a condition for church membership. Whatever your convictions, don't minimize baptism.

Baptism ought to picture the burial and resurrection of Christ. Romans 6:4 indicates that baptism symbolizes just that: "Therefore we are buried with him by baptism into death: that like as Christ was raised up from the dead by the glory of the Father, even so we also should walk in newness of life." The Greek word *baptizein* was not translated but rather was adapted into English form. The word means to "immerse or dip." The Greek word *rhantizo* means "to sprinkle" and is so translated all through the New Testament. Those who are sprinkled are "rhantized," not baptized. If these people have been born again, they will go to heaven; I don't question that. But Baptists believe to be true to the word "baptize" and to picture the burial and resurrection, a believer must be immersed.

128

Together, the Lord's Supper and baptism picture the whole gospel: the death, burial, and resurrection of Christ. This is why I listed the Lord's Supper first; it pictures Christ's death. Baptism symbolizes Christ's burial and resurrection. These three events are vital parts of one's testimony of faith in Christ and make the two Christian ordinances important acts of obedience.

The purpose. One important purpose of baptism is the fulfillment of Christ's command to baptize. Baptism is a vital step of obedience and discipleship. Many who stress discipleship minimize baptism. To do this is absolutely inconsistent. Experience has borne out that often those who profess to receive Christ but refuse to be baptized are either not genuinely born again or they don't commit themselves to a local church. Check it out with any soul-winning pastor, and let him tell you how few who renege on baptism truly commit themselves to the kingdom of God or to a local church.

Baptism pictures what one believes is necessary for eternal life: Christ's burial and resurrection. The offering of the lamb did not save anyone under the Old Testament; rather, faith in God's promise to save did. So this ordinance doesn't in itself save anyone, but rather it pictures who and what one's faith is in.

Baptism is a public testimony of one's faith in Christ. Many unbelievers will accept a secret disciple, but when a believer makes an open testimony by being baptized, he or she is suddenly ostracized by family and friends. Jewish believers who follow Christ in baptism have been disowned and mourned as dead by their parents.

Baptism is the initiation into church membership. Throughout history evangelical churches have insisted on baptism for church membership. A pastor who does not insist on baptism will be hurt by that decision. Christians who refuse obedience at this point will surely be disobedient to many other admonitions and commands of the Word of God.

The preparation. Appoint a baptismal committee of both men and women. Robes need to be stored and kept clean, and the baptistry, if there is one, needs to be filled well in advance of the baptismal service and drained afterward.

Candidates should be instructed in the meaning and purpose of baptism. I have found it profitable to meet with new converts just prior to the church service during which they are to be baptized. The purpose of baptism is explained and an opportunity for questions given. Often people express gratitude for this help in understanding what they are about to do. It makes the act of baptism much more meaningful to them. Don't take for granted that people know what baptism is all about.

Be sure people know when the baptismal service is. The time and date should be clear.

This leads to an important question. When should a new convert be baptized? Many accounts in the New Testament tell of baptism directly following the moment of salvation. Paul was baptized right away, despite his past belief in Phariseeism and his part in persecuting the church (see Acts 9:18). The believers at Damascus didn't give him a catechism or a period of waiting to be sure he was sincere. The Philippian jailor was baptized the same night he was saved (see Acts 16:33). The Ethiopian eunuch was baptized immediately (see Acts 8:38). To put off baptism is a hindrance to the process of discipleship.

Tell the candidates what to wear and to bring a change of under-clothing or whatever they will need, according to whether you provide robes for them. They should also bring towels and handkerchiefs.

Appoint several attendants in the dressing rooms to assist with putting on robes and wringing out wet ones.

Instruct each candidate on how to stand in the baptistry and how to hold the pastor's arm. He should take hold of the pastor's arm as if holding a baseball bat. The pastor will have a handkerchief in his hand and place it over the person's nose when he places him under the water. The one being baptized should just lie back and go under the water with the movement of the pastor's arms. Remind the candidate that a person is lightweight under water and need not fear that the pastor can't bring him up. With the proper guidance, every candidate should be able to cooperate very naturally through the whole process.

The church should provide adequate dressing rooms and heavy robes. Wet robes cling to a person's body, and if the material is thin it can be seen through. Don't buy thin, cheap material for robes and ruin the beauty and solemnity of baptism by embarrassment over wet robes.

The procedure. Before anyone comes into the pool, the pastor

130

should take one or two minutes to explain baptism to the congregation. Be sure to state that baptism does not wash away sins but is a step of obedience after one is saved.

Appoint people to assist candidates down and back up the steps of the baptistry. The candidate should hand his handkerchief to the pastor when he enters the pool.

The person being baptized may want to give a sentence or two of testimony. This is powerful preaching and often a highlight of the service.

Bring husbands and wives into the pool together, and children also if they are being baptized. Baptize the husband first so the wife doesn't have to stand in a wet robe too long. I have seen couples who were baptized together embrace and shed tears of joy over their reconciliation in Christ.

After the person gives a testimony, the pastor says: "Mike, my brother, upon your profession of faith in the Lord Jesus Christ as your personal Savior and in obedience to the command of Christ, I baptize you in the name of the Father and of the Son and of the Holy Spirit. May your life bring glory to Christ."

The pastor puts the handkerchief over the person's nose and holds it there securely. This is important, for if water enters the nose, the person will come up choking. Some will panic and ruin the beauty of the whole service.

As the pastor lowers the person into the water, with his hand on the person's back for support, he says, "Buried with Him in baptism." As he brings him up, he says, "Raised in the likeness of His resurrection."

Putting the person under and bringing him up should be done as smoothly as possible. (It would be well for pastoral students to go to a pool and seriously practice with each other several dozen times before they ever baptize anyone.)

Dr. Homer Lindsay, Jr., of the First Baptist Church of Jacksonville, Florida, conducts a beautiful baptismal service. After the person is brought up from the water, the choir sings one verse of an appropriate song. This fills the time when one person leaves the baptistry and the next one enters. What a beautiful conclusion to each person's baptism.

131

To conclude the service the pastor can remind the people to rejoice with those who have been saved and followed Christ in believers' baptism. Then he or someone else can close in prayer.

The question always comes up, What about someone who was baptized and joined the church but who didn't know what he was doing and was born again later? Should he be baptized again, even though he had been immersed before? In my opinion, the answer is obvious. Of course, he should be baptized. Baptism in Scripture always follows salvation. Though it may not be deliberate, baptism without salvation is a lie. It is like putting on a wedding ring when one isn't married. Never will the ring make one married. The purpose of baptism is to declare that one has been saved. After salvation, baptism will mean something. If the person lived a false Christian life, this gives testimony to the world that the former life was phony but a new life will follow.

One of the greatest thrills of my life was the opportunity to preach in Communist Romania. On one occasion I was there for a baptismal service when 112 people were baptized. It was fantastic! When people confess Christ and are baptized there, they know they will be harassed and discriminated against. You can imagine the effect when each person comes up out of the water and the whole congregation sings "I have decided to follow Jesus, no turning back, no turning back." I have never wept so much in my life as when I looked into the faces of these dear people and saw their commitment. Baptism ought to be equally meaningful to us in America.

13

Dedication of Children

"Lo, children are an heritage of the LORD; and the fruit of the womb is his reward" (Ps. 127:3). One of the reasons grandparents rave so much about grandchildren is that they are now mature enough to realize how true this verse is. New mothers are radiant and fathers are proud because nothing is as exciting as a new baby in the home. What an obligation a pastor has to etch in the hearts of parents the seriousness of a child given by God.

It only takes a few minutes on a Sunday morning to dedicate babies to the Lord, and the dividends are immeasurable. The ceremony emphasizes the home, magnifies the family, and sanctifies the marriage. The relatives are confronted with the responsibility of being godly examples to the child.

Encourage parents to do everything in their power to get every relative possible to come to the dedication ceremony. Insist that both sets of grandparents come. Emphasize the importance and sacredness of the ceremony, and establish it as a tradition so that dozens in a family will want to come. Many unsaved relatives who haven't darkened a church door in ages will come and hear the gospel when nothing else will get them to church. Many loved ones have been won to Christ this way.

Have the parents with their baby and all the relatives come to the front of the church. Let the parents introduce their relatives by name and relationship and state how grateful they are the relatives came to this wonderful and meaningful service.

The pastor then should thank the relatives for coming. He should explain carefully that dedication of children is not baptism. Rather, the ceremony is primarily for parents to commit themselves publicly to bring up their child in the nurture and admonition of the Lord. Also, the couple is acknowledging God's right to use the child and make him what He wants him to be. This parallels what each believer should do with himself in obedience to Romans 12:1,2.

The pastor should ask the parents if they will promise to do all they can to bring up their child in the nurture and admonition of the Lord. Will they live as godly parents before their child? Will they do all they can to lead their child to Christ? Are they willing to present their child to the Lord for God to have His perfect will in their child's life?

The pastor should then address the relatives, especially the grand-parents, stressing the influence each one will have on this child. They have an awesome responsibility. The most important issue for them to settle is their own salvation. The pastor can briefly and graciously present the gospel, stressing how much God loves them and wants to bless them. He should encourage them to pray during the dedication prayer and call on the Lord to save them if they aren't already. Many loved ones can be and have been won to Christ this way. When the gospel is presented joyously and graciously people will in no way be offended.

Finally, offer the prayer of dedication and ask the congregation to pledge to pray for this family as a part of the whole family of God. You may choose to hold the baby as you pray, but if more than one baby is being presented, it is best not to take time to do this.

I have seen twenty to fifty relatives come to such a service. Many have been won to Christ ultimately because of how the Lord spoke to them during the dedication. Parents and relatives never forget such a ceremony. The whole church is impressed and regularly reminded of the importance of children and how their lives affect the lives of little ones.

People should be taught to dedicate not only their children but also their homes, their businesses, and all they have to the Lord. The dedication of a home can be a God-honoring occasion, blessing friends, deacons, and loved ones who are invited to the home for this special service.

14

Deacons and Ushers

In the Baptist tradition there are two ordained officers in the church: pastors (referred to as elders or bishops in the New Testament) and deacons. In the Scriptures the men of these two offices were set apart by the laying on of hands. In Baptist churches the pastor is the "ruling elder," and the deacons are subject to the pastor's authority, just as the disciples were subject to Jesus' authority or Timothy was subject to Paul's authority.

The pastor should view these men as ". . . a band of men, whose hearts God . . . touched" (1 Sam. 10:26). They are a group of men banded together in a unique fellowship—a "fraternity"—who follow their leader, the pastor.

The Pastor's Disciples

Deacons are what the pastor makes them. These are the men, first and foremost, that a pastor should teach as admonished in 2 Timothy 2:2: "The things that thou hast heard of me among many witnesses, the same commit thou to faithful men, who shall be able to teach others also." Pour your vision, your ideas, your burden, your heart and soul into these men. Spend time with them. Make them your inner circle of disciples, your "think factory." This group then will reflect your heart and attitude to the congregation.

Magnify the office of deacon. Not everyone can be a deacon. Deacons must be men of God, filled with the Holy Spirit. Men of God are not puffed up. They do not demand their own way. The office should humble a man and make him cry out for wisdom. Deacons in the early church were chosen because they were Spirit-filled men of God, called to serve. Respect them as such. Explain and expect this of them publicly.

135

You need deacons. Let them know how much you need and love them. My, what it does to a person to be needed and wanted! A pastor should give deacons a feeling of importance by his attitude toward them. A pastor needs other Christian men who, by their loyalty, hold him accountable and, through their input, help him avoid mistakes. You will learn as much from the deacons as they learn from you. A good pastor will tell you he would never make it without godly deacons.

Love these men. If the world marvels at how Christians love one another, the church should thrill at how a pastor and his deacons love each other. Most men are starved for brotherly love. They want their pastor's love and esteem. Give it to them and they will be loyal till death.

Let no one criticize a deacon behind his back. Ask the accuser to face the deacon with his charge. This does two things. Knowing this could happen makes the deacon live right. He knows he is expected and trusted to live a moral life. Secondly, it silences false and foolish accusations. Deacons deeply appreciate your support of them in this matter of gossip and criticism.

The Purpose of Deacons

Pastors oftentimes find their relationships with deacons less than ideal. Most of the trouble can be traced to wrong philosophies about what deacons are supposed to do. Let's examine the scriptural function of deacons.

Deacons are to serve. The word "deacon" means "serve." In Acts 6 we read the account of a squabble between the Grecians and Hebrews concerning the unfair distribution of food to the Grecian widows. Godly men were chosen to serve tables so that no one would be neglected. This task wasn't glamourous! Nothing about this would have made these men puffed up. They surely didn't consider themselves big shots. They were servants.

They didn't rule the church. In no way did they tell the apostles what to do. In fact, they were chosen so that the apostles could devote themselves to the Word and to preaching, and there is no indication

136

that the apostles consulted the deacons about what or when to preach. Of course, pastors are not to be "lords over God's heritage, but . . . [examples] to the flock" (1 Pet. 5:3). Pastors should carefully study the scriptural position, power, and purpose of deacons and pastors.

Deacons free the pastor to do his work. If the church wants its pastor to pray and preach, then deacons should be his servants, not his lords. When deacons are faithful in caring for the physical needs of the church and pastors are free to care for the spiritual needs, great things will be accomplished. In Acts 6:7, after the first seven deacons were ordained, "The word of God increased; and the number of the disciples multiplied in Jerusalem greatly; and a great company of the priests were obedient to the faith." You can't beat that for results. That's what every church should want. When everyone functions properly, such results will be repeated again and again.

Finally, deacons serve as the pastor's advisory and sounding board. Often deacons are wiser about certain matters than is the pastor. They can help you achieve goals and avoid problems.

Qualifications for Deacons

The scriptural qualifications for deacons are similar to those for pastors and are listed in 1 Timothy 3:8–13:

> Likewise must the deacons be grave, not doubletongued, not given to much wine, not greedy of filthy lucre; holding the mystery of the faith in a pure conscience. And let these also first be proved; then let them use the office of deacon, being found blameless. Even so must their wives be grave, not slanderers, sober, faithful in all things. Let the deacons be the husband of one wife, ruling their children and their own houses well. For they that have used the office of a deacon well purchase to themselves a good degree, and great boldness in the faith which is in Christ Jesus.

Everyone can't be a deacon. A man can love God, serve God, and be used by God greatly, and yet not qualify to be a deacon. Let us look at these biblical qualifications.

A deacon must be "grave." He must not be flippant and frivolous about spiritual things. Churches need men who are serious about God and the King's business.

137

A deacon must not be "double-tongued." He is not to be one who, when with the saints, says one thing, but says another when with unbelievers. He must have Christian character.

A deacon is "not given to much wine." Abstinence is the standard among fundamentalists. For the sake of the testimony of Christ and the responsibility we have to a weaker brother, no deacon should indulge.

Deacons are not to be "greedy of filthy lucre." Money is not the root of all evil. The love of money is. Men who make a lot of money are not to be disqualified automatically. The stipulation is that they not be greedy.

Deacons hold the "mystery of the faith in a pure conscience." Simply, this means he knows what he believes. Belief determines behavior. A man of God must know what he believes and why (1 Pet. 3:15,16).

The above qualifications must "first be proved" before a man is asked to be a deacon. "Lay hands suddenly . . . on no man" (1 Tim. 5:22). A man ought to be saved *at least* a year before he is considered as a deacon.

To be found "blameless" does not mean he must be sinless. "No just cause for an accusation" is what this means.

"Even so must their wives be grave, not slanderers, sober, faithful in all things." Probably most churches do not examine deacon's wives as thoroughly as they should. The wife should be questioned along with her husband. She then feels more a part of her husband's work as a deacon. Also, she feels a greater responsibility to live an exemplary life.

The word "slander" is derived from a Greek word meaning "devil." Nothing is more unbecoming to a woman than a vicious tongue. Nothing causes more trouble within churches than a deacon's wife whose tongue is not bridled.

The word "sober" means calm and circumspect. A deacon's wife should be a lady in every sense of the word. She must not be highstrung and temperamental.

The deacon's wife is to be "faithful in all things." Of course, if this is required of the wife, how much more of the husband. She should attend all services with her husband.

"Let the deacons be the husband of one wife." The most common view of fundamentalist, Bible-believing Christians throughout the ages has been "not divorced and remarried." A man can be fully forgiven of divorce, but he is still disqualified from this high office and privilege.

Deacons are to rule "their children and their own houses well." A man's greatest responsibility is not to succeed in business or in athletics but in the home. If his children, by their behavior, reveal that he is not exercising his parental authority well, he is disqualified from being a deacon. In addition, a deacon's wife must be in submission to her husband. If she is not, he must not be a deacon.

Acts 6:3 lists three additional spiritual requirements for deacons: "Wherefore, brethren, look ye out among you seven men of *honest report, full of the Holy Ghost* and *wisdom . . .*" (italics mine). Deacons, then, must have good reputations, live Spirit-controlled lives, and see life through God's eyes. Most churches set up guidelines for deacons based on these biblical qualifications.

Election of Deacons

According to Acts 6:5, the first deacons were elected by the church, not appointed by apostles. This seems the best method in today's church as well.

How many deacons should a church elect? The church in Acts 6 chose seven. This is not a magic number. A rule of thumb is one deacon for every 50 members, with a maximum number often set.

How long should a deacon serve? For years it was thought that a deacon should serve the rest of his life. In some churches, seniority has been treated the same as in the U.S. Senate: the older, the more powerful. This surely is not a scriptural concept.

I recommend the "rotating system." With this set-up, a deacon serves actively for three years and then has a year off. After a year, if he still meets the qualifications, the man is eligible to be reelected to active deacon service. Three good reasons for this system should be considered.

1. It gets new blood into the deaconate. New ideas from younger men often are helpful. Sometimes deacons who serve for life get into a

rut, howbeit unintentionally. Often very godly men are shut out from being of great service to the Lord because the deaconate is a closed fellowship.

2. This system removes a tradition-bound or cantankerous deacon in the gentlest way possible. Many churches are tragically hindered by unspiritual deacons who are full of pride and untouchable because of a policy of lifetime deacon service.

3. While off the active board, a man often sees anew how the deacons appear from the other side of the fence. It can be very revealing. With that view also comes a healthy attitude when one is reelected. Also, after a year the man is reevaluated to see if he still qualifies. Sometimes it becomes apparent that he has changed and no longer should serve as a deacon.

Several different methods for electing deacons exist. The open ballot is sometimes used. In this plan, every member of the church votes for whomever he wants; if five deacons are needed, the top five vote-getters are elected. If a church is properly instructed and spiritually discerning, this can work well. The only problem is, each new deacon and his wife must be examined *after* being elected. This can be embarrassing if a man must admit he doesn't qualify.

Another approach involves a screening process by the pastor and active deacons of men nominated by the members. After the screenings, a list of qualified men is presented to the congregation for a vote of the number needed.

The process of determining who is qualified can be a highlight of spiritual joy and blessing—or it can be a fiasco. Some men considered for the position of deacon are told to read 1 Timothy 3:8–13 and then to let the active deacons know if they can serve. This is folly. In some churches a man is asked if he will serve, and nothing is said about the qualifications or requirements. This, too, is a terrible injustice.

I recommend that pastors write a series of articles for the bulletin or newsletter, beginning a month or so before the election of deacons. Church members need to be well-informed concerning qualifications and election of deacons.

Because of the importance of selecting the right men as deacons, a sermon or two should be preached about the requirements and qualifications of a deacon. At this time the pastor's vision and burden for

140

the ministry can be reiterated and updated—a kind of "State of the Church" message.

The pastor and several deacons should go to the home of each prospective deacon before putting his name on the ballot. This way the man and his wife can be examined thoroughly, and if they are not qualified or willing to serve, the man can be eliminated without embarrassment.

After stating the purpose of the visit, explain that you want to go over the qualifications for deacons and their wives carefully with them and then ask them a few questions. Spend time in prayer together before you begin. Everything about this visit should magnify the importance of the office of deacon.

Go over in detail all the qualifications as listed in Scripture. After going over each point, ask if there are questions or comments. Ask each deacon with you to give a testimony of what being a deacon has meant to him.

Finally, I always asked three questions, insisting that both husband and wife answer them audibly.

1. "Will you promise us and the Lord that you will never lower the standards we have presented but, by the grace of God, you will do all you can to live up the them fully if you are elected as deacon?"

2. "Will you promise that if you ever backslide so as to hurt the testimony of Christ and the church that, even before we find out, you will resign? If you reach a place of doctrinal disagreement or if you can no longer wholeheartedly follow the leadership of the pastor, will you resign?"

3. "Will you promise never to criticize the pastor behind his back but instead talk to the pastor personally about the problem? Will you promise to come to me and not to anyone else if ever you feel I am doing something wrong?"

With these answered, have prayer and assure the prospect the church will be praying with him. If he feels he does not qualify or cannot serve, he should call you before the election.

Discipline

We need more church discipline. It is scriptural. It prevents small problems from becoming large ones. How do you deal with a deacon or anyone else who walks in the flesh and causes problems? If you have a deacon's word that he won't do certain things, but then he does them and causes division or disturbance in the church, what do you do?

Matthew 18:15-17 tells exactly what to do. Go see him. Try to reconcile the situation. Our first motive must be to restore a person (Gal. 6:1). If he does not respond, then take one or two other persons with you. Again, go in love to try to restore the man's spiritual life. If then he does not respond, "tell it to the church." If the person still does not repent and respond, you should withdraw fellowship, and you can be sure God will deal with that person.

This applies to anyone who so blatantly lives in open sin as to cause division in the church or derision from outside the church. Don't go witch hunting, but don't run from facing a person either. Most people don't have the fortitude to come to your face about a matter. If you go in love, God will put His fear in them. If the problem is with a woman, I suggest never going alone. Take someone with you.

I have practiced this for thirty years and have seen God melt some of the most rebellious hearts. Sad to say, I have seen several who did not repent, and I believe God killed them. It's awesome to walk in complete obedience to the Word of God and see God intervene in dramatic ways.

Ordination of Deacons

According to Acts 6:6, deacons were ordained through the laying on of hands. For the most part, the ordination of deacons should follow the same format as the ordination of a pastor. Sunday morning is the best time for this ceremony. Church members see who the deacons are, hear why they are deacons, and are reminded of what the deacons are for. This service, too, is a spiritual highlight of the year.

Follow the same service as for pastors, only make all the applications to deacons and wives. The charge to the deacons and the church can be given by one of the associate pastors or an already active deacon. The pastor then brings the ordination message and invitation.

Following the sermon, have all the men of the church, representing

142

their families, come by and lay hands on the new deacons as they kneel by their wives at the altar. The men who come remain, kneeling around the deacons being ordained.

The organist should be playing very softly some appropriate hymn like "I Surrender All," "Have Thine Own Way," or "My Jesus, I Love Thee." After the ordination prayer, the pastor should shake hands with all the men and their wives and welcome them as deacons. The pastor then can bring concluding remarks or offer an invitation. After the closing hymn, the new deacons and their wives can form a receiving line at the front of the church. Encourage members to come by and express their love and prayers. This will be a sacred time neither the church nor the deacons will ever forget.

When Joshua was fighting the Amalekites, Israel was winning as long as Moses held up the rod of God. When his hands became heavy and drooped, the Amalekites prevailed. Two men, Aaron and Hur, stood by him and held up his hands and so Israel won. This is what the deacons do for the pastor today. As they hold up his hands, the church prevails. When his hands are weary, he needs help. Praise God for those men around you who hold up your hands. Great will be their reward in heaven.

Ushers

The very first person a visitor meets at church often is an usher! Is the usher ever important! What kind of an impression does he make? Will the visitor feel welcomed? Will he get the polite nod and a quick shuffle into the auditorium?

Very few ushers are ever trained or taught what to do. You will want to notice carefully the decorum of everyone in your church who has any contact with visitors and teach them how to conduct themselves and to carry out their functions in the most inviting way.

Ushers, first of all, are servants. They need a servant's heart. They cannot just stand around talking to each other and exchanging pleasantries with their friends. They are there to serve. A servant must know what is expected of him and then do it.

An usher should be a spirit-filled man of God. Two essentials for an usher are love and joy. These are not personality traits, they are

143

the fruit of the Spirit. To love people so that it shows is so important. A living demonstration of the joy of the Lord goes a long way in ushering.

As a seventeen-year-old street kid, I walked to church for the first time in over ten years. I felt so uncomfortable and out of place. A nice looking, well-dressed usher spotted me. He knew I was new and sensed how I felt. Instead of visiting with his friends, he walked up to me, stuck out his hand, and with a warm smile said, "Hi there, my name is Jake, what's your name?" I was shocked, but impressed. He really wanted to know me. The people who wanted my name usually had been the police! I felt welcome. I never forgot Jake Lyons, and for forty-two years he and his wife have prayed for me every day. He was a great deacon and usher! Next to the preacher in that church, he played the most important role in getting me saved.

The usher must be friendly. Flight attendants on airplanes are. They are trained to be. They must be friendly to get a job. Ushers who will not go out of their way to be friendly with strangers and visitors just have no business being an usher. Souls are at stake. They must realize the importance of their role.

The usher must introduce himself to visitors. The usher should try to find out a little about the visitor. It could be so helpful to introduce the visitor to several other people before they go into the service. If alert, he will get them with someone else about the same age. When he finds out the visitor's occupation, he can introduce him to someone else in the church in the same profession.

Ushers must be full of wisdom. Colossians 1:9 teaches to look for those full of wisdom to serve. It takes a lot of wisdom to do all an usher should do. What are some specific things he should do besides welcome visitors?

He must be aware of those who come with babies and small children. He needs to know how to graciously direct the parents to take babies to the nursery. This isn't always easy. Some are not sure about leaving their baby in the nursery. To get a small child to children's church or to a proper Sunday school class takes the wisdom of Solomon sometimes.

The temperature and ventilation is important in helping people to be comfortable and enjoy the service. A pastor should *never* have to ask publicly for an usher to check the heat or air conditioner. Ushers must be alert to these things.

Young people who sit on the back row and talk during the service are the usher's responsibility. They must know how to handle the situation. The lost can be hindered by talking. The pastor is hurt by it. No pastor should have to call down young people for talking. That's an usher's job. How many have you seen handle the problem?

If a church uses visitors cards and asks visitors to receive one from an usher, he must be ready and get to the people immediately. It just tears me up to be in a church and see visitors hold up their hands while ushers fumble around looking for visitors cards and then ramble down lackadaisically to give them out. There should be two ushers for every section, and they should be alert and get to the people promptly with cards.

Taking the offering is so important. Every usher knows the offering is going to be received. Why, oh, why then do they wait till the last minute to look around for the offering plates. The pastor so often has to call several times to alert the ushers it's time for the offering. Time is precious. It must not be wasted by unconcerned or unprepared ushers.

The usher is a front man. He is a public-relations man for God. He must look sharp and be sharp. His first contact with that visitor can make all the difference in the world. Teach and train him properly.

3/EVANGELISM

15

Personal Evangelism

No thrill surpasses that of seeing someone born again right before your eyes. Jesus told the apostles to "... preach the gospel to every creature" (Mark 16:15). If we are to be disciples of Christ, we must obey this command. Jesus' last words on earth were, "... ye shall be witnesses unto me..." (Acts 1:8). The Book of Acts is replete with evidence and examples of evangelism. In it we learn that witnessing played a significant role in New Testament Christianity. Just as evangelism played an important role in the life of the early church, so it must play an important role in the life of the church today. It must be part of every pastor's ministry.

I said earlier that every church is a reflection of its pastor. He is the shepherd. "Like shepherd, like sheep." Sheep follow the shepherd. He must be able to say with Paul, "Be ye followers of me even as I also am of Christ" (1 Cor. 11:1). If his people are going to witness, he must witness. Paul wrote, "... this is good ... in the sight of God our Saviour who will have all men to be saved and to come unto the knowledge of the truth" (1 Tim. 2:3,4). If this is God's desire, then every preacher should do all he can to see that "all men" come to this knowledge. "All men" certainly means those in the city where he pastors.

It is a travesty to send missionaries all over the world and do little or nothing about getting the gospel to everyone in your community. Dean Fetterhoff wrote, "If the fires and passion of evangelism die in the preacher, they will very likely burn out in the church."

"Evangelism is simply the church getting down to business about its first obligation, reaching people with the message and invitation of Jesus Christ," says Dr. Joe Ellis. He further states, "The most important tasks the church can do are those that only the church can do. Since she cannot do everything she must do first and best that which no one else in the world can do—make Christians and nurture them in the Lord.''

Of course, the ministry doesn't end with evangelism, but it has to begin there. Dr. C. S. Mueller says, "The smell of death is upon any church that ignores the elementary fact of evangelism. It hasn't long to live, not long at all." Today many pastors are not fishers of men but keepers of aquariums. If you are not fishing, you are not following, for Jesus said, "Follow me, and I will make you fishers of men" (Matt. 4:19).

It may seem superfluous to stress evangelism by the pastor, but when thousands of churches go a whole year without one person being born of God, something is wrong. Nothing excites a home like a new baby. Nothing stirs up a church like new babies being born of God week after week. Nothing motivates and drives one to holy living, Bible study, and prayer like witnessing. Pastor, make up your mind now to make evangelism a vital part of your own life and the life of your church. Heed Paul's words: "... do the work of an evangelist" (2 Tim. 4:5).

The owner of a small two-story hotel was having problems. Sheraton built a beautiful ten-story hotel right beside his on the left, and Hilton built one on the right. He solved his problem by stretching a huge sign over his hotel between the two new ones. It simply said Main Entrance. Write Main Entrance above personal evangelism. It all starts there.

The Bible is full of examples of men who practiced personal evangelism. Let's look at a few.

Jesus Himself. Jesus certainly evangelized individuals and did it consistently. In John 4 (probably the most beautiful example ever) the Lord Jesus went out of His way to reach one lonely fallen woman. Remember when the disciples returned with the food and said, "Let's eat"? Jesus wasn't hungry any longer. He said, "I have meat to eat that ye know not of" (John 4:32). He had the thrill of seeing that woman saved and cleansed. Then He told his disciples, "My meat is to do the will of him that sent me, and to finish his work" (John 4:34). Though He preached to multitudes, He was always ministering to individuals.

Paul. Paul said, ". . . I . . . have taught you publicly, and from

150

house to house" (Acts 20:20). This is the twenty-twenty vision we all should have. It is not enough to preach publicly. You must preach personally and privately. Paul did that.

Peter. Yes, Peter denied the Lord but repented and then, filled with the Holy Spirit, became an ardent soul-winner. "And daily in the temple, and in every house, they ceased not to teach and preach Jesus Christ" (Acts 5:42). Under Peter's ministry it is stated, "And believers were the more added to the Lord, multitudes both of men and women" (Acts 5:14).

Follow their examples. A burden for souls is caught, not taught. Everything rises or falls with leadership. A man cannot lead a church where he himself will not go. Dr. L. R. Scarborough said, "Many a minister is on the treadmill, marking time, drying up, not earning his salt because he has no passion for souls and no power for effective service."

Essentials for Successful Evangelism

What is going to make a church evangelistic and its people soul-winners? Here are some essentials.

One must have the love of Christ to constrain him. It did Paul as he said in 2 Corinthians 5:14. "For God so loved the world, that he gave his only begotten Son . . ." (John 3:16). If believers are full of the love of Christ, they too will give the Lord Jesus to the world. Love, *agape* love, which constrains one to be an ambassador for Christ, comes from God. It is totally unselfish and yearns to make others happy. Most don't witness because they have so little genuine love.

One needs a burden for souls. Paul had this. He wrote

> Brethren, my heart's desire and prayer to God for Israel is, that they might be saved (Rom. 10:1). I say the truth in Christ, I lie not, my conscience also bearing me witness in the Holy Ghost, That I have great heaviness and continual sorrow in my heart. For I could wish that myself were accursed from Christ for my brethren, my kinsmen according to the flesh (Rom. 9:1-3).

It has been my experience that the minute a person is born of God he has a burden to see loved ones and friends saved.

New believers usually ask you to come talk to a loved one. One day

I led a seventy-two-year-old lady to Christ. She called me the next day and in tears asked if I would talk to her ninety-two-year-old mother. "Of course," I said. Her mother had been in bed for over six months, but the daughter said, "I am going to pray she will be able to get up and come over here tomorrow."

The next day she called and said, "They are here." The mother's eighty-six-year-old sister was there as well. The ninety-two-year-old lady was very feeble. We went over the gospel, and both women bowed their heads in brokenness and invited the Lord Jesus to be their Savior. The eldest woman looked up, her face beaming, clapped her hands softly, and said, "I am without one plea. I know Thy blood was shed for me, and that Thou bidst me come to Thee. O Lamb of God, I have come, I have come!" Heaven came down and flooded all our souls. A daughter had gotten burdened for her ninety-two-year-old mother. This mother got burdened for her sister, and God saved three dear ladies who are all in heaven today.

One needs tears of concern. "He that goeth forth and weepeth, bearing precious seed, shall doubtless come again with rejoicing, bringing his sheaves with him" (Ps. 126:6). Jesus wept over Jerusalem (see John 11:35). Paul wept "with many tears" (Acts 20:19). Jeremiah wept (see Jer. 9:1). We should, too. Our tears don't save people. They show that our hearts are in tune with God's. We respond to lost people as He did, and God is now able to hear our prayers and work in the lost person's heart.

The lack of tears is revealing. It may be the greatest single barometer of our day. We have more money, better buildings, the best music, but so few tears! Oh, that our eyes were a fountain of tears (see Jer. 9:1).

We had prayed so long for Joe. He was an alcoholic. One Wednesday his thirteen-year-old daughter came to me before prayer meeting with her heart broken, weeping, and said, "Brother Wemp, when is my daddy going to get saved?" He had come home drunk and cursing the night before. After seeing her broken heart, I said, "I believe it won't be long." The next Sunday Joe was in church. At the first words of the invitation song, Joe came forward and gave me a bear hug like I had never had. Right there he was saved and never drank another drop. My preaching didn't make the difference. Some tears before God made the difference.

One needs to consider the reality of hell. "In hell he lift up his eyes, being in torments" (Luke 16:23). Hell is no joke. Never laugh at jokes about hell. Maybe we need more old-fashioned hellfire and brimstone sermons, until, as in Jonathan Edwards's day, people feel like they are slipping into hell and cry out for mercy.

General William Booth said he wished every Salvation Army preacher could spend five months in hell. If they could, he knew they would come back with a greater burden than ever before. If we really believe our neighbors, our friends, and our loved ones are going to burn in a literal hell forever if they are not born again, we will weep and witness with a consuming passion.

One needs to see soul-winning as a privilege. The biggest thing that ever happens in a city is not a multimillion-dollar deal by the president of some corporation. It is a soul won to Christ. What happens through your daily witness is more important than the president's decisions. To be a real soul-winner one must realize that. It will keep his priorities in order. What an astounding thing that God takes a hunk of dirt like us and uses us to help people go to heaven. That's fantastic. No wonder ". . . he that winneth souls is wise" (Prov. 11:30).

One must confess and forsake every known sin in order to be used by God in winning people to Christ.

He that covereth his sins shall not prosper . . . (Prov. 28:13).

Behold, the LORD's hand is not shortened, that it cannot save; neither his ear heavy, that it cannot hear: But your iniquities have separated between you and your God, and your sins have hid his face from you, that he will not hear (Is. 59:1,2).

God isn't going to take the pure water of life in a dirty pitcher to thirsty souls. Every soul-winner knows that. Jealousy, bitterness, covetousness, lust, short temper, wrong attitudes, and all forms of worldliness will keep you from being used by God. When you get right down to it, *you* don't win people—God does. But it's so wonderful to be around when He does it.

153

One needs faith. You must *expect* God to use you. The young preacher asked the much-used preacher, "Why is it every time you preach, people get saved, and when I preach nothing happens?"

The older preacher asked, "You don't expect people to be saved every time you preach, do you?"

The answer came, "No, of course not."

The wise preacher answered, "Well, that's why!"

How true that is, and it is the answer to so many barren ministries and individuals.

Here is encouragement. "But God hath chosen the foolish things of the world to confound the wise; and God hath chosen the weak things of the world to confound the things which are mighty" (1 Cor. 1:27). Isn't that great? I can qualify for both the foolish and the weak. That means God has chosen to use me. Why not claim that for yourself? "Humble yourselves therefore under the mighty hand of God . . . (1 Pet. 5:6). It works.

Not only that, but "the gospel is the power of God unto salvation" (Rom. 1:16). Rockets have enough power to get a man all the way to heaven. How thrilling! When you preach the gospel, then, you ought to expect something to happen.

". . . ye shall receive power, after that the Holy Ghost is come upon you: and ye shall be witnesses unto me . . . (Acts 1:8). When you depend on the Holy Spirit, you have the power of God behind your witness. Something ought to happen. You should be surprised and shocked if people don't get saved when you witness with such power behind you. Remember, "He did not many mighty works there [in his own hometown] because of their unbelief" (Matt. 13:58). He won't do it where you are unless, with faith, you expect Him to. He said, ". . . I have . . . ordained you, that ye should go and bring forth fruit" (John 15:16). Count on it!

One must preach boldly. In Acts 4:29 the disciples prayed for boldness at a time of persecution. God granted it, and they spoke the Word of God with boldness. "And with great power gave the apostles witness of resurrection of the Lord Jesus: and great grace was upon them all " (v. 33). This can and should be the testimony of every pastor. Pray for boldness, and preach with boldness. You will see God do great and mighty things through you.

Some don't have this boldness because of fear of people and what they might do. Too many preachers lack boldness for fear they will lose their churches. They need to hear the words of Jeremiah, "Be not afraid of their faces: for I am with thee to deliver thee, saith the LORD" (Jer. 1:8). Paul feared people so little because he feared God so much. Holy boldness, not brashness, comes from sacrificial abandonment to the Lord Jesus Christ. Are you sold out to God, or are you playing games? If God's servants were half as sold on Jesus as Communists are on Lenin, we could turn the world upside down tomorrow. If you are going to be a soul-winner and lead people to Christ, you must have this holy boldness.

One must live a Spirit-filled life. The Holy Spirit alone can convict and convert. You can't manipulate people into getting saved. The gift of gab won't do it. It takes a man of God who is filled with the Spirit of God. Someone said, "It's hard to win people to Christ today." Why, it's always been hard. It takes the power of God, and a Spirit-filled pastor knows when that power is flowing through him. Preachers used to sow seed; today they string intellectual pearls. Someone has figured it takes a thousand laymen and six preachers to win one soul per year. No—a thousand times no! It just takes Spirit-filled Christians faithfully sowing the seed for hundreds to come to Christ day after day. R. C. Worley, a lay pastor at Thomas Road Baptist Church, leads about a thousand people to Christ each year.

Every pastor must be a personal soul-winner himself. This keeps him fresh and vibrant. It makes every Sunday exciting as those he won to Christ in their homes during the week confess Christ before the church. This is the heartbeat of the ministry. This is what keeps a pastor going when the problems come. These converts won through a pastor's personal visit will be the most loyal and faithful believers a pastor can want.

Witnessing

Witnessing, or soul-winning, isn't natural. Satan fights it. The flesh doesn't want to do it. The world surely hates it. If a pastor and people are going to make this a vital part of their balanced ministry, here are some things to be considered.

Organize your time. You won't find time to go soul-winning unless you plan on it. It must be a priority. Set definite times for soul-winning visitation (see Chapter 8 on Visitation). Just as a pastor has his study time, he must have his soul-winning time, or it won't happen. Many times you will go soul-winning not feeling at all like winning souls. As you go (in obedience to the Lord), you will find someone prepared by God who receives the Lord, and it will give you the renewal you need.

Be soul-conscious. Thirty-eight years ago I was a draftsman. We built bridges and buildings out of steel. To this day, every time I see a large structure it attracts my attention. Pastors ought to be soul conscious so that every time they meet a person, they immediately think about his soul and where he will spend eternity. Every time God puts us with a person for a few minutes, we should look for the reason.

During a week of meetings I was asked to switch rooms in the motel where I was staying. At first it bothered me to have to move. The motel management had a maid move my belongings while I was eating. When I returned, she had just finished and was about to leave. I handed her a tract and began talking to her about the Lord. God had prepared her, and she received the Lord Jesus as her Savior. The next day she told my wife she had planned to leave her husband that very night, until she accepted Christ. Now she was staying with him and wanted him to accept Christ, too. God had directed the whole move.

Knock on all doors. Don't try to push the door down, but gently knock on the heart's door of every person you can. If they are unconcerned, you know God only wants you to plant the seed this time. Pastors who do this consistently find one heart after another prepared to meet Christ. Soul-winning pastors will win more people to Christ by "accident" than most other pastors win in a lifetime.

In Salt Lake City at the Temple Hotel, where the vast majority are Mormons, I was eating lunch one day. As the waitress took my order, I handed her a tract. When she brought my food, she remarked that she had already read the tract and had never thought about Christ like the tract put it. Wow! In a very few minutes she was in tears and right there prayed to receive Christ. That was one door I never expected to see open. It was a joy to give her name to a local Christian for follow-up.

Keep at it. "And let us not be weary in well doing: for in due season we shall reap, if we faint not" (Gal. 6:9). Oh, the tragedy that so many pastors give up so quickly and easily. They go out a few times and nothing happens. Then they tell themselves, "This isn't for me. I'm just not cut out to be a soul-winner. My gift is teaching," they conclude. How foolish. What a rationalization. No one is "cut out for it." It's hard work. The devil fights it. We are commanded to get the gospel to every creature (see Mark 16:15). Not to witness is rebellion and high treason. Every pastor must, to be true to his calling. God's promise is to reap.

Scatter the seed. No farmer digs one enormous hole and pours a whole bag of seed into it. He scatters it, if he wants a good harvest. Look for ways to scatter the seed into the hearts of thousands. ". . . He which soweth sparingly shall reap also sparingly . . ." (2 Cor. 9:6). Don't cry out against some pastor across town who is seeing hundreds come to Christ, saying the conversions can't be real. Don't criticize his methods or results. He probably is sowing more seed than you. Get out and keep sowing the seed, and you will see the hundreds come.

It has been my privilege to be very close to Dr. Jerry Falwell for six years. Time and time again, when driving with him down a street in Lynchburg, he has told about every house we pass—how he visited the residents and what their responses have been. You see, he has been to every house in Lynchburg with the gospel. No wonder one fifth of its population has confessed to receive Christ as Savior in his church.

Avoid detours. If Satan can't defeat you, he will suggest a detour. Don't get off on tangents. Whatever you do, don't fight some other preacher who doesn't see eye to eye with you. Don't fight some denomination or liberal preacher. Sow the seed.

A man in our church worked with a man married to a Jehovah's Witness and asked me to go see her. Of course, I went and began witnessing to her about the forgiveness of sin. She tried every way to get me talking about hell or something else so she could argue. All I did was keep telling her how Christ suffered for her sins. God entered her heart and she trusted Christ. Afterward she told how she couldn't get over the fact that I never mentioned "Baptist" or "hell" or "once saved always saved," and she found no place to trap me.

157

There is a terrible danger of a pastor's becoming an amateur psychologist who sits in his office counseling all day. Others spend all their time discipling and never balance their ministry to include soul-winning as well. Some have gotten detoured into fighting everyone who doesn't see eye to eye with them on every detail of Scripture. If you want to build a church and help change the world, keep winning souls and keep off the detours.

Never argue. Real soul-winners don't argue. ". . . the servant of the Lord must not strive . . ." (2 Tim. 2:24). You may win an argument, but you won't win a soul for Christ. If in witnessing you feel the conversation getting heated, stop. Apologize. Let the person know you don't want to argue, and you are sorry for anything you might have said or done to be offensive. If the gospel is an offense, that's all right. But if I'm offensive, that's sin. Soul-winners learn quickly that they must not strive or be offensive.

Leave the door open. Our mothers kept telling us, "Shut the door." But a soul-winner learns to leave the door open, spiritually speaking. If the person being witnessed to is not open and receptive, don't push. If the person gives or makes smart remarks, never, never give a smart reply. This is unforgivable. A Christian should never do this. If you believe God is sovereign, then understand that when He wants to use you to win a person to Christ He will have prepared that person.

My good friend Bill Pack has told publicly how he was rude to me the first time I came to see him. He didn't want to be bothered by a preacher. He was rude, but I would have sinned wickedly to have responded in like manner. Because I gently left the door open, he later received Christ as Savior, became a deacon, and then was called by God and is now the pastor of a fine church.

Be authoritative. They said of Jesus, ". . . he taught them as one that had authority, and not as the scribes" (Mark 1:22). A soul-winner must be authoritative, not arrogant. Some people witness but never see any results. They are almost apologetic in their approach. A lost person isn't going to have any confidence in them or their message. The world needs a "thus saith the Lord" kind of message.

Be serious. I cut up a lot and love to tease people, but when witnessing I am dead serious. Never joke about hell. You need not be so serious that you make a person feel uncomfortable, but he must know you are serious about leading him to Christ.

Beware of distractions. Telephones, television, and a thousand other things can distract a person from really hearing the gospel, even during one-on-one witnessing. Many times, when I've been at the point of asking a person to accept Christ, I've almost seen the devil suggest that he light up a cigarette. It's a distraction and you need to ask if the person would mind waiting until you are finished before lighting up. If a person begins to ask questions that you know will be clear after he receives Christ, ask if he minds saving his questions until you have gone through the plan of salvation first.

Use the Word of God. ". . . faith comes by hearing . . ." (Rom. 10:17). Quote Scripture. Often unsaved people have problems reading the Elizabethan "thee's" and "thou's." Too, the person might not read a verse you just pointed to in the Bible. The Word of God is the ". . . sword of the Spirit . . ." (Eph. 6:17) which brings conviction and cuts to the heart (see Acts 7:54).

Give them the gospel. ". . . the gospel . . . is the power of God unto salvation to everyone that believeth . . ." (Rom. 1:16). It is shocking to see how the gospel is left out of half of the so-called "gospel" tracts. The same is true of most sermons. Probably most witnessing is done without one word of the gospel in it.

What is the gospel? ". . . I declare unto you the gospel . . . that Christ died for our sins according to the scriptures; and that he was buried, and that he arose again the third day according to the Scriptures" (1 Cor. 15:1,3,4). The gospel must include the substitutionary death for sinners. First Peter 3:18 is the best verse to use to bring conviction to a sinner's heart: "For Christ also hath once suffered for sins, the just for the unjust, that he might bring us to God. . . ." The fact that He suffered for our sins seems to open hearts quicker than any other truth.

One day a lady, who thought she was saved, asked if I would give her some verses to make her husband go to church. I quoted Romans 3:10,23; 6:23 and 1 Peter 3:18. She suddenly burst into tears and said, "I never realized He suffered for *my* sins." Here she was writing these verses for her husband, and the Holy Spirit applied them to her own heart. If the gospel is "the power of God unto salvation," then it should be very prominent in witnessing.

If you only have a minute at the door with someone, tell him, "God loves you so much He let His Son the Lord Jesus suffer and die for your sins. The Bible says 'Christ has also once suffered for sins that he might bring us to God.' Here's a tract that tells about it. Let me leave it with you to read. You will enjoy it." Often no seed has been planted before. Now the Holy Spirit has something to convict him with and can then bring him into the new birth.

Be sure the lost person understands the gospel before making a decision. In the parable of the sower in Matthew 13, God uses the word "understand." The seed that fell by the wayside represented those who heard the word ". . . and understandeth it not, then cometh the wicked one, and catcheth away that which was sown in his heart" (Matt. 13:23). He does not need to understand the Trinity or the doctrine of election, but he must understand the gospel, the only basis on which God forgives sins and takes a person to heaven. It doesn't matter whether he is five or fifty; he must understand this.

How horrifying when a preacher says, "You don't have to understand it, just take it by faith" or, worse yet, "Take it by blind faith." No wonder our churches are filled with unsaved people who have made false professions of faith. Being sure that they understand the basis on which God saves will save you many a heartache.

Thelma came to our church from one where they didn't preach the gospel. As I presented he gospel to her one day, she suddenly said, "I've got it." When I asked her what she had, she said, "I was just saved. I see now how Christ paid for my sins, too." And saved she was.

While in seminary, I was on my way home on a bus one night, when a boy got on and came all the way to the back of the bus and sat next to me. After a few minutes of conversation, I handed him a tract. He read it. I knew we would be at the next stop very soon. Quickly, I quoted the "Romans road" passages to present the gospel.

Suddenly he turned to me and said, "Hey, I see that." Then he stood up and pulled the cord to get off the bus. Again he said, "I see that now." I was stunned as he jumped off and the bus pulled away.

Finally I realized something had happened to him. I got off at the next stop and ran back to catch him. Then I asked, "What did you mean when you said, 'I see that?' "

Just as clear as a bell he said, "I just got saved." He genuinely was and we became close friends. He understood the good news of Christ's death and believed in the Lord Jesus and was saved. His life was transformed from that moment on. Be sure to help people understand.

Don't use difficult theological terms. One must learn how to think as the unsaved do. Put yourself in their shoes. There is so much talk about being "born again," but precious few know what preachers are talking about. To talk about redemption or propitiation just clouds the issue. They will understand if you talk about the forgiveness of sin and going to heaven. The old anagram KISS, "Keep it simple, Stupid," is good advice.

Give invitations. Give people an opportunity to sign on the dotted line. Again, don't push them or try to force a decision, but do give them a chance to say yes to God. You can never see the heart. The person may be about to say yes to God. I repeat: You can never see the heart. He may be about to burst inside with conviction and not show it one bit on the outside.

Max and I were visiting with Jimmy and Isabel. I had presented the gospel thoroughly and so I asked if they wanted to accept Christ. Jimmy turned to Isabel and asked, "Isabel, do you want to?" in an unemotional, matter-of-fact way. She replied, "If you want to, I will." It was as if they were discussing buying a loaf of bread. He turned and said, "Yes, we're ready," with no emotion whatever. We prayed, and they accepted Christ. They showed no outward emotion, but their lives were transformed and they became two fine Christians. He later became a deacon. Never second guess people. Always give them an opportunity to respond, even though you may feel sure that they are not ready.

Get them to confess Christ (see Matt. 10:32). If someone is with you, get the new Christian to turn to that person and tell him what happened. Then get the new Christian to come and confess Christ publicly before your whole church. Explain how this is done. This strengthens him, glorifies God, and will bless the hearts of those who hear it.

Presenting a Plan of Salvation

Most Christians cannot give a simple, logical presentation of the plan of salvation. People often criticize a "canned" presentation of the gospel. What some fail to realize is that very few people are original enough or spiritual enough to extemporize articulately when they begin witnessing. How then, are they going to present the gospel? Too often it is uttered in a haphazard way, and then Christians wonder why they have no success leading people to Christ.

Pastors must train their people. You, as a pastor, must have your own plan for evangelizing. All effective soul-winners will tell you they have a set plan, which they usually modify for each individual. One serious mistake I made was not to give our people a definite plan. I didn't want the people to be robots who said exactly what I said. The result was that most just didn't do anything.

People need help. Most soul-winners started out using someone else's tried-and-proven methods. A pastor should use an effective method himself and then teach it to his people so that he knows what they are sharing. The majority will not make up plans of their own.

Invariably, people say the hardest part of witnessing is getting started. To me that is the easiest part. Often in seminars I'll ask, "If I can show a way to witness to a total stranger, with his permission, in nineteen seconds, how many will try it?" Most say, "I will." Here are a few approaches. The first is the easiest way.

Tracts. What a key to open the door! What a tool for witnessing! Never be unfriendly when passing out a tract. Always be pleasant, with a smile on your face. In a home, a service station, or a restaurant it really works. After paying a bill or visiting a few minutes in a home, hand a tract to a person and say, "Let me give you something good to read when you have a few moments. You'll like this."

Then pause a few seconds. Often they ask, "What is it?"

Whether they ask or not, you then say, "This just tells you how to go to heaven." Pause again. Many times the reply comes, "Is that right?" or "Really?"

Then very graciously ask, "Tell me, do you know for sure you are going to heaven?" The common replies are "I sure hope so," "I think I am," "I'm trying to," and "No, I don't." The last is the most common.

Once again ask, "Wouldn't you like to be sure?" Those who are open or prepared will say yes, and you are off.

If the person is not interested at the moment, ask him to read the tract when he has time and to think about it. (Usually this approach is used with a stranger you most likely will not see again.) When visiting the person in his home you can ask him to read the tract later and tell him you would like to talk about it with them some other time. Then later follow up the visit. Remember, you are looking for people prepared by the Holy Spirit. If they are not prepared, you simply plant the seed.

In a service station I gave a tract to the husband of a lady in our church and asked him to read it when he had time. We hadn't even been able to get Bill to come to church. A couple of weeks later, while visiting a few doors from his home, I remembered giving him the tract. In a few moments, I was in his home and found him open to the gospel. That night he, too, trusted Christ as his Savior, and he confessed Him publicly the very next Sunday. This will become rather common if you are persistent in giving out tracts.

One day I went to an address to visit a couple at someone's request. At the door I asked, "Is this Mrs. Johnson?"

She said, "No, you have the wrong house. Mrs. Johnson lives two doors down."

"I'm sorry I bothered you," I said. "But let me give you something good to read." And I handed her a tract.

She took one look and said, "That's funny, someone else gave me one of these about a week ago."

"That's great," I said. "Tell me, did you read it?"

"Oh, yes," she replied.

"Good. May I ask, have you thought much about what was in the tract?"

Tears welled up in her eyes and she soberly said, "That's all I've been able to think about all week long."

In all my life I've never found anyone more prepared than Mrs. Parker was. She wept as she accepted Christ. I don't know who gave her the first tract, but won't he be thrilled when he gets to heaven and learns that he was instrumental in her salvation? Of course, the point is not who gets the credit but that a dear lady was saved. What if we all, courteously and consistently, gave out tracts? We would find more Mrs. Parkers prepared to receive Christ, because the seed had been planted earlier.

Testimony. Very often the door will open to share a word of testimony during a conversation. When this happens ask, "Do you know for sure you are going to heaven?" The same questions then can follow, and once again you are leading a person to Christ.

In the home of a newcomer to town or a first-time vistor to church, a pastor can say, "You know, I'm preaching for one reason. I want to help people go to heaven. After I was saved, I found it so wonderful to know that all my sins are forgiven and that I'm going to heaven that I had to tell others. Do you know for sure you are going to heaven?" Literally thousands of times I've used this approach, and it works. If the person is not interested at the moment, leave a tract and an invitation to come to the greatest church in town. Then send others to visit or call.

Take-offs. The late Dr. Walter L. Wilson was the master at this. Just be alert during a conversation and look for something you can make a take off on and lead into witnessing. There are many obvious ones.

On a plane I once asked the stewardess how high we were. She said thirty thousand feet. Then I asked if she were ever going to be any closer to heaven than that. Startled, she said, "I sure hope so." From that I led into the plan of salvation, and she prayed with me to receive Christ.

You can ask a person for directions, thank him, and then ask graciously, "Do you know how to get to heaven?"

A man was complaining about how hot it was one day. I agreed and then said, "Boy, if the heat here bothers a person, think what it would be like in hell. I surely don't want to go there, do you?" The man looked shocked and answered, "No, I don't." Once again the door was opened.

Surveys. A church can take a religious survey door-to-door. After asking a series of questions, one can finally ask, "Do you have a sincere desire to know more about God?" If the answer is yes, you are in.

Trying. Just try the door and see if it opens. If you walk in the Spirit, have a genuine love for people, and sincerely want to help people go to heaven, you really don't need gimmicks or fancy ways to witness. Often on a plane, in a waiting room, or in a service station, after talking a few minutes to a person, I'll just ask, "Could I ask you my pet question?" No one has ever said no. Then I ask the same question,

164

"Do you know for sure you are going to heaven?" Some suggest asking, "If you die tonight, do you know for sure you will go to heaven?" This is a little stronger. The key is to find a way that works for you and then use it.

Instruction

Now that the door is opened, how do you present the gospel simply and logically? It is so important that the presentation is clear so that people understand what they are doing. Here are four ways to present the Word of God.

1. *The Romans Road* is probably the best known and most widely used method of presenting the plan of salvation. This plan primarily uses Scripture from the Book of Romans. Many use the outline of the Romans Road with variations of their own. It is good to have an outline to keep on track and thus be open to the Holy Spirit directing you to particular verses that fit the occasion.

After a person has said he would like to be sure he is going to heaven, turn to the Book of Romans if you are going to have them read with you. One fatal mistake is to be accusative in witnessing. Don't start out by saying, "First you need to realize you are a sinner." They immediately become defensive. Rather, read from chapter three of Romans. "There is none righteous, no not one . . . (v. 10), . . . for all have sinned, and come short of the glory of God (v. 23)."

Then say quickly, "We all are in the same boat. We have all sinned, haven't we?" They will always admit to being a sinner if we include ourselves. Otherwise, they believe that we think we are holier than they are and are accusing them. This is crucial in the opening. Next in importance is to use illustrations for emphasis and explanation. Here is the way I present the gospel when witnessing to a person.

"Suppose we had a ten-gallon jug of pure, clean, fresh water and someone poured one drop of poison into that water. Would you drink it? Of course not. Sin is like poison. One drop can pollute us and make us unclean, unfit for heaven.

"Now God says, 'The wages of sin is death' (Rom. 6:23). There is but one penalty for sin, and it is death, separation from God. In physical death, our life is separated from our body. Spiritual death means that our life is separated from God. If you pay for your sins or I pay for mine, we will be separated from God forever.

"But, you know what? God loves us and doesn't want us to have to pay for our sins. Look here. 'But God commendeth his love toward us, in that, while we were yet sinners, Christ died for us' (Rom. 5:8). Why did Christ die? Because death is the wages for sin. He didn't just die physically; he was separated from God. He cried, '. . . My God, my God, why hast thou forsaken me?' (Matt. 27:46). God also said, 'For Christ also hath once suffered for sins, the just for the unjust, that he might bring us to God . . .' (1 Pet. 3:18). That's a lot of love, isn't it? He suffered for everything we ever did or will do wrong.

"Now, suppose I owed you ten thousand dollars and couldn't pay it. Then a friend said, 'Sumner, let me pay that debt for you. You can't pay him, and so you couldn't pay me back either. I want to give it to you.' Then he counts out ten thousand dollars and hands it to you. I don't owe you one more penny, do I?

"Suppose, though, that I say 'No, I won't accept your offer. I'm going to do the best I can.' And I count the thirty-seven cents change I have and offer a comb and a knife to you in place of ten thousand dollars. Would you accept that in place of ten thousand dollars? Of course not. No bank would.

"God wants you and me to accept the offer of Christ's payment in our place. We do this by telling God that we accept the Lord Jesus as our Savior for God says, 'That if thou shalt confess with thy mouth the Lord Jesus, and shalt believe in thine heart that God hath raised him from the dead, thou shalt be saved. . . . For whosoever shall call upon the name of the Lord shall be saved' (Rom. 10:9,13).

"Do you understand that? Do you believe the Lord Jesus suffered and died for your sins, then rose again? Do you want to call upon Him and receive Him as your Savior right now?"

Briefly this is the Romans Road presentation. You can add any emphasis that you feel is important. Many pastors use this very effectively. You should teach and train your people how to use it.

2. *The Four Spiritual Laws* used by Campus Crusade can be an effective witnessing tool. In my possession are at least fifteen booklets that are spin-offs of the *Four Spiritual Laws* booklet. Major denominations have brought out their own versions of it. Campus Crusade

has proved the value of a tool that helps and guides Christians in the presentation of the gospel. On purpose, I simply read the booklet to a man one night without any comments to see its effectiveness, and the man prayed with me to receive Christ. You can order these tracts from Campus Crusade, Arrowhead Springs, San Bernardino, California 92404.

There are two key points to this presentation. First, it starts out on the positive—"God loves you and has a wonderful plan for your life"—rather than a blunt, "You are a sinner." It presents the wonderful side of God, the fact that He loves us. Second, it has a step-by-step presentation that helps guide a soul-winner and keeps him on course. The diagrams are helpful also. At the end of the booklet a prayer is presented to help the person invite the Lord Jesus into his heart.

3. *Diagrams.* Below is a diagram that can help people understand and know the Lord.

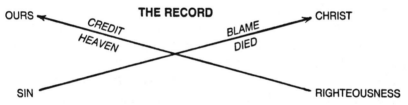

Here is one way to begin when using this method: "Let's look at our records. We are all in the same boat; we have a pretty good list of sins, isn't that right?" (Point to the diagram as each point is being presented.) God says, '. . . There is none righteous, no, not one" [Rom. 3:10]. ". . . for all have sinned, and come short of the glory of God' " [Rom. 3:23]. Continue using the same illustrations as under the Romans Road.

Here is another illustration: "If I slapped you in the face or cursed you, you wouldn't be very friendly to me. I would offend you. Sin is an offense to God. God says that '. . . the wages of sin is death' [Rom. 6:23]. Sin carries with it penalty and pollution. Now look under Christ's record and what do we see? Righteousness. He knew no sin. '. . . in him is no sin,' God says, [1 John 3:5]. He was good enough to go to heaven, wasn't He? Now let's look at the diagram.

"The whole Bible can be summed up right here. Two thousand years ago God took all our sins [point to the word] and put them under

Christ's record. He took the blame [point to the word] as though He had actually sinned. Why did He die? Because that's the penalty. But He also shed His blood, and that takes care of the pollution, for '. . . the blood of Jesus Christ his Son cleanseth us from all sin' (1 John 1:7).

"Now that's a record of history. God can actually transfer what one does from one record to another. Now God wants to take Christ's righteousness [point to the word] and put it over on our account. We get credit [point] for what He did [point to "righteousness"] and we go to heaven [point] as though we were actually righteous or perfect.

"If I deposited one million dollars in your bank account, would you be a millionnaire? Of course. God says, '. . . The righteousness of God . . . is . . . unto all and upon all them that believe" (Rom. 3:22). God deposits to our account all that Christ did when we believe in Him as our Savior. Do you understand that? This is what it means to believe in the Lord Jesus Christ."

God gave me this diagram a number of years ago, and thousands have been led to Christ through using it. It presents a side of salvation that is often left out—the imputed righteousness of Christ. Many are still trying to earn points to go to heaven. They feel they must be good enough to get there. This diagram has helped many see the fallacy of that view.

3. *The James Kennedy plan* also is effective and has been profitable. It is explained in his book *Evangelism Explosion*. Many feel this plan is too complicated for the majority to use. It takes extensive training, but it has proved worthwhile in countless churches.

4. *Invitation.* Truth transforms, not just informs. When the gospel is not responded to, it tends to harden the heart. Never try to force a decision, but always give an opportunity for a person to make a decision.

A student said she was afraid to give an invitation for fear someone would make a false profession of faith. She had never led a soul to Christ. My response was that it isn't our business to tell if it's real or not. Our obligation is to carefully present the gospel, be sure they understand it, and sincerely pray that they receive Christ. We have to leave the results up to God. He alone sees the heart.

Of course, some are not going to really mean it when they profess to receive Christ. Jesus had a Judas. Every preacher has had some false professions of faith. There will always be the tares, but that should not keep us from offering the opportunity to receive the Lord Jesus. Most commitments will be real if we are depending on the Holy Spirit to do the convicting and converting.

When the person has been presented the gospel and understands it, then what? The person needs to know how to be saved and then to be willing to be saved. Some don't believe it and some don't want it. If the person has given evidence of understanding the way to be saved, the next step is to see if he is willing to be saved.

If he is not willing to be saved at that time, you must try to find out why. Sometimes you never will learn the truth. For two years I tried to lead the husband of one of our members to Christ. He kept saying no and gave all kinds of lame excuses. Later it came out he had been having an affair with another woman for seven years. No wonder he wasn't ready.

If people are not willing, often it is simply because they love their own sin and are not willing for God to change their lives and direction. They haven't truly repented. They aren't willing to turn their backs on their old lives and receive new life in Christ Jesus. Getting to the root of the problem is often a complex challenge. It is not our purpose here to give a full course on personal evangelism. More than anything, we learn by doing. God gives us wisdom when we really seek it, and many excuses can be overcome when we are being controlled and directed by the Holy Spirit.

When the person has said "Yes, I want to be saved" and appears to understand the gospel, you can say something like this: "Bill, God says, '. . . Him that cometh to me I will in no wise cast out' [John 6:37]. How do we come to Him? Why, in our hearts, for God 'looketh on the heart' [1 Sam. 16:7]. Jesus said, 'Behold, I stand at the door, and knock: if anyone hear my voice, and open the door, I will come in.' [Rev. 3:20]. God also said, 'As many as received him to them gave he gave power to become the sons of God, even to them that believe on his name, [John 1:12]. For '. . . whosoever shall call upon the name of the Lord shall be saved' [Acts 2:21]. Would you like for us to bow our heads together while you in your heart let God know you want to receive the Lord Jesus as your personal Savior?''

He replies yes and you say, "Bow your head with me. While we both have our heads bowed and our eyes closed, pray this after me if you really mean it. 'Dear God [pause for him to pray], I know I have sinned, too. [Pause] I'm sorry for all my sins. [Pause] Lord Jesus, I accept you as my Savior. [Pause] Come into my heart and save me right now. [Pause] Change my life and help me live for you. [Pause] In Jesus' name, amen."

Ask, "Did you pray that from your heart and mean it? Jesus said, 'I stand at the door, and knock: if anyone...opens the door, I will come in.' Where is the Lord Jesus right now?" If he answers with assurance, "In my heart," rejoice with him.

A verse that is most effective in helping people gain assurance of salvation is John 3:36. "He that believeth on the Son hath everlasting life. . . ." After you have read that verse with him, the questioning should go something like this. "Bill, if God Himself were to say to you right now, 'You have everlasting life, you are saved,' would you be sure you were saved then?" He answers yes. "Bill, this is God's Word, just as sure as if He were speaking it right now. He says, 'You want to know who is saved? You want to know who has everlasting life?' He couldn't put everyone's name in here, but He says, 'He that believeth on the Son.' Bill, do you believe your good works or your church will get you to heaven, or do you believe the Son will get you to heaven?" He answers, "The Son."

You go on, "God says that he who believes in the Son *has* everlasting life. Do you have everlasting life?" If he answers, "I think so," remind him that God didn't say he would *think* he has everlasting life but that he *would* have everlasting life.

Ask again, "Do you believe the Son has saved you? Do you have everlasting life?" When he answers, "Yes, because God said so," his assurance will be based on the Word of God and not on what you might say. Faith, genuine faith, comes by the Word of God. This has proved to be of great help in giving final assurance to thousands. It works.

Indoctrination

The baby is only the beginning. It takes years for him to grow up. A newborn baby needs the right kind of atmosphere, food, and care to start off on the right foot. So does a newborn babe in Christ. You won't be able to give one all he needs the first hour he is born, but it is essential to give a few basics.

Assurance. It is most important to see that he has a genuine assurance of salvation based on the Word of God, as I have just outlined, using John 3:36.

Confession. Like the cry of a newborn baby, the first thing a new Christian should do is confess Christ openly as Savior. If someone is with you, get him to say to that person, "I have accepted the Lord Jesus, too, and I know I'm saved." Even though that other person has been sitting there all along, it is strengthening for the new Christian to look someone in the eye and in his own words confess Christ as his Savior.

A woman from the Gallup Poll came to our door taking a survey. After answering her questions, I asked if I could ask her some questions. Surprised she said, "Sure." The first question, of course, was, "Do you know for sure you are going to heaven?" In a few minutes, after I carefully gave her the gospel, she prayed to receive Christ as her Savior. My wife was in the kitchen, and I asked the woman if she would tell my wife what she had done. "Of course," she said. My wife came in. The woman looked up with tears in her eyes and blurted out, "Lady, I just got saved." Well, we were all rejoicing, and bless God, there was an abundance of joy in heaven that night. She said, "I came to ask your husband some questions, but he asked me the most important one."

If no one is around, get the new Christian to promise to tell a wife, mother, or someone when he gets home.

Then he should confess Christ publicly in a church (see Matt. 10:32), preferably yours, since you led him to Christ. You must be sold on the local church and on its importance.

Baptism. The Great Commission commands us to make disciples of all men and to baptize them. Baptism is like putting on the wedding ring. It identifies what you have done. Of course, it doesn't save you any more than a ring marries you. Baptism is important as a first step of obedience, though. Brand new converts should be told of its importance and urged to take this step very soon.

171

Bible reading and prayer. Every new Christian should desire the Word of God as a newborn baby desires milk (see 1 Pet. 2:2). This is important to stress.

Confession of sin. What happens when a Christian sins? A new convert needs to know how to confess sin and get back into fellowship with the Lord.

Incubation. Join a church. Of course, joining a church will no more make you a Christian than joining the Elks will make you an elk, but it is important. A newborn babe needs a warm incubator. That's what the church is for.

There are so many things new Christians need to know, but, like a new babe, they can only take a little milk at a time. You must discern how much you think one can take at the first feeding. You must have a good follow-up program, especially in these first and most critical days.

16

Public Evangelistic Preaching

What is public preaching for? Some say the church is a "body shop" or a "filling station" whose job is to prepare saints for the work of the ministry. Others say that the purpose of the church is to evangelize—to preach in order to save people. The truth is, both are correct and must be kept in balance.

To say the church is not the place for evangelism is unscriptural. Some even go so far as to say you should not bring the unsaved to church! Paul certainly expected unbelievers to come to church and to be saved by the preaching. He tells about it in 1 Corinthians 14:23,25.

> If therefore the whole church be come together into one place, and all speak with tongues, and there come in those that are unleavened, or unbelievers, will they not say that ye are mad? But if all prophesy, and there come in one that believeth not, or one unlearned, he is convinced of all, he is judged of all: And thus are the secrets of his heart made manifest; so falling down on his face he will worship God. . . .

Paul expected unbelievers to come to church. They came and heard prophesying and preaching. They became convicted, fell on their faces, worshiped God, and were saved.

Paul says plainly, ". . . it pleased God by the foolishness of preaching to save them that believe" (1 Cor. 1:21). The obvious conclusion is they were saved through the preaching. Why have preaching in a church? One reason, surely, is to get people saved. God uses this great art of preaching. Romans 10:13-17 stresses that people are to call on the Lord for salvation through preaching. When and where? Why, anywhere when ". . . the whole church be come together into one place. . ." (1 Cor. 14:23).

The balance between evangelism and edification, which is desperately needed, is given in the Great Commission of Matthew 28:19,20.

The church should evangelize, baptize, edify, and then teach its new members to do the same things—evangelize, baptize, and edify. What a beautiful cycle. When the cycle stops, the church stops.

Some pastors never give invitations for lost people to trust Christ. Obviously, they don't expect them to be in their churches nor are they trying very hard to get them saved. Not only that, but they don't invite those won to Christ in their homes to confess Christ publicly. When do they expect them to confess Christ? Often records show that such churches baptize precious few. Where are their converts? If they have them, why aren't they being baptized? This is not said to criticize or castigate anyone but to face reality.

Why do some churches have a host of visitors and unsaved in attendance Sunday after Sunday, and some have people confessing Christ week after week, while other churches have neither? There are definite reasons. And there are some valid ways to get the unsaved to come to church and to come to Christ, without neglecting to feed the flock of God. Both can and should be done.

Nothing keeps a church alive like seeing people saved week after week. The crowning finish of a Sunday morning service is seeing someone who is brokenhearted over his sins come to Christ. Nothing is more deadening than to preach truth week after week and to see the same saints commit the same sins and to hear the sinners all around cry out, ". . . no man cared for my soul" (Ps. 142:4). Now, of course, every church that doesn't give an invitation is not guilty of this, and for those who are winning people to Christ we shout, "Hallelujah." But there is a place for evangelistic preaching in the church, and I want to talk about it.

Preparing Your Congregation for Evangelism

If the unsaved are not in the church, then evangelistic preaching is unproductive. That we should expect them to be there seems clear from 1 Corinthians 14:24. Why do some churches have so many and others so few? Here are a few of the reasons and some ways to lead the unsaved to accept Christ.

Your people must be burdened for the lost. Experience has shown that a new Christian has a burden for his unsaved family and friends.

This burden is often squelched in a dead church. If no exhortation to win the lost is presented, the burden is soon stifled. Believers are to be exhorted daily lest they be hardened (see Heb. 3:13). This every pastor knows. The believer must be exhorted to pray, give, feed, fast, and, of course, to witness as well. The lost get saved when the found get burdened.

Christine is a beautiful example of this truth. Christine had been saved only about six months when she came to me and asked me to pray for her mother. She was so burdened for her. Her mother was coming to visit her in about a month. We shared her request with our people to pray for Mrs. Grey. They did. One Wednesday I walked into the service, and there sat Christine and her mother. From the pulpit I could see the look of loneliness and unhappiness on Mrs. Grey's face. She had a miserable life.

That night I was teaching Isaiah verse by verse, but I know how to run to Calvary from any verse and pour in the gospel. Our people were aware I was fishing. We gave the invitation. She did not respond. After the service Christine introduced me to her mother. I began to witness to her.

She said, "Preacher, I don't believe in God. There can't be a God who loves me, not with the kind of life I've lived."

It broke my heart. I wept and told her God did love her and Christ died for her, but I was getting nowhere.

Suddenly I looked around and saw a beautiful sight. All over our church, people had gathered in little groups of six and seven to pray for this woman, because they knew I was witnessing to her. Christine stood aside, the tears pouring out. I said, "Mrs. Grey, look around. See those people? They love you and are praying for you to know God's love and His Son." She still did not respond. We all left.

An hour later at home our phone rang. It was Christine's husband. I knew what had happened. He said, "Brother Wemp, Mom just got saved! She wants to see you."

I rushed over, walked in, and saw the same woman with her face glowing. "How did it happen?" I asked.

Her son-in-law said she asked, "Why was that preacher crying? Why were all those people weeping?"

He said, "Because they love you, Mom."

"But they don't know me," she replied.

"No, but they know Jesus and that makes them love you."

It broke her heart, and he led her to Christ. Glory! Genuine love and a burdened heart won that dear faithless woman to Christ.

Create an atmosphere for evangelism in your church. It is obvious when churches try to create an atmosphere for worship during the service. But some churches never attempt to create an atmosphere for evangelism. A few can even be accused of never attempting to create an atmosphere for worship.

Encourage your people to bring the unsaved to church. Christians should be winning the lost and bringing them to church. Keep a record and see how many are won during the week by your people. Nothing prepares a preacher or people for an evangelistic service like knowing there are people present who were won to Christ in their homes during the week. Thirty years ago a fellow led a deaf man to Christ and brought him to church. Though we had no one to interpret for him, he read lips well. Our member introduced the deaf man to several people before the service. The news spread throughout the church, and everyone could hardly wait until the service was over and for him to confess Christ publicly. When he did, many tears flowed at the goodness of God.

Invite the unsaved to come. Lost people seldom come unless invited. Jesus said to go into the highways, and compel them to come to my house! (see Matt. 22:9).

Put the gospel in every message and give the unsaved an opportunity to be saved. If you do this, people will bring the unsaved to your church. If people know that no matter what service it is—even Wednesday night Bible study—you will specifically bring out the gospel in your message, they will be much more likely to invite lost friends and family.

Teach your people to pray, and expect people to be saved. We should expect something as powerful as the gospel to work. If a church doesn't expect people to be saved, then there is a definite lack of faith, and that is sin. In the churches I served it was rare to have a service and have no one accept Christ. Somebody in our church would always come to me with a shocked look and ask what happened when no one was saved. With faith and expectancy like that, no wonder we had people saved week after week.

Conducting an Evangelistic Service

How do you have an evangelistic service? How do you create an evangelistic atmosphere? Here are some ideas I've found useful.

Music

Have good gospel music played by the organist for the prelude. Larry Mayfield played a special arrangement of a gospel song before chapel at Moody Bible Institute one day. When he finished, our hearts had been so turned to the Lord Jesus the whole student body burst into applause and many were in tears. A good, warm service of any kind starts with the right kind of music.

Open the service with special music. Who said every Sunday morning service has to begin with the Doxology or some "worshipful" hymn? Starting differently usually wakes the congregation up so that they listen more carefully during the rest of the service.

Use the right kind of music. If the service is specially designed to reach the unsaved on Sunday or during a week of evangelistic meetings, use familiar gospel songs.

Don't teach a new song out of the hymnal unless it is a very singable, easily learned evangelistic song you plan to use often during the campaign.

The music director who is also a soul-winner knows how to plan and present appropriate music that will prepare lost people for the gospel. His part in winning the lost is immeasurable. Those who remember Dr. Charles E. Fuller on *The Old-Fashioned Revival Hour* will never forget the hundreds of times he gave an invitation in the middle of the song service for people to be saved.

Sidelights

Minimize announcements. If you do have announcements, preach them. That's right, preach them. Make them a challenge and an exhortation. This is an art, just as preaching a sermon is an art. The way prayer meeting is usually announced doesn't get one more person out on Wednesday night. You need to persuade people of the benefits of being there.

Make prayers brief and alive. Droning the same old clichés week after week in heartless prayers is also wicked. Prayer ought to reach God. It ought to move people. Like Hannah, those who pray publicly ought to pour out their souls to God and not try to impress people or God with flowery words (see Sam. 1:13).

Train people to say "amen." According to 1 Corinthians 14:16 people are expected to say "amen" in church. Done in the spirit, it is electrifying. People will become used to hearing themselves and not be self-conscious about it when it bursts out from the overflow of the heart. After a beautiful solo or choir special, say to the people, "If you enjoyed that, say amen." Ask your people privately sometime, and see how many have felt like coming out with a hearty "amen" but held back because it wasn't done in your church and they were self-conscious. As the old cliché says, saying "amen" is like saying "sic 'em" to the preacher. It really encourages him to preach.

Have testimonies. With Sunday-morning time limits, plan ahead for someone to share briefly an unusual conversion experience or blessing. This should be the sharing of an experience, not a sermon. On Sunday evenings, Wednesdays, or during week-nights of evangelistic meetings, testimonies can be effective. Instruct the people giving testimonies to say they are saved and tell their story briefly. Testimonies give the unsaved the opportunity to identify with those who are saved.

Use the offering time for another musical special. People can be ministered to while glorifying the Lord with their offerings.

Have special music before the message. The music and announcements should hold the interest of the congregation. Many times the pastor's message accomplishes nothing through no fault of his. It is a grievous sin to bungle through forty-five minutes of inappropriate music or tedious announcements and turn over the service to the pastor fifteen minutes till twelve. He can't win, no matter what.

178

Preaching

Well-known preachers used to be identified as "great gospel preachers." They had a powerful ability to preach Christ. The grace of God in saving sinners was proclaimed in power and clarity. People were stirred by the story of Jesus and His love. One rarely hears this label any more. Many have placed a stigma on gospel preaching, calling it shallow. In reality it takes a deep man of God to preach the kind of message that moves sinners to come to the foot of the cross. The old rugged cross is not shallow in any sense of the word. The ". . . grace of God that bringeth salvation . . ." (Titus 2:11) is deeper than the human mind can ever fathom. The kind of preaching that moves men's hearts to God is the kind of preaching that needs to be done.

Evangelistic preaching must present the gospel. Again we remind you, it seldom does. Listen with discernment; count the times it is omitted from sermons, tracts, and books. The recounting of the vicarious suffering of Christ and the victorious resurrection of the Savior is essential if people are to be saved.

Make it clear and simple. People really aren't impressed with a man's wisdom and eloquence if Christ isn't exalted. High-sounding phrases usually go over people's heads. The gospel must be made simple so that little children can come to the Savior. The deep things are for the spiritual man, but the unsaved need all the help and light one can give them.

Use illustrations. The Savior did this. During college and seminary training, a student can glean a wealth of illustrations from his teachers, preachers, books, and experiences that, if filed on cards, will be worth a fortune. Use illustrations and stories that help explain the gospel story. Non-Christians will listen to stories and get the point more easily than if you quote to them from a theology book. Use doctrine and theology, but don't let it use you. Great doctrines need to be stated in plain language.

Preach from your heart. If the message hasn't gripped your heart, you can be sure it won't grip the people's hearts. Get carried away when you preach. A man needs to be so caught up in his preaching

179

that he becomes uninhibited and unconscious of the people and place. Self-consciousness and people-awareness distract from getting the message across. As the wise old preacher told the young preacher, "Just get your heart full of Jesus and cut loose raving about Him."

Use humor. Humor can help convey an important point concerning a delicate matter, but without offense. People are sad enough, and most of the humor on TV is sick. People need to experience real joy. Used correctly, humor can add another dimension to preaching.

Be authoritative. Evangelistic sermons must be given with sincerity and authority. There are a few passages of prophecy that we don't have clear interpretations of. But when it comes to the gospel, we need to have that clear, ringing authority of "Thus saith the Lord."

Be yourself. Be concerned with the message, not the mechanics. It's hard to understand how someone can paint the picture of Christ on the cross without a broken heart and a wet eye once in a while. The worst thing in the world you can do is to try to preach like someone else. Some try to preach like Billy Graham, but they don't have Billy Graham's power or his commission. Just pour out your own heart for the lost and dying people. They will get the message.

Giving the Invitation

Some fishers of men don't pull in the net. How sad. An evangelist told me about a disaster he recently experienced. He had preached his heart out and had felt there was deep conviction in the service. At the close he turned the invitation over to the pastor, and he never even gave one. He simply commented on the message and closed in prayer.

How do you give an invitation?

Here are some don'ts.

Don't use deceptive methods to get people down the aisle. Trickery never works, nor does it glorify God. Be honest with people about the invitation.

Don't embarrass people. Never put people on the spot with hand-raising techniques. If you say you won't embarrass them, keep your word. One preacher asked all who were sure they were going to heaven to raise their hands. Then he told them to stand. Those who were

180

standing were told to look around and talk to those who were seated. Nothing but anger and embarrassment resulted.

Don't use high-pressure methods. If you get people down the aisle because of pressure, nothing will be accomplished. If the Holy Spirit moves people, eternal results will occur. Long, drawn-out invitations do little more than harden hearts and sear the conscience. Someone wisely said, "If you don't strike oil in five minutes, stop drilling."

Recently we had a time of invitation at Thomas Road that lasted one hour. Over one thousand people came to the prayer room or knelt at the front making decisions. There was no pleading from the pulpit. Nothing much was done except singing and crying "amen" as the people came weeping to get things right with God.

Don't tack the invitation onto the end of the message. Preach for decisions. Make the invitation an integral and vital part of your message. The message should demand a decision. We are to be ". . . doers of the word, and not hearers only" (James 1:22). Every message should vitally affect a person's life. The unsaved know they need to be saved. Satan does all he can to discourage them. We need to do all that's possible to encourage them to make the right decision.

Here are some dos.

Do have everybody bow their heads and close their eyes. Assure them you will not embarrass anyone, and be sure you don't. No one should be looking around. This helps people get close to God. Distractions are less apt to happen. It saves embarrassment when hands are raised.

Do ask all who know without a doubt that they are going to heaven to raise their hands. It helps you to know if any unsaved are there. Often someone uncertain can be spotted and helped by the pastor. He can ask privately, "I noticed you didn't raise your hand. Was there a reason? May I help?" Many will open up and tell of doubts. This also causes a non-Christian to acknowledge to himself without public embarrassment that he isn't saved. This is one method the Holy Spirit uses to bring conviction to the lost.

Do thank those who were honest and didn't raise their hands. Let them know you have genuine respect for them.

Do ask those who didn't raise a hand and who want to be saved to

181

raise a hand for prayer. Assure them again that you will not point them out in any way. As hands are raised simply say, "Thank you" or "Amen."

Do train your people to pray earnestly for those people as you say "amen." My wife always counts how many raise a hand by how many times I say "amen," and she prays for each person. Your people can have a vital part in a person's salvation. Remember, the battle for their souls is real as you wrestle in prayer against spiritual powers.

Do ask anyone with a spiritual need who wants prayer to raise a hand also. The Christian Life class I teach numbers seven hundred students each day. I ask everyone who is burdened or has a special need to raise his hand if he would like for me to pray for him. Always there will be at least two hundred hands raised. Many come up later and tell me how much it has meant to them to be prayed for on that particular day.

Do ask people to pray for those seated around them. Have them pray specifically for the one in front of them, then for the ones on the right and on the left. People are comforted with the knowledge that they are being prayed for personally.

Now you can say, "With our heads bowed, let's everyone stand for prayer." Be sure to pray for those who raised hands. The prayer should be brief and to the point, but fervent and from your heart. You can be sure Satan is mad and at work.

Do train the song leader to be ready to start the invitation song immediately upon your signal. The pianist or organist should only play the chord and not a line or two of introduction. The choir should lead out the singing. A good procedure is to begin with "Just as I Am," so that you don't have to announce a hymn number and distract those who are making a decision. After a few verses you can ask them to turn to another song. As they are turning, you can exhort the people briefly. Never just stand with a long pause between verses. Remember, Satan will do all he can to blind the minds of those who believe not (see 2 Cor. 4:4). Don't underestimate the power and work of every demon of hell. He will use anything to get their minds off the Lord.

Do have personal workers ready to go to the prayer room with people who come forward to make a decision. The personal workers

182

should slowly and quietly come forward at the first notes of the invitation song. The pastor should meet those making decisions first and turn them over to a personal worker. If the church has quite a few coming for each service, then the associate pastors or deacons should meet them while the pastor stays in the pulpit.

One Sunday, as a guest speaker, I preached, gave the invitation, and adults came forward to receive Christ as Savior. The church wasn't used to invitations and had no personal workers ready. The pastor counseled with each one personally and very awkwardly. The congregation stood and sang "Just as I Am" for over thirty minutes. The people who came forward couldn't have been counseled as they would have been if trained soul-winners had taken them aside individually.

Do exhort and urge people to obey the Lord and do what the Holy Spirit prompts them to do. This should be a soft and tender exhortation. A pastor can say, "Won't you come? Do what you know you ought to do. Obey the Lord. You will be glad you did." What a thrill when the Holy Spirit is moving to see people come, one after another, with only a few words of encouragement from the pulpit. Many times as you urge people to come, you will unintentionally catch someone's eyes, and they immediately move out to make a decision for the Lord. How graciously God can use every word and movement of a pastor.

Do have a comfortable place for the newly saved to kneel, In many churches the ones who come to the front kneel on a one-step kneeler or on the floor or at the front pew. At one church we built a new auditorium with a carpeted kneeler in front of the platform all the way across the front. Soon after it was installed, the best-dressed, most elegant woman in our church came forward and felt free to kneel before the whole church without one bit of embarrassment and made a decision with the Lord. This is the way it should be.

Do include an invitation for young people to surrender to full-time Christian work. This is vital. A church can have no greater honor than sending out scores of young people all over the world to preach the gospel.

Do make much of the decision. Let the church know what the decision was and get the people rejoicing with the ones who come forward. Have Sunday school teachers or deacons come stand next to those accepting Christ as you tell the church of their decisions. Train your people to be responsive and rejoice with each decision. Make a great deal of each one. Don't ever underestimate any decision. Get the people to rejoice, and promise to pray for young people who are called by God to Christian service.

After the people who have made decisions are introduced, say, "All those who rejoice with each of these people, let it be known by a hearty 'amen.' " Isn't it tragic to see and hear people get more excited about a homerun than a soul saved? Which is more important? People want to rejoice and show emotion. Give them a dignified opportunity.

Train your people to come by afterward and shake hands with those who made public decisions and assure them of their love and prayers.

The night I, as a seventeen-year-old boy, was saved, I'll never forget the five men who waited until all the others had shaken my hand and then personally came by and assured me of their love and prayers. Jake and Dolly Lyons have faithfully prayed for me for the past thirty-eight years. Probably this is the greatest source of power and victory in my ministry. Great will be their reward in heaven. There is great blessing in teaching your adults to pray daily for young people who are special to them.

The key to profitable evangelistic preaching is a church that has been taught to enter into evangelistic work through witnessing, getting the lost to church, praying like mad for them to be saved, rejoicing when they confess Christ, and then following up with prayer for new converts and new members on a regular basis.

17

Evangelistic Meetings

Today most people are familiar with the week-long campaigns of evangelists like Billy Graham. Mainline churches used to have at least one week of evangelistic meetings every year. Many churches still have "revival" meetings that feature guest evangelists.

There are several reasons for having evangelistic meetings. First, it stirs the fires of evangelism. No church is winning too many people to Christ. You just can't do that. Too, such meetings give you the opportunity to get the gospel to every person in your area. And a concentrated emphasis on evangelism is healthy for any church.

People will visit a special meeting more easily than a regular service. With special attractions, special music, and a special speaker, many will come who otherwise would not. Your own people will put forth extra effort for a special meeting. You will then win people to Christ whom you have been trying to reach for a long time.

When people hear a different voice preaching the same gospel, it has a healthy effect. Using men called by God to be evangelists is a good way to complement your own ministry. Being evangelists, they can be used to win many you would never reach.

There are reasons why many churches don't have evangelistic meetings. Probably the most common is that many people have been turned off by high-powered, high-pressure evangelists. The Elmer Gantry stigma, unfortunately, has been attached to evangelists. Thankfully, today there is a new breed of evangelism, which does not utilize high-pressure methods.

One practice that hurt so-called evangelistic meetings in the past was the use of pastors who were not evangelists. God didn't use them as evangelists, and the meetings were fruitless. There is a vital place for evangelists, and they should be recognized and utilized. Mass

185

evangelism is still in vogue. People will come out to mass meetings, as witnessed by the Graham crusades.

Evangelism is on the upswing. Now is the time. Pastors are finding it works to have protracted meetings. The results are lasting and uplifting.

The Length of the Meeting

How long should a meeting be? Much depends on you and your church. If your congregation is not accustomed to campaigns, start out with a short series of meetings.

Friday night through Sunday is good for a weekend meeting. If properly planned, prayed for, and preached, it can be very profitable. Many times we have seen from ten to fifteen people saved in churches of only two hundred at weekend meetings.

Sunday through Wednesday can also be an effective time to have a revival. Starting on Sunday gives you an advantage. More people will be introduced to the evangelist, so they will be able to tell friends and relatives about him and get them out for the meeting.

Sunday through Friday is better than a four-day meeting. It usually takes a few days for people to become burdened for the lost or for their own souls, unless the pastor has prepared his church weeks before.

Sunday night through the next Sunday morning is the best. This gives the evangelist maximum exposure to the church. During an entire week, interest and concern build up and often explode on the final Sunday morning.

Two to three weeks, if properly planned, can totally transform a church and community. Life Action Inc., with Del Fehsenfeld, goes to a church with no set time to leave. Calvary Baptist Church of Covington, Kentucky, had a three-week meeting, and well over one hundred people were saved. There was a purifying and unifying of the church that was rich. The pastor, Galen Call, said it was one of the greatest things he had ever witnessed. This church was totally unaccustomed to lengthy meetings but responded beautifully.

A number of revival teams are going into churches on such a basis and having the most wholesome results their pastors have ever seen.

Weekend youth revivals are effective. Invite young adults from

186

Christian colleges to conduct the meetings. One of the young men can do the preaching and others can lead the singing. They should visit all day Saturday. People will turn out in large numbers if the meeting is properly planned and promoted. This will be an invaluable experience for your young people.

Choosing an Evangelist

Nothing is more important than choosing the right evangelist. The wrong choice here has been the downfall of many. Too often a pastor asks a pastor friend to do the preaching. The man may be a jewel of a pastor but not an evangelist. I am not an evangelist. God seldom has used me as an evangelist who sees a large number of people saved in a week of meetings. Consequently, I don't accept invitations for evangelistic meetings at all now. I try to be honest with pastors. Yes, I witness a lot and see people saved through witnessing, but I'm realistic. I'm not an evangelistic preacher. If pastors who don't have this special calling would turn down these invitations and force preachers to get evangelists, it could change the whole picture.

Invite a full-time evangelist. There are many being used by God. Doing this may cost a little more, but evangelists are worth their hire. More would stay in evangelism if they were used more frequently and supported better. Contact the great schools that emphasize evangelism for the names of evangelists.

Music can make or break the meeting. It is second only to preaching in importance for the success of evangelistic meetings. Many evangelists travel with a full-time music director. Those first thirty to forty-five minutes of the service are crucial. Music can drive out the evil spirits as it did for King Saul when David played his harp (see Sam. 16:23). The right kind soothes the fevered brow and prepares hearts for the Word of God. Don't get just anyone to lead singing.

In one meeting at a large church the pastor led the singing and joked about how he wasn't a musician but said, "We'll make out." He killed the meeting. The people were not prepared to listen to the evangelist. Get a good team. It will pay off in every way. A skilled music director can bring a revival to most hearts even before the evangelist gets up to preach. This is the way it ought to be.

Get soul-winning pastors who are used as evangelists. There are

187

many pastors who are frequently used in evangelism. These understand a pastor's heart and a church's need, as do evangelists who have been in evangelism a good while.

You may wish to invite a lay evangelist. A meeting led by a good layman can be very effective. There are laymen who are being greatly used in evangelism.

Many Christian colleges have evangelistic teams who serve churches for weekends and during summer vacation. At Liberty Baptist College there are some students who have the hand of God on them. God is using them greatly. Preachers are intimidated by them sometimes, but they have the fire and zeal that is desperately needed. However, if you have doubts about a student evangelist, check out his credentials by calling the college he attends or a pastor who has had him preach in the church. You don't want someone who might do more harm than good.

Provision for Guest Speakers

"Of course the speaker would rather stay in a home than in a lonely motel," says a sincere church member. The truth of the matter is, most preachers would rather stay in a motel, especially if they are in full-time evangelism or conference work.

One reason that most evangelists would rather stay in a motel is because they need time to be alone and pray. You just can't do that in a home. An evangelist will lose his fervor if he doesn't have this time. In a home you might be disturbed by crying babies, disruptive children, and barking dogs.

Another reason evangelists usually prefer motels is because they need to study. Very few homes have a desk in the guest room where the visitor can spread out his books and write his sermons. Motel rooms do have desks. Preparing new messages requires concentrated study. One must be alone in order to get this done. The visiting preacher is considered odd and unfriendly if he isolates himself in someone's house to do this.

A speaker needs time to relax. This is quite hard to do in a home where people want to visit with him. Have you ever been staying in a home where you had to listen to an hour of family history just before going to preach? The evangelist needs the time right before a service to be quiet and get the message fresh and burning on his heart. Very well-meaning hosts sometimes keep a speaker up until the early morning hours talking. Of course, they tell him he can sleep late the next day, but this just can't be done night after night. Most of us need regular hours, and it is quite hard for a preacher to adjust to different hours and routines in one home after another.

Watching TV is the favorite American pastime. I like to watch sports and the news. This is my relaxation when staying in a motel. It is quite frustrating when a guest is expected to sit with the family and watch an endless succession of TV programs that he does not enjoy. If you excuse yourself and go to your room, they think you are rude and have no taste for the finer things. Then if you are watching a sports event and really want to enjoy it, there will be inevitable interruptions so that you can't relax.

Most guest speakers like to exercise by walking, sight-seeing, or shopping at places near the motel. If the host pastor can provide the speaker with a car so that he can drive to a nearby shopping center, this is very helpful. I often walk and get much-needed exercise and relaxation by shopping.

A motel provides excellent opportunities to witness. I've led many maids, waitresses, and desk clerks to Christ. This always inspires me to preach better. One Saturday in a motel, the maid came to clean the room. I was studying, and at first I told her not to bother with cleaning it. She insisted on providing clean towels and making the bed. Then the Lord reminded me that He had brought her there. I began witnessing to her. Her heart had already been prepared by the Lord, and she prayed with me to receive Christ. She left rejoicing. Thirty minutes later she knocked on my door again. She said, "Sir, I don't mean to disturb you, but I was cleaning a room down the hall and told a lady in there how you talked to me. I told her how I got saved. She said, 'I want to be saved, too. Do you think he will talk to me?' Sir, could you talk to her?"

Well glory! She brought the woman to my room and in thirty minutes, with tears running down her face, she, too, trusted Christ. My day was made. My preaching was freshened by that experience, and the whole church was blessed by the testimony.

Most preachers are isolated from many of the harsher realities of the world. In a motel you often see sights that break your heart and awaken you to the destructive existence of sin. Several times I've been approached by call girls in motels. It makes you weep. Just to walk by a bar or hear the music outside the dancing room makes you sensitive to the emptiness of this world. Looking at the faces of those coming from these places can stir your soul with a much-needed burden for people. You don't get these insights when you're sheltered in someone's home.

The bathroom privileges alone almost demand that you put a guest speaker in a motel. Many a preacher has had embarrassing incidents and inconveniences in private homes. In one home, I stayed in a room upstairs and had to go through the daughter's bedroom to get to the bathroom during the night. It was absolutely ridiculous. A pastor should never be put in that kind of situation.

If a church wants a speaker to be at his best when he preaches, then it should do all it can to help him. If the church has to cut corners financially, this just isn't the place to do it.

The pastor should make all the arrangements for the evangelist's meals. Usually preachers don't want to eat two big meals a day. If he is to eat in homes, it is best to let him eat the noon meals there so he won't be rushed before the evening service. But remember that the visiting speaker should be consulted as to his preferences before meal arrangements are made.

Financial arrangements are important. A church, of course, should take care of all travel expenses including tips, meals, taxi fares, and mileage for his car if he drives. If a full-time evangelist comes, the church is responsible only for his travel to their church and not to the next one as well, unless he is going back home. Then they should pay expenses to and from their church.

Stinginess is not becoming to a Christian or to a church. The laborer is worthy of his hire. In thirty years of ministry only a couple of times have I not been treated fairly. I've never demanded money for my ministry. Most preachers don't. Sometimes, though, churches have been unfair to evangelists. Too many times, I've heard of a church not giving the guest speaker all of the love offering when an unusually large amount comes in. This is stealing. If an offering is announced as a love offering, every dime must be given to the speaker.

Occasionally a speaker is in a church for just one service. It is sad to say, but some people think that a dollar a minute for a thirty-minute sermon is pretty good pay! What about his study time, travel time, having to stay overnight, being away from his home and family? All this costs and not just in dollars. Many preachers quit taking extra meetings, for it just isn't worth the wear and tear on their bodies.

Preparation

Preparation is half the battle. The most common cause of failure during evangelistic campaigns is lack of preparation. Hundreds of stories could be told about evangelists who arrive to conduct meetings only to find that nothing has been done to prepare for them.

Promote Your Meeting

Plan ahead. Line up the meeting a year or so ahead. Most men being used by God as evangelists are booked one to three years ahead. Many preachers plan their evangelistic campaigns two to three years in advance. Large churches often have evangelists scheduled five years in advance.

Begin promoting the meeting among your people at least two months before it is scheduled. Check the church calendar, and make sure nothing else is scheduled for that time. Make everyone conscious of the meeting and keep it before the congregation through announcements.

Publicize your revival. Use radio, TV, newspapers, posters, handbills, and mailings. Find the kind of publicity that is most profitable in your area and use it. Every Sunday school boy and girl is a super promoter. Those children whose parents aren't saved can tell their parents about the meetings. Send them home with novel ideas to entice parents to come. This should be done for several weeks before the meetings begin.

Buttons, bumper stickers, and billboards are invaluable advertising aids. Sending home a button on every child usually gets good results.

Have a phonothon. Assign a page or a part of a page in the telephone directory to each person who volunteers. Have them call and invite people to the meeting. Done graciously, this can bring in dozens of new people. If only one family came to Christ, it would be worth it. Many shut-ins, elderly persons, housewives, and teen-agers will volunteer to make calls if you ask them.

Get people to pledge that they will come. Cut paper into 1" x 11" strips for people to sign, pledging to come every night unless providentially hindered. Make a chain of these and hang it in the vestibule of the church. Do this for a couple of weeks before the meeting, getting new names at every service. Members can get visitors to sign up for the first Sunday only.

Often people will say, "I plan to come to some of the meetings," but they will put if off until the last night. If you can get them there the first night, you can get them back again.

Some churches are afraid of promotion. If done graciously, it can make the meeting. Proper promotion creates enthusiasm. We have had members get a hundred people to come to a week of meetings, with many saved as a result. Do it on a soft-sell basis. You will be amazed at how well it works.

Form Committees

Have the nursery well-planned and staffed before the meetings begin. Top-notch nurseries are a must if you want to reach young couples. Understaffed nurseries will drive them away quicker than anything. Don't ever turn the nursery over to teen-age girls, no matter how good they are.

A committee should arrange for the transportation, meals, and other needs of the evangelist. If possible, you should provide him with a car so he can have some personal freedom. Many churches have a basket of fruit sent to his room. This is a gracious gesture and provides him with something fresh to snack on during the week. A super extra is sending flowers to his wife back home. This is small remuneration for the price she pays by being left alone.

Put a committee in charge of visitation. Several weeks before the meeting, the congregation should be encouraged to visit in their neighborhoods, inviting people to the meetings.

Pray for the Revival

The formula is in 2 Chronicles 7:14. When God says, "If my people, which are called by my name, shall humble themselves, and pray . . . then will I hear from heaven . . . and will heal their land." Dr. Jerry Falwell says so often, "Nothing of eternal value happens apart from prayer." It's an absolute fact. Throughout history the great revivals that swept across nations were preceded and accompanied by fervent prayer. Revivals are truly prayed down. It is always so. Little prayer brings little power. Much prayer brings much power.

Here are five plans for prayer meetings:

Cottage prayer meetings. People gather, usually five to ten couples, in homes and pray especially for the meetings. You have to be careful that you don't have too many meetings before the revival, or your people will be drained of their enthusiasm. Home prayer meetings don't seem to be as popular as they were twenty-five years ago, but some churches still use them effectively.

Around-the-clock prayer meetings. Have people sign up to pray for fifteen minutes each day for a week. Make a large pie-shaped poster divided into fifteen-minute segments that span a twenty-four-hour period. Have people sign up to pray during each time slot. Many will get up all through the night to take their turns in prayer.

All-night prayer meetings. These meetings probably have produced more results over the years than any other type of prayer meeting. Many great evangelists have had at least one all-night prayer meeting during a campaign. There have been many times when such a prayer meeting turned the whole revival around. In such a meeting people often will come and go. Some come in off night shifts. A surprising number of people will stay all night.

Pray until. Life Action teams do this a lot. After a night meeting ask those who want to pray to meet in a room. Don't set a time to stop, but pray until a burden is lifted or a peace comes assuring you that this is all God wants of you that night. This can be done on several nights.

193

Pray from 7:30 P.M. until midnight a Wednesday or two before the meetings. This is a plan I have used and have found to be the best and most effective. This prevents the problem of wearing people out with too many meetings. More people will stay for this specific time if you challenge them.

Here is the plan:

7:30–8:00.   Have singing and testimonies. Testimonies always bless and speak to people's hearts. The testimonies should be fresh, recent causes for rejoicing.

8:00–8:15.   Preach a message on the Christian's responsibility to the lost. A strong emphasis should be placed on the power and purpose of prayer to get people ready to pray.

8:15–8:30.   Ask for names of people your members want to win to Christ in these meetings. Get several large chalkboards or an overhead projector and list the names so people can see them. As people request prayer for loved ones, it is good to stop and pray immediately. During this time a burden for people begins to build up.

8:30–9:00.   Pray. Have everyone bow their heads and call on one or two to open the prayer session. People should look up at the names and pray for different ones as the Lord guides them. Instruct people to stand and face the largest number of people when they pray. They should pray loud enough so everyone can enter in with them.

9:00–10:00.   Repeat the cycle. Have everyone stand and sing an appropriate hymn. Bring in a neighboring pastor to speak for no longer than ten minutes on prayer. Ask for prayer requests again.

10:00–11:00. Start the cycle again. Have another pastor in for a ten-minute message on prayer. If the people know the meeting will last only until twelve o'clock, very few will leave.

11.00–12:00. Once again go through the cycle. It is amazing, but people will still be adding names to the prayer list.

Keep the whole list before them. At twelve o'clock sing a song and urge the people to list names to pray for throughout the upcoming campaign. Provide paper. If you start out with one hundred in the prayer meeting you usually will have eighty or more still with you at twelve o'clock.

At this kind of prayer meeting you have more total hours of prayer by more people than in any other kind. A genuine burden for souls is encouraged and reinforced. When the evangelistic meetings are over, you will find that the names of most of the ones who come to Christ were on the prayer list.

Prerevival Preaching

The most important preparation for the meetings is in the preaching. Pastors prepare the people in heart and attitude. This is vital.

Preach about the sins of Christians. The church needs to be of one accord. If there is bitterness or jealousy among some of your members, tell them to ask God to remove these feelings from their hearts. Get people to confess their sins to God and to each other so that they will be cleansed for the meetings.

Emphasize prayer at all times, but especially when you have a revival. We all need to be stirred to pray more.

Impress upon your people the fact that witnessing is essential if the lost are going to be there. People need to be encouraged to plant a lot of seed before the meeting.

Genuine revival, with Christians being renewed and the lost being saved, is the goal of the meeting. This needs to be preached about.

Subjects such as these should be included in your sermons for several weeks before the visiting speaker comes. When the seed has already been sown, the evangelist can begin reaping sooner, and more people can be won to Christ. It just makes sense for a pastor to do the groundwork ahead of time so that the meetings will be more effective.

Suggestions for the Service

Singleness of mind and purpose is essential this week. Call off all other meetings. Nothing should interfere with the revival.

Some churches have an early morning service featuring the evangelist. If the meeting lasts from 7:00–7:45, school children and working people will have a chance to come. Be sure to dismiss on time.

A ten o'clock Bible study used to be a standard part of every meeting. This gives night workers an opportunity to get in on the meetings. Vistors will come from other churches too, if it is advertised properly. These meetings have proved very fruitful in many churches.

Have a theme chorus or hymn. If the chorus of a hymn seems to be particularly popular, start some of the evening services with it. In the Moody-Sankey meetings, songs would catch on, and they were heard in the shops and on the streets all through the day.

Begin the service with a familiar, singable hymn. This sets the pace for the whole service. Don't let the hymn drag or the whole service will drag.

Use plenty of special music. Special music has a special ministry. Use a music minister who is able to communicate with people. Revivals have broken out during a special solo. We have seen people open their hearts and receive the Lord Jesus during a hymn. Many times my own soul has been revived just from listening to inspirational music.

Create a friendly, relaxed atmosphere for the meetings. "Where the Spirit of the Lord is there is liberty" (2 Cor. 3:17). People need to feel refreshed. They often come to meetings in a state of tension. Hearts are heavy. The service should not be a formal affair.

People are faced with excitement everywhere but in church. People flock to musical concerts where emotion can be released. Of course, the purpose of the church is not to entertain, but it is important to have a relaxed atmosphere so that people can enjoy the sermon. It isn't a sin to enjoy church. There *should* be joy in the house of God. Humor and informality can transform an evangelisitic meeting.

Be sensitive to the Holy Spirit. Let Him change the direction of the meeting by choosing a song or even a sermon. Spirit-used men of God are receptive to the power of the Holy Spirit and have seen many meetings transformed when the Holy Spirit interrupted the service and changed the plans.

Take up an offering every night. If only one or two offerings are

196

taken up all week, pastors tend to overemphasize them. If people are taught properly all year long, they will be accustomed to giving generously and joyously for special meetings.

Recognize visitors and have them fill out visitor cards. These will be some of your best prospects in the weeks to come.

The invitation is the ultimate purpose of the meeting. If no one does anything about the message you have failed. ". . . Choose you this day . . ." Joshua said (Josh. 24:15).

Postrevival Plans

You don't "dip them and drop them." You don't count nickels and noses to measure success. The ultimate end is to see new converts grow into mature Christians. How do you do it?

Have a warm, Spirit-filled, friendly church. A new babe is kept in a warm, sterile environment in the hospital. New Christians need the right atmosphere too. You have to work at creating this atmosphere in the church.

At one church I pastored, a young couple had an evangelist and my family over for lunch. Another lady was helping the hostess. The evangelist thought the two women had been childhood friends or neighbors and asked about it. The woman helping said, "Oh no, we didn't know each other until three weeks ago when my husband and I were saved. That night Ron and Wynelle invited us over after church, and we have become good friends since then." It was impressive. The couples remained friends and grew spiritually because of this encouraging relationship.

That one hour after church can be the most profitable time for follow-up. Just going out for coffee with several couples and experiencing true Christian fellowship helps strengthen the newly saved. In New Testament days Chrisians visited from house to house. It works today as well.

Training classes are essential for those who have just found Christ. A special ten-week training class for new converts can be conducted during the Sunday school hour. After the designated period of time, these Christians move into a regular Sunday school class. You need a trained teacher for this in order to get them started out right. Some have training classes an hour before the evening service. Baptists have called it the Training Union. A special class is most helpful at this time.

18

Practical Means of Evangelism

There are many ways to reach people for Christ that can become extensions of the local church ministry. Time has proved that ministries not linked to the local church are ministries that are not complete. Many ministries cease to function, or they depart from their original purposes. They cease to be evangelistic. Our nation is filled with schools, once fundamental and evangelistic, where now religion is virtually banned. One such great evangelistic ministry that is now nothing but a social organization is the famed YMCA. We must remember that Jesus founded the church (see Matt. 16:18). Organizations that begin in the church should never sever their ties.

Breakfast Clubs

The breakfast club is one work that can be sponsored by a church and can be very effective in reaching people for Christ.

The primary purpose of a breakfast club must be evangelism. It is a great tool for that. Keeping evangelism foremost keeps it from becoming a gossip session or a hothouse of dissention. Men will come to a breakfast who would never come to church. A breakfast club meets at a good time for people who have to work on Sunday. It secondarily provides fellowship for men. Men become encouraged when they hear the testimonies of other Christians.

Meet in a nice restaurant where a room can be reserved for privacy. It doesn't have to be the most expensive place in town. Many "family restaurants" have private rooms.

Each member of the club should invite a friend, colleague, business associate, or neighbor to be his guest for breakfast.

After the meal, introduce the person or persons who will give testimonies. Perhaps ask a prominent Christian businessman or local celebrity to share his personal testimony. Usually there are local people whose names are known and who would attract new people. This can help to get the unsaved there. Sometimes the testimony can be the only message (if the man is the type to use his testimony as a message). Al Worthington, a major-league baseball player for eighteen years and one of the more consistent Christians I know, is superb at giving a testimony-message. People like him are frequently used as speakers for informal breakfasts as well as in the pulpit.

Have a brief Bible study or a message by a good speaker. The Bible study can be on current topics of interest. It can be a message to help Christian businessmen meet the problems and temptations they are faced with. Of course, the gospel should be presented carefully so someone there who is not saved can have the chance to believe in Christ. Then an invitation to trust Christ at the table must be given lest Satan snatch away the seed that is sown.

I spoke at a breakfast early one morning. A man brought his unsaved friend. At the table the man prayed to receive Christ. He came to me and told me that he was now saved. "For fifteen years I have been putting it off, but when you asked us to accept Christ here and now, I knew that this was my time and I did it. I want to thank Fred for bringing me," he said. We all rejoiced.

Child Evangelism

There are 41 million children under the age of twelve in the United States. Most have never been reached with the gospel. Multitudes do not have parents who will take them to church. They must be reached. They can be reached. Most of them will respond to the gospel if it is presented clearly and in the power of the Holy Spirit.

A Good News Club run by a local church can be an effective means of evangelizing children and eventually reaching the whole family. Child Evangelism Fellowship, Warrenton, Missouri 63384, has the plans that have proved to be effective in thousands of homes. Write them for information.

The Awana program is another very effective means of evangelism and Christian growth for children. Usually this will reach an older group than child evangelism.

Awana stands for "A workman and not ashamed." It is an exciting evening of games and Bible programs. A gymnasium or large room like a fellowship hall is needed for the games. The games are exciting, and Awana even promotes regional and national olympics and competition between churches. The Awana program is growing by leaps and bounds across the nation. There are regional workers who will come in and help you get your program going.

Another feature of Awana is the Bible-study time. There are verses to be memorized and a system of awards and ranks similar to the Scouts. It is a real challenge for boys and girls. Hundreds of children can be won to Christ through Awana. You also can have an Awana night once a year and get the parents to come see their children perform and receive their awards. We have seen over twenty parents saved on such a night.

The Awana headquarters are at 3215 Algonquin Road, Rolling Meadows, Illinois 60008 (312/394-5150). Write them for information.

Word of Life Clubs

Word of Life Fellowship began back around 1940 when newly saved Jack Wyrtzen and a small band of men took a stand for the Lord in New York City. Bible studies and evangelistic rallies grew to ministries in radio, television, camps, clubs, literature, Bible institutes, and Word of Life ministries around the world.

The Club ministry began in 1959 through the direction and leadership of Paul Bubar, Clubs Director. His early philosophy of developing patterns of godly living in the lives of young people has been the foundation stone of the club ministry ever since. It is also the foundational philosophy that the gospel-preaching church is God's ordained means of reaching a lost world and that it must be accomplished through dedicated laymen at the local church level. This has brought great acceptance of the Word of Life Club ministry by pastors. In Paul Bubar's words, "If we are not helping churches build an aggressive and strong youth ministry through their own people, we aren't doing the job!"

Regional directors and area representatives located across the United States and Canada are trained to help the local church establish a strong and dynamic youth program with capable lay leaders within that local church. Lay leaders are trained through leadership conferences and monthly grass-roots leadership institutes throughout the year.

The *Bible Study* is highly doctrinal with enough topical studies to meet the needs of the young Christian and his daily walk with the Lord. It follows a six year cycle and is built around group dynamics.

A *Quiet Time Diary* teaches the teens to daily search the Scriptures, apply the truths to their lives, and be organized in prayer.

A *Scripture Memory* program is correlated to the doctrines being studied and is attractively packaged for easy use.

Christian reading is encouraged throughout the club year and does much to expand the teen's thinking and way of life.

The teens are trained in mass and personal evangelism through conferences, round ups, regular Christian service projects and the example of their leaders.

More recently, Word of Life has developed two more programs giving the local church the potential for a complete youth ministry from ages six to thirty.

The *Word of Life Olympian Program* is written especially for boys and girls in grades one through six to establish godly ideals in their lives.

A very meaningful system of Bible study, a unique, illustrated Scripture memory program, First Steps in Quiet Time Adventure (one for grades 1 and 2 and another for grades 3 to 6), plus a super new type of Bible Land floor game are all a part of the learning and fun times for the Olympians.

It's an exciting way to teach primary and junior age children how to reach their generation with the simple gospel and build spiritual maturity and character into these very impressionable young people.

The *Word of Life College/Career Fellowship* is written to reach and teach those ages eighteen to thirty, establishing godly *goals* in their lives.

The program gives organization structure and curriculum content to establish a young adult College Career Bible Institute right in the local church. The program is strong in discipleship, leadership training, and Christian service.

The leadership of the College Career Fellowship needs to be a spiritually mature couple that is attractive to Fellowship members.

The College Career Fellowship program is designed to reach post high school career young adults, college students, military personnel, and professional young adults that are in the community and needing someone to help them establish their priorities and a system of godly goals.

The potential reached through the College Career Fellowship can be limitless. Individuals discipled through the College Career Bible Institute can help reach the entire community for Christ.

Most importantly, *Leadership Training* is provided for the leadership teams through the Institute of Youth Leadership (IYL). This training vehicle is designed by Word of Life Clubs and geared to the busy lay leader. It is developed around a six-year curriculum that deals not only with leading the various age groups but offers much general leadership instruction as well.

The IYL has been developed and has become the top leadership training course for church leaders offered in America. It is automatically available to anyone in the church using the Word of Life Club ministries. For information, write to Word of Life Fellowship, Inc., Jack Wyrtzen, Harry Bollback, Directors, Paul Bubar, Director of Clubs, Schroon Lake, New York 12870.

Special Ministries

There are so many other ministries that can be added to the church. These must be taken one step at a time as a church grows and the needs arise. There are experts in specialized fields, and they should be contacted to help set up ministries. Most of the larger soul-winning churches will have such ministries, and their staffs can usually help.

Deaf ministry. This is one of the most rewarding ministries in a church. Sue Willmington, who signs for *The Old Time Gospel Hour* on TV is fabulous. She has helped many churches get started. The Bill Rice Ranch in Murfreesboro, Tennessee, has a most unusual deaf ministry and offers sign language classes twice yearly.

Senior Saints. Older Christians will make a powerful prayer band for the church and pastor as they are ministered to and given the opportunity to minister. They are usually hungry for love and for an opportunity to serve.

Bus Ministry. In heaven there has to be a special place of honor for bus workers. What a ministry! In many places it has been dropped, but it is a rich and profitable ministry, especially in isolated areas. There are thousands of children who will be in heaven because they were reached through bus ministry. We have students studying for the ministry now who were won to Christ by a bus captain.

Go to a bus conference, or contact some church that has an effective bus ministry. They will help you start one.

4/PREACHING AND TEACHING

19

The Pastor-Teacher

Preaching and teaching the Word of God is a vital part of the ministry. To stand in the pulpit and preach in the power of the Holy Spirit and see God transform lives is just short of tasting heaven itself. It is astounding how God uses the preaching of His Word. The preacher always must remember that " . . . we have this treasure in earthen vessels . . . " (2 Cor. 4:7) and that God gets all the glory. Place a high premium on preaching. God does!

Plan your preaching. You must not wait until Saturday night to decide what you will preach on Sunday. It is a sin to do so—besides, it will give you ulcers. To wait until Saturday night usually means several things:

First, you are not spending enough time studying and praying. A pastor should have dozens of messages burning in his heart to be preached. If one studies enough and prays enough, he will.

Second, it means a pastor doesn't know his people and their needs well enough. Sermons ought to meet needs. Knowing where people are hurting should supply a pastor with messages by the dozens.

Third, it means a pastor is choosing the subjects of his sermons on the spur of the moment instead of giving them deep thought. Too much is done on impulse. Not enough pastors chart their courses. A good shepherd knows where he wants to lead his flock and very carefully and prayerfully does much of it through his planned preaching.

Keep records of each message. It can save you embarrassment. If you preach in places outside your own pulpit and go back to the same churches for more meetings, this is essential.

Review regularly what you have preached. You will detect it if you have stumbled into a rut. Neglect of the Old Testament, the Psalms, prophecy, or doctrine can be detected as you review.

Consider preaching about every book in the Bible. This probably has been the single most significant change in preaching in the past twenty-five years. Dr. W. A. Criswell of First Baptist Church in Dallas, Texas, preached about the whole Bible, starting with Genesis and going right through consecutively. It took him seventeen years, but it had a profound effect on his church. Of course, not everyone can do this, and some pastors shouldn't attempt it.

Preaching about the entire Bible obviously saves you from wondering what to preach about next. You can study more deeply and farther ahead when using this method. It forces a variety of subjects. You will preach on every subject, including those you normally would avoid. People cannot accuse you of picking on them and their pet sins. It is astounding how often the right chapter comes up at the right time. But feel free to interrupt the series with a special message God may put in your heart for a particular Sunday. The change causes no problems, and you can go right back where you left off the next Sunday.

Beware of becoming too detailed and technical when preaching through the Bible, especially when you first begin. You could, of course, preach a whole sermon on any verse. You could become laborious and get bogged down quite easily. I attended the services of Gillis Partin, a pastor at Dothan, Alabama. He preached about the whole New Testament in two years. He had a fabulous ability to pick out the important words, ideas, and verses in each chapter. His church members were the most knowledgeable about the Bible of any people I have ever met. His accomplishment was most impressive.

Without realizing it you can get in a rut even using this method, unless you learn how to cover more ground in less time. About four times I started to preach through the books of the Bible and gave up each time, because I would stay too long on one theme such as "suffering" in 1 Peter. I finally caught on and passed over or summarized some of the verses. Dr. H. A. Ironside was a master at preaching about the books of the Bible. Get his books. They are excellent. His books consist of his sermons at the great Moody Memorial Church in Chicago. He packed four thousand people in to hear him every Sunday back in the thirties and forties when one thousand was considered an enormous church.

If you decide to preach through the entire Bible, start with a short book to get your feet wet.

Beware of preaching through the books of the Bible at all three services—Sunday morning, Sunday night, and Wednesday evening. It can become too heavy a diet. This became a problem for me, and I had to change quickly.

Another way to plan your sermons is to preach in series. The possibilities of a series on doctrines is excellent. Or you can have a series of sermons on several Bible characters, showing contrasts and comparisons. Systematic theology makes excellent preaching. Present the theology of Christ, His preexistence, birth, life, death, resurrection, ascension, and second coming. A sermon on each helps people understand the whole theology of Christ. Preach in a similar way about the Holy Spirit or the Father. People hear bits and pieces of every subject and often never get a whole view of most doctrines.

When feasible, use charts to help illustrate your message. One of the most profitable charts I ever used was the Tabernacle. On Sunday evenings I used a large cloth chart I had made. It always built up attendance. The response was overwhelming, for almost no one preaches on the Tabernacle. People think you are really smart to be able to preach on a theme hardly anyone else uses. You can cover so many wonderful truths in picture form. These messages resulted in my book, *Teaching from the Tabernacle,* published by Moody Press, which went into the third printing in two years.

The feasts of Jehovah, from Leviticus 23, is another superb subject to illustrate on a chart. People know precious little about the feasts. They illustrate great truths and make fascinating preaching. The same is true of the Levitical offerings. Don't miss these neglected teachings. Your ministry will be unique.

Charts on prophecy are classic. Yes, this subject often is misused. Some people set dates and go to extremes, which hurts the cause of Christ. Prophecy makes great preaching, though. Don't neglect these subjects.

An overhead projector is a good teaching aid also. It is especially good in the pastor's Sunday school class or for Wednesday evening Bible study. Diagrams and charts prepared for the overhead projector help people to see truth in a fresh light. People are more attentive when you use visual aids, and they often take notes. Teaching in this way also resulted in my writing *How on Earth Can I Be*

Spiritual? The charts and diagrams, students said, opened their eyes as nothing had before.

Be conscious of four groups of people in your audience as you preach. This awareness will transform your preaching and give it variety.

The unsaved need the gospel. Never take anyone's salvation for granted. There are unsaved preachers, according to Matthew 7:22,23. We have all seen deacons, Sunday school teachers, and church leaders get saved. If you always include parts of the gospel that help the unsaved to become true believers, your people will bring non-Christians to church with them.

Babes in Christ need tender loving care. It is so easy to preach over the heads of these babes. Be aware of them even when you ask the congregation to turn to different passages. In one church I pastored, everyone had a Scofield Bible. When people were saved, I would help them get Bibles wholesale. When I asked the congregation to turn to a passage, I often told what page it was on. Hundreds have thanked me for helping them get used to finding the references. Be sure to provide tender loving care for these babes.

Carnal Christians will be there. Don't preach at them but for them. They need help. Preach to restore them. Be aware of them and include them in your sermon preparation.

Mature Christians love some steak so that they can have something to chew on. Explain the Greek and Hebrew when appropriate. Don't avoid the tough commands of God and the passages that are more difficult to understand. At the same time, don't make a sermon sound so esoteric that only a few will comprehend it. Speak on a level they all will understand.

The Scriptures were given for doctrine, reproof, correction, and instruction in righteousness (see 2 Tim. 3:16). Include all of these things in your sermons. Remember that sheep need shepherding as well as shearing. Positive preaching is a must. Negative preaching produces negative attendance. On the other hand, some reproof and rebuke is needed to keep a church clean.

Three elements that should be in every message are evangelism, exhortation, and edification. Traditionally, the worship service has been on Sunday morning and the evangelistic service on Sunday evening. Churches that no longer have the Sunday evening service usually have no evangelism either. This tradition should be reexamined. Years ago the non-Christians hardly ever came on Sunday morning but would come on Sunday evening. Realistically, this is no longer true. The unbelievers are there Sunday morning. So why do so many feel bound to follow a tradition when there is no longer any reason for it?

Many pastors have faced the facts and changed the Sunday morning service to an evangelistic service. In order to make this change, a pastor needs to win the understanding and support of the deacons. One can, little by little, educate people by pointing out the facts and mentioning the need to reevaluate all methods of the ministry.

Many pastors have found that Sunday evening is the time for special emphasis on exhortation. The ones who will be challenged to do more for Christ are there then. But a healthy church will have the unsaved here as well. Keep your message well-balanced.

Edification and education should be emphasized on Wednesday night. The faithful folk are there then. These are the mature Bible believers who love the taste of steak. Feed them. Put out the best you have. They will warm it over in the Sunday school classes. Here is where 2 Timothy 2:2 sees its finest fulfillment. Don't forget that even here you need to be aware of ministering to all the flock.

The Delivery of Your Message

Stop and let the message grip your heart before you preach it. Here is the ultimate secret of successful preaching. Like Jeremiah (see Jer. 20:9) you must have the Word of God burning in your bones. When it burns in your heart, it will strike the hearts of the people. They will respond as the two on the Emmaus road, who said, " . . . Did not our heart burn within us, while he talked with us by the way, and while he opened to us the scriptures?" (Luke 24:32).

Do you remember professors in school who spoke the deepest truths but failed to interest the class? Have you heard preachers who preached profound messages and nothing happened? You wondered if the preacher believed what he said. You can tell when the message has gripped the speaker first. He needn't be a Bible-banger or pulpit pounder, but the message must touch him first or it won't touch others.

This is what divides the inspiring preacher from the tedious preacher. This is what makes the difference. Here lies the reason why sometimes a pastor who is much less endowed intellectually can fill a church while a more learned preacher has only the faithful few.

Soak your soul in the Word of God. Saturate yourself with the blessed Book as Jeremiah did. He said, "Thy words were found, and I did eat them; and thy word was unto me the joy and rejoicing of mine heart . . . " (Jer. 15:16). Absorb it until it seeps into your every conversation. Let it flow out of your message as naturally as breathing. The Word of God will burn like a fire. It will break the hardest heart. It will cut to the quick.

Bathe yourself in prayer. There is power in prayer. If you want to preach well, pray well. You can analyze a preacher's sermons all day and not find the secret of his success until you find out how much he prayed over that sermon. A sermon can be polished but powerless. How often you hear someone say of a pastor, "He's just not a great preacher. I know many preachers who can outpreach him." You want to cry. The mechanics don't make the message. The power of heaven does. Learn to pray before you learn to preach, and you will preach with power.

Preach with love and compassion. If you don't you will become "sounding brass or a tinkling cymbal" (1 Cor. 13:1). Dr. S. F. Dowis told of the dear old lady who responded to his message one day, saying, "You can preach *for* me now; you have preached *at* me long enough." Brokenheartedly, he admitted he had preached at her and not for her. If preachers were completely honest, they would admit that this is true of a lot of messages they have preached. And herein lies the reason for their fruitlessness.

Preach with authority, not arrogance. There is a vast difference between these two attitudes. In graduate school I had a professor who was constantly saying, "I'm not attached to this view," "It seems to me," "In my judgment. . . . " He impressed me. He impressed me with how little conviction he had. He never taught me a thing. I never knew if he was right or wrong, or if I should believe his view—whatever that was. People need and want an authoritative word today.

212

Some will try to water you down and say, "Don't be dogmatic or authoritarian," but don't you believe them. This was the difference between Jesus and the Pharisees. He spoke with authority (see Mark 1:22).

Preach with a smile, not a scowl, on your face. What a difference. "A merry heart maketh a cheerful countenance . . . " (Prov. 15:13). There is something about a face that glows that makes the message glow with it. Part of what some call "charisma" is simply that cheerful countenance that comes from a heart that is filled with the love of the Lord. When the glory of your message is real in your own heart, it will show in your eyes and on your face.

Preach with enthusiasm. Enthusiasm is not a personality quirk. It is a lack of self-consciousness. The word "enthusiasm" comes from the Greek *en theos,* meaning "God in you." A pastor whose heart is overflowing with love for God will let it spill out in his speech. Why is it that some preachers, who practically burst with excitement over a football game, can seem so bored when they preach about the glory of God? It doesn't make sense. We have let those who decry emotions set the standards for our preaching. There are those who call a pastor who gets excited about preaching a fanatic. Someone said, "A fanatic is someone who loves Jesus more than you." Soul-winning, sin-hating, Christ-loving people want an enthusiastic preacher.

Preach with spontaneity. Be free. Be loosed from the mechanics of preaching. Forget yourself and what the people are thinking about you. Don't try to impress your congregation with your diction, delivery, or decorum. Be concerned about one thing only. Get the glorious, wonderful message God has laid upon your heart into the hearts of your listeners. How many times I used to pray and weep over a message, then freeze on Sunday because I was self-conscious.

Preach as to a dying man. Some people will attend your services only once. Pour out your soul for them. You must, or you must not preach. Something ought to go out of you, just as when the woman touched Jesus and he felt "virtue" (power) go out of Him (see Mark 5:30). If you put nothing into your message, nothing will come out of it. Preach with power.

Outline your messages. Give listeners something catchy that will help them remember each portion of the message. Many use allitera-

213

tion for this. It will make the message stick in the minds of listeners, making it easier for them to repeat to someone else. Isn't that one purpose of preaching? That is putting 2 Timothy 2:2 into practice.

Use your Bible and train your people to follow along with you. You can do this in several ways. Note words and phrases, and ask the people to underline them as you preach. Tell them to write another meaning of a word in the margin. This helps keep their attention and makes the information more usable. Teach and train them to take notes and mark their Bibles.

If you read a reference in another place in the Bible, tell them the page number and give them time to find it. While they are looking it up, make some remarks that will connect the reference with what you have been saying. Of course, you can't do this with every verse you use outside your text, but with the key verses and longer passages, you can. By doing this people will learn how to find references and learn the books of the Bible.

How Does It Sound?

Your voice is very important. Learn to use it well. Listen to others' voices. Listen to radio preachers. Some voices captivate your attention; others turn you off. Why? Learn what makes you listen and what turns you off. A radio preacher cannot catch your attention by his appearance, facial expression, or gestures. His voice plays an enormous role. Subconsciously, people are turned off by a voice more than preachers might realize. Here are some things to consider.

Preach to the person on the last row. Nothing is worse than having to strain to hear the preacher. Learn to project your voice. Don't just talk to the people. Herald out the message. Preach it. It takes energy, it costs you, but preach it. If you are conscious of speaking to the person farthest away, you can be sure all will hear. When you lower your eyes to those directly in front of you, you automatically lower your voice as well. Preachers need to lift up both their eyes and their voices.

Learn to keep your voice under control. You can speak loudly and with great force without losing control. Don't speak in shrill, piercing tones. Many have ruined their voices by straining them.

If your voice is high-pitched, learn to lower it. My voice used to be very high-pitched. I've lowered it quite a bit by consciously working at it. Be careful about speaking fast; it always makes your voice get higher.

Try to create a resonant, warm sound when you speak. A singer works at the way he opens his mouth and holds his tongue in order to improve his singing. You too can improve the sound of your voice by genuine effort. Above all, don't have a nasal twang in your voice and don't have a whining voice. Make a tape of your sermon, and listen to your voice objectively.

Learn to modulate your voice. You may be speaking in a monotone without realizing it. How boring! And don't let your voice trail off at the end of your sentences. The joy in your heart that puts a smile on your face can also put a beautiful sound in your voice.

Articulate your words. Don't slur them. Learn to pronounce words clearly and correctly.

Use good grammar. It is absolutely unpardonable for a preacher to say, "He don't." Learn to speak correctly. You cannot reach successful people by using poor English, but you will never lose poor people by using good English.

Sharpen your tools, develop your skills, master the art of preaching. Preaching is unique to the ministry. You must be at your best in these few moments. The power and product of preaching is awesome. Don't neglect it.

What to Expect

When Christ preached, something happened. Paul produced a spiritual revolution when he preached. Something always happens when we preach, though it isn't always evident at the moment. If you expect nothing, that's exactly what you will get.

Preaching is powerful. God ordained it. " . . . how shall they believe in him of whom they have not heard? and how shall they hear without a preacher?" (Rom. 10:14). This is the way people are to hear—through a preacher. Music is wonderful. Christian films, drama, and cantatas are all fine, but " . . . it pleased God by the foolishness of preaching to save them that believe" (1 Cor. 1:21). What can you expect, then, from preaching?

Some will scoff. "...there shall come in the last days scoffers..." (2 Pet. 3:3). "And when they heard of the resurrection of the dead, some mocked . . . " (Acts 17:32). You might as well be prepared. You may be the most eloquent, the most fervent, the most sincere preacher, but some will not hear you or like you. Your reaction? "Be not afraid of their faces: for I am with thee to deliver thee . . . ," the Lord said to Jeremiah (1:8). Keep loving them. Don't be discouraged. Don't react negatively and try to retaliate. That only fosters hostility.

Some will ponder your message in their hearts. They just don't react as quickly as others. They sincerely think things through carefully before making decisions. To try to force an immediate decision could be disastrous. It is good, at the close of the service, to let people know they can receive Christ all by themselves at home. A man who had been to our church did this one night while his wife slept beside him in bed. He lay there thinking about the message and knew that if the Lord came he and his wife would be separated forever. Not wanting this, he prayed in his heart and received Christ as his Savior. He confessed the Lord publicly the next Sunday. We have known of several similar experiences.

Others will procrastinate, saying, I'll hear you again later (see Acts 17:32). Some will want to hear you when it is convenient for them. Sometimes that convenient time never comes. Satan snatches away what was sown in their hearts (see Matt. 13:19).

Some will do absolutely nothing and harden their hearts (see Prov. 28:48). This is sad, but it is not our responsibility. To some "we are the savor of death unto death..." (2 Cor. 2:16). God ordained preaching. It must not be taken lightly by the preacher or the hearer.

A common response to the Word of God is a glib agreement, with no depth of meaning (see Matt. 13:20,21). A person will say with a smile on his face that the message was wonderful, that he enjoyed it, and yet not mean a word of it. Yes, some actually lie. There will be no change in these people. This is disappointing, but it must not throw you.

Those who rebel and fight you probably are the worst. When Stephen preached " . . . they were cut to the heart, and they gnashed on him with their teeth" (Acts 7:54). This wasn't the end, for "They stoned Stephen . . . " (v. 59). No, they don't stone the preacher today; they just persecute him. "All that will live godly in Christ Jesus shall suffer persecution" (2 Tim. 3:12). Think it not strange (see 1 Pet. 4:12) but "count it all joy" (James 1:2), and you will be the victor. You must not get discouraged. God never uses a discouraged preacher. You cannot get bitter. That is a worse sin, and many become defiled by it (see Heb. 12:15).

Here is one final thought that can save a preacher from a devastating shock! Where were all Jesus' followers at the end of His life? Where were the blind He healed, the dead He raised, the multitudes He fed? Peter is often reprehended because he denied the Lord, but where were the rest of His followers? Mark says of Jesus, "They all forsook him" (14:50). Where were all of Paul's converts? He tells us " . . . Demas hath forsaken me . . . Only Luke is with me" (2 Tim. 4:10,11). Paul felt all alone in that dungeon in Rome. Every pastor has had the crushing blow of some of his most loved and faithful converts forsaking him. He has seen some who were once on fire for God die out in a smoldering ash heap.

Thank God, it isn't all bad. Some will believe (see Acts 17:34) and cleave to you. There are those who hear the Word, understand it, believe it, and bring forth fruit. But here is where many preachers get thrown for a loop. They will all bring forth different amounts, " . . . some a hundredfold, some sixty, some thirty" (Matt. 13:23). No matter how dramatic the conversion, some will never produce more than thirtyfold. Two people can receive the same amount of discipling and one bring forth a hundredfold and the other only thirty. Another may not receive any follow-up and bring forth much more than a person you spend hours on. You must not blame yourself because of this enigma. No one followed me up at all. I had never been to church until I was seventeen years old. Don't ask me why I went on with God.

There are many things about how God works that we will never understand. He said, " . . . my thoughts are not your thoughts, neither are your ways my ways . . . " (Is. 55:8). This does not mean we shouldn't do everything in our power to follow up and disciple everyone who professes to receive Christ. It does mean we should not allow ourselves to be frustrated because of the great differences in response and growth. Some who start slowly, end quickly. Some who start out the Christian life like a house afire fizzle out like a Fourth of

July sparkler. The solid, mature man of God goes right on, unhindered.

Bless the Lord, there are always those who will produce one hundredfold. These make it all worthwhile. There will be the Mikes and Bills and Melvins who go on with God, are called to preach, and build great churches. Many will not pastor or go to mission fields but will be soul-winners who help *you* build a great church. Paul had his Timothys and Onesimuses. So will you.

20

Bible Conferences

We should be thankful all the time. Thanksgiving Day accentuates the importance of thanksgiving, so it is good to have this special day. The Jewish feasts of Jehovah were given to accentuate special events and truths. Bible and missionary conferences can be used in the same way.

Some pastors are leery of Bible conferences, and justly so. Bible knowledge as an end in itself can be deadening. There must be an application of the truths of Scripture to daily life, or we will become like the Pharisees. Everyone is aware of those who flit from one Bible conference to another yet haven't won a soul to Christ in a lifetime. Pastors have been hurt by those who go all over the country to hear their favorite Bible teachers, only to come back critical of their own pastor because he doesn't preach the "deeper things of God."

An excellent way to deal with these problems is to have a Bible conference in your own church, with the right speakers preaching and making the correct application and emphasis. A Bible conference ought to place strong emphasis on applying the Word of God to one's personal life. The New Testament epistles were written to local churches. Local bodies of believers are emphasized throughout the Book of Acts. Believers today should love their local church and help to make it strong, so that it can carry out the Great Commission. If the congregation has this love, it will become a place where the whole family can be nurtured in fellowship with the dear Lord and each other.

Special conferences can and should complement a pastor's ministry. New faces and voices in the pulpit can reinforce in fresh ways what the pastor is trying to do. Bringing in someone who has given himself to mastering certain books or studies will add immeasurably to the spiritual life of your people.

When Should You Have a Bible Conference?

Summer. Having a Bible conference during the summer slump can revitalize your church. Promoted properly, it can practically do away with the big dip in attendance that occurs in the middle of the summer. Don't expect all of your people to put off their vacations for the conference, but some will stay for it. It also can be used to renew the interest of those who have lost their zeal. In the middle of July or even into August it can give your people a big boost. If you have top-notch conferences over a period of years, they will attract people from far and wide.

January. Some pastors like to start the New Year with a Bible conference. For years I conducted a January prophecy conference in my own church by using a large, beautiful, colored cloth chart to teach from. Our people looked forward to it. We also had a large number of visitors who hungered for this neglected teaching.

Easter or October. Many churches have an evangelistic meeting in the spring and Bible conference in the fall or vice versa. This makes a good balance.

How long Should a Bible Conference Last?

Sunday through Sunday. An eight-day Bible conference is the most productive. If you are able to employ several nationally known Bible teachers, it can be a time of revival in a church.

Sunday through Wednesday or Friday. Three one- or five-day conferences are best for some churches. Or, if your church has not yet come to love and appreciate such conferences, a shorter time might be more widely accepted.

Friday through Sunday. Weekend conferences can be very good, also. It has been my privilege for eighteen years to hold hundreds of weekend conferences. We've had family-life, soul-winning, and spiritual-life conferences. It is common to see ten to fifteen people saved and a church spiritually renewed in a weekend meeting. Recently three wives saw their husbands saved in a three-day family-life conference. Don't minimize a short conference like this.

How Do You Choose Personnel for a Bible Conference?

How do you select speakers? Where do you find them? The choice is unlimited. Pastors, Bible college professors, and full-time Bible and conference speakers offer plenty of options.

A church that has never had a Bible conference and is limited in finances can use local pastors. Several pastors who are gifted teachers can share the time. Two or three pastors can help each other and put on conferences in each other's churches over a period of a couple of months. This has been done very successfully.

As you progress, you can use a Bible teacher for your principle speaker and supplement with local pastors. Have the pastors speak in the early services and the Bible teacher deliver the main message each evening.

You may want to have a well-known Bible teacher speak the entire week at every service. There are many excellent conference speakers available. You can get names of speakers from Christian colleges and fellow pastors.

Ask the pastors of large churches to come in for one or two nights each. Dr. Jerry Falwell, of Thomas Road Baptist Church, Lynchburg, Virginia; Dr. Lee Roberson of Highland Park Baptist Church, Chattanooga; Dr. Jack Hudson of Northside Baptist Church, Charlotte, North Carolina; Dr. A. V. Henderson, Temple Baptist Church, Detroit, Michigan; and many others are often used to help pastors challenge their people to greater heights.

How Do you Schedule a Bible Conference?

The needs of every church are different. The working conditions of the people can dictate the length and style of your conference. Here is a suggested schedule.

Morning services. Morning services are good, especially if some of your people work at night and can not attend evening services.

10:00–10:45 A.M.   Have a Bible study series. It might be the study of one book led by a pastor or teacher.

10:45–11:30 A.M.   Have a series of individual messages to chal-

221

lenge and exhort. These should be especially designed to apply biblical truth. A balance of teaching and application will keep the conference interesting.

In the morning meeting sing only one song, make announcements, and have one musical special. Time is of the essence and should be used wisely so that the speakers will have as much time as possible.

Evening service. Two messages can be given each evening as well. Like the morning meetings, the two services should be different in type of message and emphasis.

7:00–7:45 P.M.	This again could be a series or a study of a book of the Bible. The same person could plan the entire series.
7:45–9:00 P.M.	Have more singing, an offering, and special music. This is the service at which you should have outstanding pastors who will challenge your people. Churches need to catch the vision and burden of these great men of God. Hearing these men can, and often does, revolutionize a church.

There are many gifted Bible teachers. Just as an evangelist has a special place in the ministry so does a Bible teacher. They can whet the people's appetite for the Word of God. They can teach deep truth to the believers. There should be no jealously or rivalry between them and the pastor. A good Bible teacher will be an asset by building up the pastor in the eyes of the people. Don't neglect this special ministry for your church.

21

Foreign Missions

Missions are our mission. The Great Commission to the church is to get the gospel into all the world to every creature (see Mark 16:45). The task is great, but God is greater. God is interested in people, not programs and promotions. You must be, too. If you are not a missionary, you are a mission field.

Pastors have found that God particularly blesses churches that are vitally involved in missions. The pastor sets the pace. He is the leader.

How can you make your church missionary-minded? You don't do it by bringing in a missionary once a year. Just as with anything else that is successful in a church, the missions program takes work. Here are some suggestions.

Have a missions chairman. This person can have a tremendously successful ministry by keeping missions fresh before the people. He should keep the bulletin board up-to-date and neat. Enlist someone who is creative to enhance the displays. The missions chairman will probably need to have a committee to help him.

Have missionaries often. Mission boards will be happy to send missionaries to your church. Churches are finding that housing a missionary family on furlough is a fruitful ministry. They make the church their headquarters while in the United States. The people get to rub shoulders on a daily basis with "real live missionaries." They have them in their homes for meals. What a profound effect this has! Sometimes they will only spend a month or two with you and then another missionary family will come. Missions becomes real to the church. The missionaries can teach Sunday school and speak on various occasions. A vital by-product of housing missionaries is that the young people get to know them. Many will be influenced to go into this field because of these contacts.

Read letters from missionaries. Excerpts from missionaries' letters

223

can be read from the pulpit every week. Special victories and needs should be kept before the church. The bulletin can print portions of letters and help promote missions.

A well-kept bulletin board can be effective. The main hallway of the church can be made into a Hall of Fame picture gallery of the missionaries. Along the hallway you can have a small, separate bulletin board for each missionary. Display 8″ x 10″ pictures of the missionaries and their prayer cards. Post their letters regularly. Underline pertinent statements so people can catch the important facts at a glance. Include pictures from their mission fields and a small map showing where they are. All this information will help make the missionary more than a name on a board.

In the vestibule of the church have a large map showing the locations of all the missionaries the church supports. A picture of each missionary placed on the map will help people identify who is where.

Have a display cabinet showing artifacts from each mission field. Most missionaries bring souvenirs home just for this purpose. Costumes and artifacts will create much interest. These displays are often of interest to visitors. A different missionary can be featured each month, with special displays presented.

Write the missionaries regularly. The pastor ought to write once a month. He can dictate one letter to all the missionaries and add one paragraph with something personal to each. Most missionaries have learned how to pray. A smart pastor will share his prayer requests with them.

Missionaries love to receive even brief notes from people back home. These personal notes are invaluable. The missions committee can have envelopes already addressed and pass them out in Sunday school classes each Sunday. A family who receives personal responses to their letters will soon be missionary-minded.

Pray for missionaries regularly. Pray for them as you do for the sick in your community. This keeps their names before the people and helps in the missionaries' ministry.

Pray for the vocation. Pray the Lord of harvest to send forth laborers from among your people.

Support individual missionaries. Supporting individuals makes missions far more real. Sending sums of money to a board depersonalizes missions.

Have missionary "outfit showers" when you have missionaries in your church. If someone is just going out to the field, get a list of their needs and have people sign up to supply the various articles. Have a party one evening when all will bring their gifts.

When my wife and I were going to Brazil as missionaries, a church did this for us. To this day, we recall that party with great joy, and it was over thirty years ago. It made a profound impression on us. Don't let people bring shoddy or secondhand things for missionaries. The old day of the missionary barrel is over. It just isn't right to expect missionaries to take worn clothes to a country where clothes are hard to get. They will have enough hardships; they don't need things that need fixing.

Have a commissioning or dedication service for missionaries before they leave for the field. This powerful service insures that your people will never forget them. We've had such services and closed with "God Be With You Till We Meet Again." We almost went up to glory singing it.

Go to the airport or ship to see them off. This is the capstone. Six carloads of our people drove to New Orleans to see Tom and Betty Young off to Brazil twenty years ago. With Tom and Betty standing on the ship and us on the dock singing, there wasn't a dry eye. They were just like our family. Our people not only supported them but, oh, how they prayed for them!

Preach on missions. If getting the gospel to every creature is our commission, then a pastor must preach it as intensely as he preaches the gospel. What a thrill to preach missions and have God call dozens of your young people to carry the gospel themselves. This adds a zest to a church that nothing else can.

Visit a mission field. While in seminary, I had the joy of hearing Jack Wyrtzen preach as he was on his way home from his first visit to a mission field. It was the most powerful sermon we had in my four years there. Go visit a missionary at work if you possibly can. It will make a lasting impression on you.

Have a Missions Conference

This can be the highlight of every year in a church. If you have never been to a successful missionary conference, you have missed one of the greatest events of life. The great Peoples Church of Toronto, Canada, is the grandfather of missionary endeavors. They had over one million dollars promised by their people last year. The great Urbana Conference in Urbana, Illinois, brings in hundreds of missionaries and future missionaries. A pastor would do well, if he needs a fresh vision of missions, to attend such a conference.

A week-long meeting is best but, as in a Bible conference, even a weekend meeting is effective.

Have veteran missionaries and a new recruit or two at your conference. Be sure you have some good speakers. Missionaries who are on the field as teachers, translators, or medical personnel are not always good speakers. You want some who will challenge your people. Sometimes those preparing to go for the first time are more enthusiastic than veterans and can be a real blessing.

Have films and slides from mission fields. A picture really is worth a thousand words. These can be presented at the early hour each night.

Have mission fields from more than one continent represented. Be sure to have some missionaries who have been successful planting churches and training national pastors.

Emphasize Missionary Support

Give generously to each mission you help sponsor. If each church only gives twenty-five dollars, missionaries have a frantic time trying to get enough money to support their fields while on furlough. When they are home, they need a little rest. Today, one hundred dollars a month is considered minimum support for a missionary.

Give a set amount per month per person. Missionaries have a hard enough time without having to juggle their budgets because of income that varies each month.

Send your support on a regular basis. If a church has to hold back paying any bills, it should never be missionary support. They are at your mercy.

The Faith Promise Plan has been very effective for churches who use it. Weeks before the conference, you challenge all your people to pray about how much they want to give to missions during the coming

226

year. Tell your people, "Ask God how much He wants to send to missions through you." This is to be given above their tithes. Christians pray and God seems to put in each person's heart an amount they believe they can expect God to give through them each month. Often someone will faintly promise to give five dollars a week and find God sending them an unexpected ten dollars a week. The next year their faith becomes bolder, and they give a faith promise of twenty dollars a week. Again, more than that comes in extra. It is a thrilling experience that thousands have had when they have made faith promises.

At the close of the conference, faith promise cards are filled out and turned in. People promise the amounts by faith, believing God is going to send what is needed during the year. If for some reason they don't get it, the matter is left with the Lord. No one should say a word about it. Hardly ever does the money not come in. The experience of most churches is that much more than is promised comes in.

The pastor and missions committee should then prayerfully consider how to divide the money among the individual missionaries and choose new ones to support. This is a time-honored plan that has been successful in thousands of churches. For further information you should write to the Peoples Church of Toronto, Canada. Dr. Oswald J. Smith and his son, Dr. Paul Smith, can give you much help.

The New Testament is filled with exhortations to be actively involved in missions. The Lord Jesus was the greatest missionary. God honors an unselfish church that actively supports those who are evangelizing in other lands. Be sure you get in on your share of the joy and privilege.

22

The Pastor's Study

"Study to show thyself approved . . . " (2 Tim. 2:15) is as true today as in Paul's day. You can neglect your study a few days and be the only one who knows it, but neglect it a few more and your whole church will know it. Slothful study produces shallow preaching, and shallow preaching produces empty churches. Don't just open your mouth and expect God to fill it. All you will have is hot air. That's good to fill balloons but not churches.

One night I was visiting my neighbor, Al Worthington, who pitched major-league ball for eighteen years. He told me about an evangelist friend who said that almost every pastor he preached for would ask the evangelist to recommend him to another church because he was ready to move on. Al asked me why that was. One reason is that preachers exhaust their resources. They preach all they know in a short period of time. This is because they have not spent enough time in the study to keep their own selves inspired, much less their people, and both are discouraged.

Remember in Luke 11 the man asked his friend for three loaves because he had a visitor. The man said, "I have nothing to set before him." This is the pitiful condition that many pastors are in on Sunday morning. If the truth were known, too many sermons are thrown together on Saturday night, or rather the ideas from a previous message are hastily rearranged. Because of a love for the pastor and church, the people don't say much about it. But they go home unfed and unfulfilled in the worship of God.

A pastor will never be caught up with his duties. He will never have enough time to do all he wants to do. In spite of everything, though, he must not neglect his study—for his soul's sake and for his people's sake. Study is a must.

The haves and the have-nots can be traced to the dids and did-nots.

228

God has no loaves for the loafers. As a pastor, it's terribly easy to become lazy and neglect your study. Too many books of sermons are available for you to skim through on Saturday night. But it's like grabbing something out of the freezer and warming it; too often the pastor's oven is not hot enough to make it enjoyable. God certainly doesn't add much fire to pastors who neglect the things of God to that extent.

"Genius," someone said, "is the infinite capacity for taking life by the scruff of the neck." Take control of your time. Use it wisely. Learn to study and study well.

Here are some suggestions for your study.

The study should be private. Your home may be the best place for it. Your office is usually at the church. Unless you can shut yourself up at the office to study, it becomes useless. Most pastors find it almost impossible to spend extensive time studying at the church. Too many people drop by "for just a minute" when they see your car or know you are at the church.

No room is more important than your study. Here is where you meet God. It is in the quietness here that He speaks to your heart. The message from God is hammered out in this sacred place. Wherever you have it, do all you can to make it a convenient place to study and seek the face of God.

Keep your study exclusive. If at home, don't use it for anything else but a study. Do your counseling and office work at church. If your study is at church, then you must set hours apart when you are not to be interrupted except in emergencies. This some find almost impossible. Nothing will be harder to arrange than extended time for study and personal fellowship with God.

One advantage in having a study at home is that you have access to it at all hours of the day and night. If you are a night owl, you can shut yourself up after the children and wife are in bed and study until the wee hours. If you are an early riser, it is easy to go there and work a couple of hours in the morning before the others get up. Wherever you have it, be sure it is convenient and that you use it. No matter what tradition says or what any other pastor does, make your study the place where you can best meet with God and have long sessions with Him.

The study should be quiet. If in the home, the children should be taught the importance of not interrupting Dad. Some pastors like soft music in the background to help them study. Fine, then put in a stereo system. Do all you can to make your study time most productive.

Make your study cheerful and well-lighted. It should be decorated in a way that is pleasing to your eye. Look at a pastor's study, and you can just about tell how well his sermons will be prepared. Heating and air conditioning are a must, not a luxury. You can be sure Satan will do all he can to distract you. Don't give place to the devil in this area.

Have your books handy. Install plenty of bookshelves. It is a big mistake for a pastor not to have a place for his books. Have your reference books within arm's reach. A large enough desk to spread out several books and the Bible is also important. Don't cut corners on equipment for the study.

Your library is like a doctor's instruments or a carpenter's tools. Without the proper instruments a doctor would have problems operating; without tools, a carpenter would have problems building a house. Likewise, a pastor without the right books will never gain the insights necessary to feed the flock.

Buy books, and buy good ones. One of my professors in graduate school said that he never bought a book to add to his library if he did not feel it was worth reading at least twice. A powerful thought. There is a proliferation of books. How do you choose good ones?

Buy reference books. A good Bible dictionary, encyclopedias like *International Standard Bible Encyclopedia,* a concordance, an atlas, a word study like W. E. Vine's *Expository Dictionary of New Testament Word Studies* or Robertson's *Word Studies* if you are a Greek student. If you are a student of Greek and Hebrew, there are many books in these areas you should have. Commentaries are essential. Many writers have mastered one particular book and written commentaries that are superb. Find these commentaries. Most whole sets are not as helpful in dealing with every word. A pastor should have four or five commentaries on each book.

Get the classic books on prayer and holy living. Books like E. M. Bounds' *Power Through Prayer, Praying Hyde,* or John R. Rice's *Prayer, Asking and Receiving* are jewels. Get books by F. B. Meyer, Andrew Murray, and Watchman Nee. Read the biographies of great men of God. The lives of men such as Spurgeon, Moody, David Brainerd, and George Mueller will stir your soul and let you know you aren't alone in times of trial.

Listen to your professors. Write down the title of every book they think is important. Ask them to recommend books in their fields. Ask pastors to tell you the ten most important books they have read. You have only so much time. There is no need to waste it reading hundreds of pages to find one sentence, when there are so many books filled with truths and insights you can use over and over.

Make a schedule and stick to it. Unless you have a schedule, you will probably be robbed of your study time. Budgeting time is one of the easiest things to put off. Don't sacrifice your study time for something unimportant. Fiercely guard that time alone with God. Be jealous of it. Plan on it just as surely as you plan on eating dinner.

Don't try to fit yourself into the mold of someone else. This almost ruined me. How often I would hear some speaker tell about great pastors who rose before daylight to meet God. Some would say, "No minister should be in bed when the men of his church are at work." Then I found out that each person has a metabolism that functions differently. Mine doesn't work at all until about nine o'clock in the morning, and it functions best late at night. My best study time is at night, so I schedule it for then. Study when it is best for you, not to impress someone else.

A Suggested Schedule

6:00–10:00 A.M. Be in your study. If the study is in your home, this is much easier. You can take a break for breakfast and get in a good three or four hours of study—if you are an early riser.

10:00 A.M.–12:00. Be in your office. Learn to get the things done that need to be done. Let your secretary, janitor, associates, and deacons all do their own work. If you teach and train your people properly, you can do what you are called to do and let others fulfill themselves in doing what they are supposed to do. Most preachers are guilty of letting themselves become errand boys.

12:00–2:00 P.M. Have lunch with your wife or with businessmen. This period can be used to spend a little extra time with your wife. Go

231

on a picnic, get in a little recreation, go shopping—do something you enjoy. This can be a good time for a fifteen-minute nap. Studies have shown that fifteen minutes of total relaxation can rejuvenate you for the rest of the day. In the spring and summer have a quick game of tennis or bowling with your wife or children. Many go for a quick dip at the Y or some other convenient place. There are many ways to spend this time wisely.

2:00–6:00 P.M. Go visiting.

6:00–7:00 P.M. Have dinner. In fairness to your wife and family, you should have a set time for dinner.

7:00–9:00 P.M. Attend meetings or visit.

9:00– ? Study. If you are a night owl, now is the time. After all the children are in bed and the phone has stopped ringing, study. This has always been my best time. Hundreds of times I have gotten inspired by a message at one in the morning. Sometimes I've spent all night in my study and gotten more done than I could have in a week of mornings. Find your time to study and do it!

This might seem to be an ambitious schedule, and it is. Adjust it to suit your own personality. If you aren't an early riser, study later. If you are an early riser, you may study little or not at all at night.

Family time is vitally important. You must have time for all members of your family. Family devotions must be scheduled. Family recreation also needs to be included in your schedule. Some pastors like to take Monday off. Do whatever works best for you.

Be systematic. Don't pass the time in your study accomplishing nothing. Set times for various aspects of study. Your own personal devotions and development are of utmost importance. Sermon preparation is obvious. Keeping up with theological trends is basic. Reading to broaden your general knowledge of the Bible is important. One needs to keep up with what's happening in the world. Social trends, current events, and moral issues need to be studied. The whole field that needs to be covered during a pastor's study time is enormous. You cannot expect it just to happen. There must be scheduling and planning.

Personal devotional time is your most important hour of the day. It takes a lifetime to fully equip the minister. If the minister isn't prepared, he can't deliver the message. Don't forget " . . . one day is with the Lord as a thousand years, and a thousand years as one day" (2 Pet. 3:8). Spend your time with God, and things that could take hours will be done in minutes. Neglect God and you will be bogged down and take hours to do what ought to take minutes. God is God. Jesus is Lord. Apply yourself wholly to the Scriptures and the Scriptures wholly to yourself.

The temptation will be there every day for you to cut short your time with God. When you do, you cut your own throat. Nothing, absolutely nothing, is as important as time with God *every day*. This is the secret behind great preachers and pastors. It will show up in the results of your ministry. Often someone will ask, "What does he have?" He may not be a dynamic preacher. He did not win the prize for scholarship. No one chose him the most likely to succeed, but succeed he did. Why? He knows God. He is on intimate terms with Him. Every day he has an audience with the God of the universe, and because of that things happen that God alone can do. The Bible is not only to be appreciated but appropriated.

Read through your Bible at least once a year. The more Scripture you have at your fingertips, the richer your preaching will be. There is much more for the Holy Spirit to bring to your mind. It is exciting when the Holy Spirit prepares your messages by reminding you of incidents in the Bible or verses that fit into a message.

Memorize Scripture. Psalm 119:11 is gloriously true. Hide the Word of God in your heart and it will keep you from sin. Begin while in school. Make it a regular part of your life from there on. You should have hundreds, even thousands, of verses committed to memory. Plan to memorize several a week, review them daily for two months, and they will stay with you for life.

Meditate. The "M and M combination" is a great winner—memorize and meditate. Learn to spend hours in meditation. It will surprise you how much the Holy Spirit will teach you. This is how you keep your mind on the Lord and thus have perfect peace (see Is. 26:3). Here is the secret of renewing your mind (see Rom. 12:2). How do you dwell in the secret place of the Almighty and abide under the shadow of the Almighty (see Ps. 91:1)? Memorize and meditate on the Word of God.

There will be times when you will be overwhelmed with His presence as you practice this. Whole messages will come to you in a moment's time. Nuggets of truth more real than you ever dreamed will pop into your mind. Preaching will be the overflow of these great times. God will be so real that you will feel like reaching out and touching Him. You will walk with God. What an astounding thought. Enoch did in his day. We surely can today. Don't miss these moments. Nothing is as important.

Pray. Pray fervently (see James 5:17). Pray in the Spirit (see Eph. 6:18). Pray in faith (see Matt. 21:22). Pray morning, noon, and night (see Ps. 55:17). "Pray without ceasing" (1 Thess. 5:17). Oh, brethren, pray. " . . . without me ye can do nothing," Jesus said (John 15:5). He means it. Don't kid yourself into thinking you can neglect Him. Try the pray-as-you-go plan.

Have a prayer list. "Keep on praying and you will receive" is what Matthew 7:7 means. If you haven't learned it yet, you will. It's the things that you really pray to God for that happen. Our memories fail us. Satan snatches names from our minds unless we make a list. What a thrill it is to have a prayer list and jot down the date and answer beside it as it is fulfilled. Have a lock on the door of your study so you can pray without fear of interruption. Some have agonized in prayer until great things have been accomplished.

Read one book of the Bible each day for a week or a month. Talk about a living Bible! It will be living to you before the month is over.

Read and meditate on the passage you are writing your sermon on. Before you go to the commentaries, let the Holy Spirit enlighten you. It's much more fun having Him bring out in advance what you'll see in the commentaries.

Study for your message. Look up the words in Greek and Hebrew or in a Greek word study if you are not a Greek student. Find the Greek nuggets and you will be in a gold mine.

Read the commentaries. They will add historical background, customs, and many other facts that enrich the message.

Study subjects that particularly interest you until you become an authority on them. My study on the Tabernacle resulted in my book, *Teaching from the Tabernacle,* now in its fifth printing. It is my desire now to write a series of messages on the feasts of Jehovah. The fields are wide open. One day you, too, will be amazed when you write books and hear from hundreds who meet the Lord through them.

Write. Write out your messages. Writing out at least one each week will immensely sharpen your ability to express yourself. It will help you to say what you want to say much more succinctly.

Write a tract. Every pastor ought to write a gospel tract. Your people will use yours more—and you will too. It's great publicity. Best of all, you get the gospel to people you otherwise wouldn't reach.

If you have the proper skills, write articles and submit them for publication. There are many magazines looking for that special article you have been wanting to write for a long time. Have it edited by a good English teacher or someone who teaches writing. The power of the pen is overwhelming. It can lead to a broader ministry in years to come.

Not everyone who wants to write ought to write. Writing well is a craft that only those who have time to master it do well. But not every book has to be a masterpiece to be helpful. So, if you have a book burning in your heart, write it.

Of course, you will wonder, "Who would ever read what I write?" We all wonder the same thing. But bless God, when He is in it and it's done for His glory, great numbers will read it.

Study for years ahead. Sometimes you will become deeply interested in one particular book of the Bible, and you will want to master it. Do it. Read everything ever written on that one book. Delve into it until you have thoroughly explored every hidden message. No, you won't exhaust it, but you will be much richer.

No one has enough time to read all he needs to. Hidden in books is a treasure trove of information that is at your fingertips if you want it. Get people to read for you. Presidents do this. Many renowned people do it.

Homemakers, retired people, shut-ins, deaf and handicapped people can all read for you. Give them magazines to read like *Moody Monthly, Christianity Today, Sword of the Lord,* or whatever you subscribe to. Also give them books to read. Instruct them in what to look for and how to underline information. You especially may want them to mark good illustrations, meanings of Greek words, definitions, historical facts, biblical customs, and unusual statements. They can be coded and marked in the margin of the book or magazine. Later, your helpers can put the information on index cards and file it alphabetically or under the appropriate Bible reference. Some can do

235

the reading and underlining; others, who may not be fast readers, can put the information on cards. In a matter of time you could have every book in your library read and indexed. Think what a store of information you would have at your fingertips.

Magazines can be cut up and articles filed in manila folders, labeled by subject or Bible book. This saves enormous amounts of space. The potential of this program is astronomical. This is a tested, proven plan. And the readings will feed your people as well. Many will find fulfillment in serving you and the Lord this way.

Acquire the habit of writing down information for future reference and filing these notes appropriately. All of us have heard innumerable illustrations and truths that we wish we had stored away. Begin writing them down and filing them now while you are in school, or one day your heart will ache at the wealth of material you are not able to recall and use. It was my privilege to sit under men like Dr. Harry Ironside, Lewis Sperry Chafer, and many others. They told many personal stories that I should have recorded. What an abundance of material I missed. You don't have to. Get stories down as you listen to the great preachers and teachers of today.

Cut out portions of Scripture from an old Bible, and paste them in the middle of a sheet of notebook paper. Then when you come across an illustration or statement that helps illuminate a particular passage, write it on the page beside the verses. Pertinent information can be cut out of magazines and papers and glued on the appropriate pages. These then can be kept in a loose-leaf notebook. You can have this handy as you prepare to preach a passage. Over the years you could have the whole Bible covered this way and have a wealth of material conserved. Dr. Harold Willmington, Dean, Liberty Bible Institute, has done this for years and has notebooks filled with these pages.

As you study and meditate you can jot down ideas, references, and illustrations that the Holy Spirit brings to your mind. The notebook can be used to store those ideas while you formulate your message on another piece of paper to insert in your Bible to preach from. Both should be kept together for future use.

Read informative secular material. You are not of this world but you are in it. Separation is not isolation. No minister wants to be so heavenly minded that he is no earthly good. You must not speak like the world but you need to be able to speak to the world. Television loves to distort the image of the pastor. Often it makes him look like an insipid little pip-squeak who doesn't face reality. He is a man who spends his days sipping tea in the parlor with people as silly and helpless as himself. You need to dispel this image. You need to be able to converse with the man on the street about the major issues of the day.

Read the newspaper. Keep up with world events. Know what's happening in your city and state. Be aware of the business world and basic trends. The political world is big and powerful. You should know the politicians in your area and where they stand on major issues. Sports are on the lips of most men. You don't have to know all the details, but you should be knowledgeable about national and local news.

The *Reader's Digest* covers a variety of subjects. There are many conversation-piece articles each month.

A major news magazine is a must. You can get a brief summary of world issues without reading all of the details. Reading movie reviews will stir your soul with anger at sin and let you know what is shaping the minds of the day.

Book digests are informative. Secular books on history, science, and politics usually are a change of pace for pastors and help keep you abreast of new developments in science and current thought.

This secular material is easy to read. Many find that reading it in bed at night relaxes them and helps put them to sleep. All the details don't have to be remembered, but it keeps the pastor from being uninformed. Keep up with the world, or it will pass you by and you won't reach the man on the street.

Shocked is a mild word for my reaction to a statement by a pastor. He said, "I have never had an original thought come to me in my study. I have to get all my information from the commentaries of other men." What a tragedy. Being alone with God in your study ought to produce sweet, precious insight that will feed and fascinate people and make them come back for more.

Your study is vital. It is the main artery of preaching. Guard it well.

23

Sunday Morning Service

This is your hour! Don't blow it. Like the trumpeter in an orchestra when it is time for the trumpet solo, you must be ready. You have that one moment to be at your best. All the week's endeavors should be climaxed in the Sunday service. Too many Sunday services are poorly planned. This ought not to be so. A pastor would be wise to analyze every minute and activity of his services and be sure they are all conducted effectively.

The prelude. The organ prelude sets the stage. It is not a performance. It is not to fill in the time. It should minister to the hearts of the listeners.

Some music, we know, stirs up the flesh. All music in church should minister spiritually. The prelude should consist of music that touches the minds and hearts of the listeners and prepares them for the service. Greatly to be praised is the organist who is sensitive to the Holy Spirit and plays music that ministers spiritually and makes the people alert to the presence of God.

Beginning the service. It is an insult to those who are punctual to begin the service late. Also it teaches people poor habits. To start on time is a mark of character. Everything is to be "done decently and in order" (1 Cor. 14:40). You must train yourself to be punctual.

Churches try everything to create a worshipful attitude for the service. Many put in their bulletins such tips as: "If you must whisper, whisper a prayer" or "Enter to worship, depart to serve." Often you read an admonition to cease talking when the organist begins playing. People who are trying to pray are bothered by noisy chatter before the service.

We found a way that worked wonders, but it may not be adaptable in every church. We made an altar with a carpeted kneeler on the floor across the front of our auditorium. About two minutes before the ser-

238

vice was to begin, I would come to the front, kneel, and pray for the service. Many of our men would come from their seats and kneel with me. We would have about twenty people praying at the front. Without saying a word, the people in the pews would stop talking and pray. It always came about in a natural way. Visitors were deeply impressed. Everyone spent that minute preparing his heart.

The choir would come in about one minute later and bow their heads to pray also. They came out, stood, and prayed in a very orderly fashion. Precisely on the hour, the choir began singing a chorus or verse of a song such as "Turn Your Eyes Upon Jesus," "My Faith Looks Up to Thee," or "My Jesus, I Love Thee." The song varied each Sunday. This was a powerful moment.

Immediately after that chorus the song leader stepped to the microphone and announced the first hymn. I went to the platform, and the men returned to their seats. It was an opening that compelled attention.

The element of surprise is powerful. There is no law that says you have to open the service with a congregational hymn. Start with a solo or the choir singing a special that relates to the theme of the whole service. We have seen this electrify the entire church and make the service come alive.

How important the beginning of a service is. Above all, you should open with a familiar song—one that is easy to sing, not draggy. A service will be ruined before you know it if the first song is unfamiliar or difficult to sing. How many times I've seen this happen, and no one knew why the service was so lifeless.

Poorly done directions are one of my pet peeves. Never say, "Let's all stand and sing number 354." Usually one or two persons jump up and then quickly sit down when they find themselves standing all alone. The proper way to introduce a humn is to say, "Let's sing together. Would each of you get a song book and turn to number 354. Hymn number 354." Then, with a motion of your hands as though you are lifting the audience, say, "Let's all stand together as we sing." When people are trained this way, all will stand at the same time. In this way you are fostering unity. It can be used to get people not only to stand together but to sing together, and that's what it's all about.

239

Exhort your people to sing. Time is precious. The song leader can say too much or too little. He should leave the preaching to the preacher. On the other hand, a word or two from him can focus attention on the message of the song. The song leader should have a " . . . merry heart [that] maketh a cheerful countenance . . . " (Prov. 15:13). He sets the pace. If the song moves his heart and it shows, it will most likely move the people's hearts.

An accompanist can waste a lot of time with a long introduction to a song. Time is of utmost value, and every second must be used wisely. When the organist plays the verse all the way through, you have wasted the time the congregation could have been singing. The song leader should start by singing out strongly himself. He should get close to the microphone and sing right into it so the people don't hear themselves sing that first note. This encourages them to raise their voices. The beginning can make or break the song service. Some song leaders only move their lips and don't sing at all. In that case, unless the congregation is unusual, people will not sing nearly as well as they can. After the first phrase or two the song leader should step back a little from the microphone so that he isn't heard above the voices of the congregation.

The song service should make people aware of the presence of the Holy Spirit. It should prepare them to listen to the sermon and to be receptive to the will of God. The music is simply a tool. A song may be technically correct but may not be singable or really communicate a message. Sometimes a music director is more concerned about the mechanics than the ministry of the music. Thousands of songs have been written by sincere Christians, but that doesn't mean that God inspired the writing or wants to use it. A wise song leader will know which songs to choose.

New songs do need to be introduced to congregations. This is what will make the difference between success and failure. Teach the choir the new song during rehearsal. Next it could be used Wednesday evening and taught to a large number. Then, when you present it on Sunday, it will go over much better. A song must not be forced on a church just because it is a pastor's or music director's favorite. But if a song is well-received, keep using it.

In one church where I pastored, "Let the Lower Lights Be Burning'' was the favorite hymn. When we sang it, the faces of the congregation lighted up. No other church I pastored ever really cared for it. My favorite song is "Make Me a Blessing.'' While on the faculty of Moody Bible Institute, I taught a class of all first-year students, which I always began with a song. I taught them this song, and they loved it. At no place else has it caught on as it did at Moody. For some strange reason, one song is a favorite of each church, and it seems to ignite the service as the people sing it.

I think it is better to sing two verses of three songs than five or six verses of one song. If one song doesn't enthuse the people, maybe the next one will. Also, one song may be a special blessing to some and the next one to others. A variety will mean that more people are touched by the music. However, if the people really seem to enjoy singing a certain song, you can sing it through. Because hymns are poems set to music, often the full message of a song will come through better if sung in its entirety. But nothing takes the life out of a service quicker than singing four or five verses of a song that people don't know or don't like. Sometimes a song leader may begin a song, find that the people don't know it, and change after the first verse. This is better than dragging through it.

Welcome visitors. Next in importance to the presence of the Lord is the presence of visitors. That's what the whole ministry is about— reaching others. If this is not done, a church becomes stagnant. It is shocking to see the way in which visitors are welcomed in many churches. They are either made a spectacle of or ignored.

The unpardonable sin is to ask, as I often hear, "Do we have any first-time visitors this morning? We want to give you a card to fill out and put in the offering plate.'' Analyze this and see how cold and selfish it really is. Worse yet is to ask them to stand. No wonder pastors say they have a hard time getting visitors' names.

Consider this approach: "It's so good to have all of you here this morning. Visitors, we are especially glad to have you. You honor us by being in our church. I hope our people give you a warm welcome. We want you to enjoy the service, and we pray that God blesses you for being here. Thank you so much for coming. We want our people to know you and welcome you, so would you remain seated while our members stand and welcome you?'' As you say, "While our members

241

stand," motion for your people to stand. Teach members to speak to those seated around them. Immediately the ushers must get to those seated and hand them visitors' cards and pencils. Then explain that you would appreciate it if they would fill out the cards so that you can write to them this week.

Often I used to add a little humor and say, "Tell me what day you are going to have fresh home-baked pie. I'll drop by and eat with you." It always got smiles and chuckles. Most people respond to a bit of humor. The unsaved man in the back of the church may feel out of place to begin with and may have a tie on for the first time in a month. Make him feel relaxed. Let him know that it is all right for Christians to laugh and enjoy themselves.

Announcements. Announcements should be preached. I mean it. If the announcement is important enough to take up Sunday morning time, then make it alive and exciting. Don't just announce Wednesday evening prayer meeting. Arouse an interest in it, and make people want to come. Stating "Prayer Meeting is Wednesday at 7:30" will not get one more person to come, and isn't getting people to come the purpose of your announcement?

Commend your people for their work. Paul mentioned people by name and praised them. The Word of God does this. Pastors should, too, giving " . . . honor to whom honor" is due (Rom. 13:7). People are starved for a little praise and attention. Choirs work hard and long hours. It is a mistake to take them for granted. They should never sing without a word of thanks, praise, or appreciation from the pastor.

Often as a guest speaker, I've turned to a choir and thanked them for ministering to me before the sermon. I have seen tears well up in their eyes. Afterward, many have said that's the first time in months they were recognized. "Like pastor, like people." A thankful and appreciative church starts with the pastor.

A church had a large and successful youth program during week nights. The new pastor dropped in on the meetings and greeted the youth. He then commended the workers. The next Sunday the pastor raved about the youth program and the workers. It was the first time there had been any public recognition of them. The youth pastor was in tears. Needless to say, the youth pastor thought the new pastor was the world's greatest. This began a sweet relationship and ministry that lasted for years. Probably most of the friction between Christian workers could be eliminated if there were more appreciation for one another.

Love your people. Most people are starved for love. Just as some parents constantly scold, some pastors constantly scold their people and never tell or show that they love them. Tell them you love them. It will help them and you too.

Smile at your people. It should not be a plastic, forced smile but should come from a merry heart (see Prov. 15:13). A smile is contagious. People will respond in like manner.

Stand with authority. One should approach the pulpit with authority and not in a careless, slovenly manner. Stand directly behind the microphone as though you own the place, not with arrogance but with authority. It creates confidence. One who stands too far back from the microphone or off to the side does not appear to be in command.

Speak with authority. One who mumbles out announcements will be ineffective. A pastor must learn how to speak into a microphone. Television announcers and singers speak directly into the microphone. In too many churches, the PA system is weak and the pastor speaks in a soft, mild manner. This does not create confidence and establish authority. Speak up so that your voice is heard with ease. A speaker should learn that when he turns to look to the side he must move his body so that the microphone is still able to pick up his voice. In other words, stay behind the microphone and use it.

Public prayer. Say short prayers in public, long prayers in private. Prayers should be to God and not for the people. (Always have those leading in prayer come to the microphone so that all can hear and enter into the prayer.) If the church is small, people should be taught to stand, face the congregation, and pray loud enough so that all can hear and pray with you. People should be taught to pray with the one leading

Prayer is talking to God. Clichés and trite religious phrases should be avoided. Have you ever heard someone stumbling around trying to pray, "Bless those who give and those who don't have wherewith to give"? It sounds utterly ridiculous, doesn't it? If someone talked to us the way some prayers are said to God, we would think the person had lost his senses. Public prayers must be stated in language that is easily understood.

One should not try to impress God with his prayers. You can't con God. He sees through the false front. My first year home from college, my pastor called on me to lead in public prayer. It was the first time I had done so in my home church. My heart was full and burdened. I poured out my heart, totally oblivious to where I was and who was around. In every sense of the word, I talked to God. After the service at least a dozen people came to me and said, in effect, "I've never heard anyone pray like that." It deeply impressed upon me that prayer should come from our true feelings.

Reading Scripture. Never read the Scripture from portions in the back of the hymnals. You invite people not to use their Bibles by doing this. Don't provide Bibles in the pews. Teach your people to bring their own Bibles and use them. Always read the Scriptures from the Bible. We always read from the King James Version. This is the most-used Bible. If everyone has the same Bible, then more people can participate when you read in unison or with responses. Teach the people to read slowly and pause at punctuation marks. Be sure the one leading the Scripture reading has gone over the passages, so that he doesn't hesitate to pronounce words and can read with feeling and understanding.

Offering. Giving is a joy and a privilege. Jerry Falwell is the master at taking an offering. He makes you want to give. It is common for him to take a second offering at the close of a service for some special need. Never have I heard the people complain. He actually is doing his people a great honor, for they are storing more treasures in heaven. What a wise thing to encourage.

Be positive when taking an offering. Never scold the people for not giving. They need to be encouraged and praised for their giving. People need to be taught the joy and privilege of giving. Moses had to restrain the people, for they brought more than enough (see Ex. 36:5,6). The people gave freely, because their deliverance was still fresh in their minds. Good gospel preaching, making much of the Cross, and keeping people aware of the grace of God in their salvation always causes people to give more freely.

Ushers should be trained to be ready for the offering. The plates should be at hand. It is inexcusable for ushers to scramble around looking for offering plates when the pastor announces that he is going to receive the offering.

Use enough ushers. Churches sometimes use only two men to pass the plates. The people at the end of the row then have to pass the plate over their shoulders to the ones behind them. There should be someone at each aisle to receive and pass the plates. This allows more people to participate in the service. If the church is very large, have men stationed halfway up the aisle to take up the offering in the back of the church. The larger the church, the more plates you will need to use. There should be at least two plates per section. Remember, time is important. To use an extra minute taking the offering takes time from preaching.

Special music during the offering uses more people and adds extra blessings during the service. A good singer doesn't enjoy going to a church and only getting to sing once every six months. Using good musicians often is one way to attract them to your church. An instrumental solo is enjoyable to listen to during the offering.

Special music. Have two or more specials every service. Have only two verses in every special. It is better for people to want to hear more of a soloist than to hear too much. You can have more specials that way also. Always leave the people wanting more. It is effective to have a package of three specials with no introductions or breaks between them. Remember, the pastor should always thank the soloist or choir for the music.

The sermon. The sermon should transform people, not just inform them. This must be your goal in preparing a message. Preaching should be relevant to life. People know how to make a living but don't know how to live. All theology and theory should apply to everyday living. The result should bring joy to the Christian and glory to the Lord Jesus. The message should end on a high note, never on a negative one, nor should it just taper off like the preacher has finally run down.

Preach for a decision. Non-Christians harden when they hear the gospel over and over and do nothing about it. Christians become hardened when they hear the truth over and over and do nothing about it. Always give an invitation. It doesn't always have to be to

245

come down the aisle; a decision can be made in the heart in the pew. But always give people the opportunity. Not to do so hardens people. As James 1:24 describes, they behold themselves in a mirror and go away and forget " . . . what manner of man . . ." they are. If people are challenged to make a decision in their hearts in the pew first, they will be more likely to make a public decision later.

The invitation is so important. The congregation should be taught to pray earnestly when it is given. A battle rages in every heart. You can be sure the imps of hell will do all they can to discourage people from making the decision they ought to. Fervent prayer during invitation makes an enormous difference. Christians won't always do it, though, unless they are taught and encouraged.

Minister to new Christians. Teach and train people to make public decisions. It is scriptural to confess Christ before men (see Matt. 10:32). In the Old Testament they " . . . stood to the covenant" to make a public decision (2 Kin. 23:3). Make it easy for them. The pastor and associate pastors should stand at the front to meet the people immediately as they come forward. Never stay behind the pulpit and wait for a person to move into the aisle before you come down from the platform. Remember, we are wrestling against principalities and powers. Satan uses every hindrance to keep people from responding; we should remove all we can. Someone should already be at the front to meet a person before he even steps into the aisle.

If a person is led to Christ by someone other than the pastor, several good things occur. First, that soul-winner has the satisfaction of leading someone to Christ. He then feels a responsibility for that person and will pray for him more and be concerned about his spiritual growth. The person saved has someone to look to for guidance besides the pastor, though he will love and respect the pastor and know that God used his preaching to bring him to Christ. It prevents building the church around the pastor, so that when he leaves the flock does not scatter.

Tell the church what happened when a person gets saved. His testimony should not be for the counseling room only. The shepherd called his friends and said, " . . . Rejoice with me . . . " (Luke 15:6) when the lost sheep was found. We should too. What a climax to a service to let someone stand before the whole church, with the joy still showing, and tell how he was just saved. Equally thrilling is when God calls some young person to Christian service, and the whole church is given the opportunity to rejoice over it. We should make much of it—the angels of heaven do, and God does. Testimonies let the people know that the gospel really works. If someone were led to Christ at home, tell the people about it. Let them see that visitation works.

Give God the glory when decisions are made. Get the people to tell others about what God did. When Jesus healed someone, He said, "Go home. . . and tell them how great things the Lord hath done. . ." (Mark 5:19). If people would tell about these blessings instead of complaining and gossiping, we would have a real revival.

A lady who had been a barmaid got saved in our church. A few months later, after Sunday service she said, "Brother Wemp, I hate this time of the week."

I asked, "Why?"

She said, "Because it is so long before we are back in church again to see all God is doing. I can hardly wait until next Sunday to see who is going to be saved next." What a wonderful way to live! What a great attitude to have toward church.

The postlude. The organ postlude sends you home with a hymn ringing in your heart. A Spirit-led organist will be sensitive to the message delivered or to something special God has done and play the appropriate song. At a service I recently attended the message was on the Holy Spirit. As He moved, so sweetly, many decisions were made. There was a feeling of love and warmth among the people. At the close the organist played, "There's a Sweet, Sweet Spirit in This Place." Nothing could have been more fitting. Dozens of people commented on it. It was the icing on the cake.

"I was glad when they said unto me, Let us go into the house of the LORD." (Ps. 122:1). What a testimony is the church that has people who say this. It ought to be so everywhere. You have to work at it, but you can make it happen.

24

Wednesday Evening Service

The Wednesday evening prayer meeting is wisely called the Hour of Power. This is not just a cute way to put it. It should be powerful, and in a good church it is. How disappointing it is to see most churches closed on Wednesday night. No one can be healthy eating one or two meals on Sunday and nothing else all week. Most of the people who don't attend a Wednesday night service have precious little, if any, spiritual nourishment during the week. A survey taken in an exceptionally devout church showed that each person averaged four minutes a day in Bible reading and prayer.

It was my joy as a pastor to have the largest prayer meeting attendance in the city. It wasn't an accident—I worked at it. The first essential is a warm, exciting service. Good singing, special music, and fresh messages from God are a must. Last week's message warmed-over won't do; a dry, sterile Bible study won't do. People need to know they are going to be fed and drawn closer to the Lord. If they know this, they will come. I've proven it over and over.

What an oasis Wednesday can be. Much planning should go into it. Nothing should be spared to make it as good a service as the one on Sunday morning. People should be encouraged in every way to attend. Here is a list of some things to make the Wednesday evening service inviting.

If the attendance is small to begin with, get the people to gather closely on several pews in the center toward the front. People will not sing or listen as well if they are scattered out. Rope off the sides and back pews, if need be.

Have good singing. Make the same effort to have excellent music that you do for Sunday morning service. Plan on it!

Have special music. Use people's talents. How foolish not to. Don't judge a person's motives. You hear people say of a soloist,

"Oh, she only goes there because they let her sing." Well, if a church wouldn't let preachers preach, they wouldn't go either. Singers don't want to just sit. If God gave them good voices, they should be allowed to minister, too! Use them. Have several special songs. Use that trumpet or violin player. Use them or or lose them. It's as simple as that. If you don't use them, you don't deserve them.

Have a good nursery and nursery staff. Don't come in and ask for volunteers at the last minute. No mother wants to leave a baby with a halfhearted volunteer. Young mothers won't come back if they find, at the last minute, that they have to keep their own baby and a couple of others during the prayer service. No wonder many young couples do not come to church.

Have a prayer list mimeographed. Instruct people to write their requests for Sunday on prayer cards and put them in the offering plates. Tell them that they may call the office to add to the list. Keep good records of illnesses, those in hospitals, and shut-ins. Add the missionaries to the prayer list. Keep future meetings and needs before the church. The pastor should point out special requests. Tell last-minute requests from the pulpit. These lists help people to pray more specifically.

Pray. One of the most effective prayer times we have seen is at the Thomas Road Baptist Church in Lynchburg, where there are three to four thousand people on Wednesday nights in the main auditorium alone. People are asked to huddle together in three's and each pray out loud briefly. They are asked not to pray loud or long. The pastor should specifically state, "If you prefer to pray alone, say so. Many prefer to. Just tell the one next to you, 'I would like to pray alone tonight,' and do so. We want no one to feel obligated to pray aloud." It is amazing, but with about one thousand people praying at the same time, it is not disturbing to the individual groups. You are unaware of those praying around you in other groups.

Close the prayer time by having the song leader begin singing "Sweet Hour of Prayer." People close their prayer sessions and join in as you go along. The music continues to swell until all are singing. It's a beautiful closing.

Take an offering. You just can't give God too much. People should be taught to give offerings above their regular tithes. This is a good time for people to give God that extra that brings greater blessing. There are always some on Wednesday who were out of town or ill on Sunday and will give their tithes on Wednesday.

Bring a solid message or Bible study. Be prepared. Don't give a carelessly prepared message. Some pastors hastily write down a couple of thoughts as they glance over a few Bible verses. That's a shame. Feed the people. Include the gospel in your message, and your people will bring their unsaved friends.

Give an invitation, even if the attendance is small. You don't need to ask people to come forward every time. You may have them pray silently or raise their hands while all heads are bowed, but do ask for response to the message. What a joy when you begin to have people saved regularly on Wednesday as well as on Sunday. It is exciting to have people coming back to the Lord or called into His service on Wednesdays. God doesn't work only on Sundays. It is great to see the results of preaching His Word in every service.

Stress the importance of the Wednesday evening meeting. Many will love Wednesday services more than Sunday ones. Wednesday evening can be exciting. People will come if there is something there for them. You have to work at it and promote it.

Attendance at prayer meeting can be greatly increased if a pastor will work at it. Prayer meetings must be as well-planned as a Sunday service. It should be as joyous and desirable as any service of the church.

In one church I pastored I saw the Wednesday prayer meeting attendance jump from an average of thirty people to over two hundred in two months' time. Here is how we did it.

During the Sunday school hour I went to two men and gave them a genuine pitch for prayer meeting. My opinion was that prayer meeting should be one of the most blessed services in the church. I wanted people to come in the middle of the week and get a spiritual boost to keep them going the rest of the week. I told them that I needed their help and asked if they and their families would be my special guests the next Wednesday night. Both readily consented. Their combined families meant eleven new people already planning to come. During the announcements in the morning service, I once again gave the sales pitch for Wednesday night. I asked all who attended the week before

250

to stand. All twenty-three stood. Then I told of my special guests who were going to be there. Finally, I asked who else would come the next Wednesday and help us build a great Wednesday evening service. A couple of other families stood. The next Wednesday we had fifty-seven in the service. It was the most ever in that church on Wednesday evening.

The next Sunday I followed the identical procedure during Sunday school and church service. All who were there the Wednesday before stood. It was quite impressive. Many were surprised to see who was coming. In two months we were having over two hundred come, and it never went below that number.

A promotion like that can be used for about two months and then another project should be pushed. You can promote Sunday school or visitation or even tithing the same way. It works if the pastor is sold on his program and will get excited about it. Of course, the Wednesday service must be worth the effort for them to come again. To say the least, anything like this must be bathed in fervent prayer. Here is where the balance of faith and works brings great rewards. Prayer meeting then becomes a powerful and effective force in the life of the church.

25

Young People and Christian Service

At the Central Baptist Church, over thirty young people went off to Christian colleges to prepare for Christian service within five years when not one had done so for thirty previous years. Why this sudden turnaround? Why is it that some churches never have one young person enter full-time Christian service while other churches seem to have a steady stream entering?

When I became the pastor at the Mount Prospect Bible Church in Illinois, there was not one young person in a Christian school preparing for Christian ministry. Six months later there were twenty-five. Today there are twenty-seven from that church preparing to serve the Lord. Why this sudden shift?

One church may support a dozen or more missionaries on the foreign field while another church—just as fundamental, just as large—will support only one or two. It is no accident. It is a matter of different emphases and priorities. These things don't just happen; they are worked at and planned for. The matter of youth being called by God into Christian service reflects the priorities and goals of a church and a pastor.

Every accomplishment begins with a vision. Great accomplishments come about only when someone lets a dream become a burning desire and then works at making it happen. Seeing young people find God's will for their lives begins with a deep desire in the pastor's heart. It has to become one of the primary goals of his ministry. Paul had this goal and shared it with Timothy in 2 Timothy 2:2 when he said, "The things which thou hast heard of me among many witnesses, the same commit thou to faithful men who shall be able to teach others also." Every pastor needs to have the same goal that Paul had. This is one of the most satisfying results of the ministry. Here are some suggestions for getting young people into Christian service.

252

Pray. The most important factor behind seeing young people called by God is prayer. This would seem obvious, and yet in reality it is not an actual part of most churches' programs which help young people find God's will for their lives. God says, "Pray ye therefore the Lord of the harvest, that He will send forth laborers into his harvest" (Matt. 9:38). If a church wants to see young people going into His service, then they must get serious about it and obey this admonition. God tells us, ". . . ye have not, because ye ask not" (James 4:2). The main reason many churches have never had any young people enter the ministry is because they haven't asked God for it.

First, prayer must be made from the pulpit. In the Sunday morning prayer, the pastor very dutifully prays for the sick and shut-ins. Then he prays for the bereaved, for those in authority, for the missionaries, and for the needs of church members. All of this is scriptural and right. But when does one hear a pastor regularly praying for God to send forth laborers from among his own young people? You must pray for it every Sunday before the whole church.

Second, the desire to know God's will should be a subject of prayer in every assembly of the church. This means that every youth worker, youth pastor, and superintendent must make this a part of his thinking and pray specifically for God to call the young people of his church.

The desire to know God's plan for us should be a subject of prayer in every class. Down to the lowest age level, every teacher should pray for God to send forth laborers into His harvest. This makes even the smallest child become aware of the fact that God has a plan for his life and that he should seek to know it.

Prayer for God's direction in the lives of the youth should be offered at all youth meetings, whether services or socials. It makes every gathering sacred and God's will of paramount importance.

The home is one of the most important places where such prayer should be offered. At every family altar the father and mother should consciously pray to know the purpose God created their children for. It is obvious that the impression this has on children will be profound. In the two churches mentioned, many families began to pray for this. They even included this petition in private devotions.

Present the need. A main avenue to seeing young people called by

God is presenting the need. In Romans 10:13-15 Paul says,

> Whosoever shall call upon the name of the Lord shall be saved. How then shall they call on him in whom they have not believed? and how shall they believe in him of whom they have not heard? and how shall they hear without a preacher? And how shall they preach, except they be sent. . . .

The need for preachers, missionaries, and Christian workers is enormous, for ". . . how shall they believe in him of whom they have not heard? . . ." There is not only the need for preachers, but a need for them to be "sent" by the Lord. This need must be presented from the pulpit.

Another way to present the need is through missionaries. Youth need to see them and hear them in person. Do everything you can to make this a vital part of the young people's thinking. Need does not constitute a call, but often God uses needs to awaken concern so that one can begin to consider his place in helping to spread the gospel.

You can also present the need for young people in Christian work by having gospel teams and chorales from Christian schools come to your church. Some youth have a false impression of Christian schools and those going into full-time Christian service. They think Christian schools are overly strict and that the students do not really enjoy attending them. Also, some speakers emphasize how they fought the will of God and how much they gave up to serve the Lord. This gives the youth a false concept. To actually see radiant Christians in teams and singing groups from Christian schools often has a profound effect on the church, especially on the youth. When they hear their own peer group all excited about serving the Lord, many false concepts are dispelled. During the summer, when teams will be traveling from schools, the pastor should have his youth exposed to this ministry.

Have testimonies from young Christian college students. A weekend youth revival led by one of those young people can make a profound impression. Just having a young person home from school to preach can be very productive as the youth hear one of their own with whom they can readily identify.

Having someone from different Christian organizations (such as Child Evangelism, the deaf ministry, or the bus ministry) speak to the youth can be used by the Lord to direct young people into His service.

Such leaders coming into a church and presenting their work in a new light often helps young people recognize their own gifts and callings. Many are unaware of the many places of service open to youth in the areas of radio and television. Many churches need someone called by God to direct these ministries.

Preach the call. Preach the call of God to service just as you preach the call of God to salvation. If the prime objective of the church is to get the gospel to every creature (see Mark 16:15) and ". . . The harvest truly is plenteous, but the laborers are few" (Matt. 9:37), then preachers must preach the call of God to Christian service. Acts 13:1-4 has an important message about God sending forth laborers:

> Now there were in the church that was at Antioch certain prophets and teachers; as Barnabas, and Simeon that was called Niger, and Lucius of Cyrene, and Manaen, which had been brought up with Herod the tetrarch, and Saul. As they ministered to the Lord, and fasted, the Holy Ghost said, Separate me Barnabas and Saul for the work whereunto I have called them. And when they had fasted and prayed, and laid their hands on them, they sent them away. So they, being sent forth by the Holy Ghost, departed unto Seleucia; and from thence they sailed to Cyprus.

This passage points out that God works in and through the local church. This is emphasized all through the Book of Acts. Jesus is building His church. He established it to carry out the Great Commission. No doubt God has used many works and ministries, but He first and foremost established His church to carry on His work.

"As they ministered to the Lord and fasted" God called Barnabas and Saul to do His work. Two things here need to be noticed: They were busy—they ministered to the Lord, and they were serious—they fasted. God does not call young people from a sleeping church. You must be serious about this matter of young people finding God's will for their lives and being called into His service. It must not be taken lightly or entered into halfheartedly. It is a blessing and a privilege for a church to have people sent from it into the world to do God's work. They also must understand the awesome responsibility of getting the gospel to every creature. One primary means a church has of doing this is by using its young people.

The final thing to note in this passage is that "the Holy Ghost said, Separate me Barnabas and Saul for the work whereunto I have called them." The work of calling people into the service of the Lord is done by the Holy Spirit. It cannot be manipulated by men or directed by parents or preachers. There must be a conscious dependence on the Holy Spirit to carry out this ministry among God's people.

Preaching about the call of God should be included often in your sermons. Seldom in the average sermon do you hear even a mention of the call of God for young people. It should not be spoken of only once-a-year during youth week. Emphasize it whenever you preach.

Include the call of God in the invitation. Just as there is a human response to the call of God to salvation, there is also a human response to the call of God to service. In a church where there is seldom an invitation to Christian service, very few will respond to full-time service.

Preach the will of God for everyone. Many do not realize that God has a definite will and plan for each life. No one should decide to be a carpenter or a lawyer on the basis of skills or aptitude alone. Thinking that the will of God is only for those in full-time Christian service is a disastrous view to take. Many people wait for some unusual sign from God to call them into His service. Confronting the entire congregation with the will of God has very sobering effects. This snaps them out of the passive attitude and makes them actively seek to know God's plan for their lives. Another valid reason for preaching about the will of God is that Sunday school teachers, bus workers, or ushers will be inspired to serve the Lord totally.

Publicly commend youth who are called to serve God. Let them know how proud the church is of their commitments. All of us have seen some young person surrender to preach and the fact hardly receive mention at the close of the service. Just as a church should get excited when someone is saved, so Christians should be aware of the great honor bestowed on a church when the Holy Spirit calls one of their young people to serve Him. When his married son was called to preach, a father said, "Son, you mean you are going to become a burden on society?" A church should make such a one feel he has been honored more than if he had become a king. In the world today the ministry is no longer at the top of the list as the most honored profession. In the church it must be presented as the most desirable vocation a person can have. Some parents are not overjoyed when a son or daughter announces a call to become a missionary. This attitude must be changed.

Post an honor roll in a conspicuous place that lists the names of young people who have been called into Christian service. (Many churches do this for servicemen.) This will cause people to pray for these young people regularly.

Form a Future Pastors Club to create comradeship and give the pastor the opportunity to teach and guide these young men in their development. It can also be used to give them experience by planning visitation and other forms of service. The girls in the church who are called to Christian service should have a club also, appropriately named, to provide experience in Christian service for them.

Challenge Youth Personally. The key to this program is for a pastor to deal individually with his young people. The world is so big now, America is enormous, cities so large. Churches also have become giants. Many people feel like a number on a Social Security card. Young people feel this.

Isn't it wonderful that God deals with us one by one? Remember when Isaiah saw the Lord "high and lifted up" (Is. 6:1)? He saw himself as undone and unclean (see v. 5). Then God showed him the world and asked, ". . . Whom shall I send, and who will go for us? . . ." Isaiah replied, ". . . Here I am, send me" (v. 8). If we are going to see our young people answer God's call, we must speak to them individually.

You have to get the young person alone and ask if he knows what he is going to do when he gets out of high school. Ask if he knows what God wants him to do with his life. It is amazing how many do not know and are terrified of getting out of high school and facing the world. Many are longing to talk to someone who will not embarrass them if they admit their fears and doubts about the future.

Going to them individually is probably the most important step in the whole program. It is like anything else. People can come to church Sunday after Sunday and somehow not feel it is personal. They never really catch on that the message is for them and that they must do something about it. However, if someone goes to them personally about being saved or teaching a Sunday school class, they can't get away from the fact that they must make a response. The same is true about going to young people personally about God's plans for their lives. Satan will do all he can to keep them from thinking seriously about it or doing anything about God's will.

The next step is to ask young people to pray very specifically the same prayer Paul prayed when he met the Lord Jesus in Acts 9:6. He asked, ". . . Lord, what wilt thou have me to do? . . ." Young people can be asked to type or print on a 3″ x 5″ card this very prayer and put it on their mirrors, so that every day when they look into the mirrors they are reminded to ask the Lord about this.

It is good to ask the young people if you can have the privilege of being the first to pray with them about this matter. If they say yes, pray with them right then and there. It has been my privilege to do this with hundreds of young people all over the nation.

Often as guest pastor in a church I have asked youth if they know what God wants them to do when they get out of school. Very few do. When I ask if they will begin to pray about it, most say yes. Then I ask to pray with them right there. The results are amazing. Sitting with them, I pray and often when I finish I find them in tears. Most will thank me right away. Many go home and tell their parents in amazement that the visiting preacher took all this time with them and even prayed with them.

Young people are starved for attention. The least little attention a pastor can give them will be met with the most rewarding response. The key is for the pastor to take the initiative by having a one-to-one talk.

The next thing needed is to teach young people, as well as adults, how to find the will of God. Most do not know how. They need to have pointed out to them that the will of God is first and foremost (see Rom. 12:1,2). There is the mistaken idea in the minds of so many that if they surrender their lives to God He will send them to the worst place in the whole world to be missionaries and from then on their lives will be miserable. In sixteen years of teaching in Bible colleges, this writer has found this belief to be prevalent among young people.

Two things you should emphasize to people are that, first, God wants people to have life and have it more abundantly (see John 10:10). It sometimes is hard to convince them of this when they do not see any examples of Christians living the abundant life and being thrilled about it all. Second, they need to be shown that all God's

Word was written "that your joy might be full" (1 John 1:4). This is hard to prove by the lives of most Christians. One could easily ask "Where is the joy of the Lord?" in most churches and in most Christians' lives. It should be pointed out that God wants the Christian life to be filled with joy, whether many experience it or not. With this attitude, it is much easier to expect Christians to want to discover the purpose God created them for.

In finding the will of God, the key is to ". . . let the peace of God rule in your hearts" (Col. 3:15). If one is led by the Spirit, he will have "the fruit of the Spirit" which is "peace" (see Gal. 5:22). The word for "rule" in the Greek is the word that means "to umpire, judge, or arbitrate." The peace of God is the umpire that tells a Christian what is right or wrong, what the will of God is and is not.

It is important to realize that God wants us to know His will for ". . . The God of our fathers hath chosen thee, that thou shouldest know his will . . ." (Acts 22:14). Many feel that finding the will of God is very difficult, that God is somewhat reluctant to reveal it to every Christian, but that just is not so. This truth needs to be emphasized.

Finally, great stress needs to be placed upon the joy and rewards of doing God's will. How fulfilling and rewarding it was to Paul at the end of his life to be able to say,

> For I am now ready to be offered, and the time of my departure is at hand. I have fought a good fight, I have finished my course, I have kept the faith: Henceforth there is laid up for me a crown of righteousness, which the Lord, the righteous judge, shall give me at that day: and not to me only, but unto all them also that love his appearing (2 Tim. 4:6–8).

Too many come to the end of life with many regrets for a wasted and unfulfilled life. Paul summed it all up in Philippians 3:13,14 when he said,

> Brethren, I count not myself to have apprehended: but this one thing I do, forgetting those things which are behind, and reaching forth unto those things which are before, I press toward the mark for the prize of the high calling of God in Christ Jesus.

Young people need this presented to them. They will respond, for most are looking for a purpose in life. If the church does not lead the way, they are going to take up some cause much less rewarding and often contrary to God's will.

What happened at the Mount Prospect Bible Church in only six months was unusual. God took over in a very different way. In that short ministry, I really went after the youth.

One Sunday night I called several of them into my office after the service, because they had been talking and not paying attention. I poured out my heart to them and really dressed them down for their attitude. While doing it, I began to weep and told them I did not want their lives wasted and wrecked. Afterward, one of the girls, now a student at Moody Bible Institute, summed it all up when she said, "I never knew a pastor really cared that much about me." It transformed her life. She then began to think about God's will and has answered the call to go anywhere He leads her.

Any pastor who is really right with the Lord himself, loves the Lord Jesus with all his heart, and loves young people can adopt this whole plan and see scores of youth being "sent by the Spirit" into the world.

Years ago I led a teen-age boy to Christ. Today that boy, Mike Cocoris, pastors the great Church of the Door in Los Angeles, California. What a thrill. No wonder John wrote, "I have no greater joy than to hear that my children walk in truth" (3 John 4).

5/CONCLUSION

26

A More Excellent Way

If I were able to say only one thing to preachers and would-be preachers, what would it be? What do preachers need above all else? What is that edge that some preachers have that makes them stand out? It can be summed up in one word.

Love. "Though I speak with the tongues of men and of angels, and have not charity [love], I am become as sounding brass, or a tinkling cymbal" (1 Cor. 13:1). In God's name, love your people. People all over the world are starved for genuine love. Preachers all over the world get angry with people and preach like it. People aren't stupid. They know if a pastor really loves them.

Love is kind, not mean. Love suffers long. Love is not puffed up. It doesn't expect people to bow at the shrine of the pastor because he is "God's anointed." Love does not seek special privileges. Love doesn't behave unseemly; it has good manners. It seeks not its own but is unselfishly concerned for others. Love is not easily provoked; it's not touchy. Love thinks no evil. It sees the best and the potential in others. Love doesn't fault find (see 1 Cor. 13:3–8).

Preacher, get a heart so full of love that you weep over souls, you weep over sins, you weep over sinners. Not a feeble love that stands for nothing and preaches against nothing. Not an egotistical love that preaches against sin to prove that you are right. Not a jealous love that preaches against sin because you can't do the same things that libertines do. But a love that hates sin because it hurts God, pollutes the world, and destroys people. Your motives have to be pure.

Stay in love with Jesus. Everyday renew and restore that first love. Keep that sweet, pure, childlike love for the blessed Savior who suffered and died for your sins on the cross. Love Him. Tell Him so. Let it show, and people will flock like bees to nectar.

A preacher needs wisdom.

> Get wisdom . . . Forsake her not, and she shall preserve thee: love her, and she shall keep thee . . . Exalt her, and she shall promote thee: she shall bring thee to honor, when thou dost embrace her. She shall give to thine head an ornament of grace: a crown of glory shall she deliver to thee (Prov. 4:5-9).

There are many highly intelligent preachers who don't have any common sense. Preachers don't have trouble in their churches because they can't marry or bury, but because they lack wisdom in dealing with people and their problems (see Prov. 3:13-18). Look around you and see if it isn't so.

Preachers go to churches, and in only a few weeks they are ranting and raving about pantsuits, movies, and people puffing on cigarettes. You might as well scream at babies for sucking their thumbs and wetting their diapers. For God's sake, feed them, nurture them, love them, teach them, and train them. Have you seen the bumper sticker that says, "Have you hugged your kid today?" People need a spiritual hug.

Cry out for wisdom. It is more precious than silver, gold, or rubies (see Prov. 3:14,15). If you are going to make an issue out of something, be sure it's big enough to merit your precious time. Wisdom is simply common sense, and it makes good sense to seek it. Solomon admitted he didn't know how to judge God's people, and he cried out for wisdom when God told him that he could have anything he wanted (see 1 Kin. 3:5-9). That was wisdom. Be sure you do the same. Study, learn, cram your head and heart with knowledge, but then cry out for enough sense to know how to use it.

A preacher needs humility. "And Samuel said, When thou wast little in thine own sight, wast thou not made the head of the tribes of Israel, and the LORD anointed thee king over Israel?" (1 Sam. 15:17). God is the one who promotes. Let Him do it. Don't you try it. The key is what you really think in your heart. God and you alone know what's there. Be honest with yourself. Every person in the world is superior to you in some area. Treat people with genuine respect. Don't lord yourself over anyone. Big people can be measured by how they treat little people.

Don't push yourself. Don't grab the best place. Don't seek top billing. "Humble yourselves therefore under the mighty hand of God, that he may exalt you in due time" (1 Pet. 5:6). You can be sure He will. He exalted Joseph, Daniel, Esther, Peter, Paul, and, bless God, Jesus, who has a name above every name. Let Him do the exalting. He will give you a name, and it will be pure, pleasant, and permanent.

A preacher needs to be God's anointed servant. ". . . God anointed Jesus of Nazareth with the Holy Ghost and with power . . ." (Acts 10:38). Great preachers know what this anointing, this filling with power, is. Don't quibble over the experience or the expression of it. You can't photograph it. You can't define it exactly. You can't buy it. But you can seek it and pray for it until you see God move in and you stand amazed at His miracles in your ministry.

The amount of power God gives your ministry is in direct proportion to your surrender of self and your cleansing of sin. There is no substitute for doing the work of God. You can be sure that many substitutes will be offered to you. In a carnal state you may try them all. You will come up empty-handed, trying to rationalize and find an alibi for a barren ministry. Get serious about your ministry. It's God's business. Ten billion years from now you will wish you had junked everything to seek the power of God for your ministry. Eternity is at stake. Heaven is at stake. Christianity's reputation is at stake. Your whole ministry is at stake. Don't miss it. The price is too great. The joy and glory of doing God's work is too majestic for words.

A preacher needs faith. The storm was raging, the ship was sinking, the sailors were shaking, and Paul said:

> And now I exhort you to be of good cheer; for there shall be no loss of any man's life among you, but of the ship. For there stood by me this night the angel of God, whose I am, and whom I serve, Saying, Fear not, Paul; thou must be brought before Caesar: and, lo, God hath given thee all them that sail with thee. Wherefore, sirs, be of good cheer: for I believe God, that it shall be even as it was told me (Acts 27:22-25).

I believe God—that's it. Many do not. Some cannot. Some will not. But you must. Faith can make a man God's man—a man who does God's work and sees God's blessing and power. When the going gets rough, say, "I believe God." When you are misunderstood or misused, say, "I believe God."

"He did not many mighty works there because of their unbelief" (Matt. 13:58). Never let this passage apply to your ministry. Don't tie God's hands. His arm is not short. His power is not short. The dead need raising. The blind need seeing. The lost need saving. Let Him do it.

A preacher needs hope. "Looking for that blessed hope, and the glorious appearing of the great God and our Saviour Jesus Christ" (Titus 2:13). What a hope. What an expectation. Jesus is coming. We win! Read the end of the Book and see how it all turns out. Glory! We are on the winning side. Don't quit. Don't be discouraged. Don't throw in the towel. Jesus is coming.

"Beloved, now are we the sons of God, and it doth not yet appear what we shall be: but we know that, when he shall appear, we shall be like him; for we shall see him as he is" (1 John 3:2). We shall see Him. The one who loves us. The one who bore our sins. The one who suffered and died for us. The one who rose again. We shall see Him as He really is, in all His glory. We shall see Him in all His splendor. We shall see Him in all His majesty. And when we do it will have been worth it all.

As you walk with Him now, may your heart burn as the hearts of those on the Emmaus road. As you look for Him, may your face glow as Moses' did. Keep that hope ever before you. Let it bless you. Let it comfort and purify you.

One day Jesus is going to come with His great ring of keys and say, "Gentlemen, it's closing time." Be ready. Be busy. Be awake. It may be sooner than you think.

How to Keep Your Enthusiasm

What fires you up? What stirs your soul? What turns you on for God? What keeps your heart right? What keeps you going? What puts gas in your tank? I suggest incorporating the Word of God in your life as a means of ministering to yourself.

Listen to the music. The right kind, that is. Music drove the evil spirit from Saul (see 1 Sam. 16:23). Rock music or any fleshly music stirs the wrong spirit as it and the wine did Belshazzar at his feast in Daniel 5. But music with a message from God can bring the hand of God upon you as it did Elisha. "...And it came to pass, when the minstrel played, that the hand of the LORD came upon him" (2 Kin. 3:15). We all need that. Get music that stirs you. Listen to it until God gets hold of your heart and soul and the hand of God is upon you.

Recently, I bought a stereo cassette player with the headset. I have tapes that really minister to me. Sometimes I shut myself up for an hour and listen until my heart is blessed and broken. What a way to minister to yourself. Music singing in one's heart is one of the results of the spirit-controlled life (see Eph. 5:18,19). Have a tape player in your car, your office, your study, your home, and keep your mind "stayed on" Him (Is. 26:3) through the great medium of music.

Memorize and meditate on the Word of God. Joshua 1:8 assures you that you will prosper and "have good success" if you "meditate" on His word "day and night."

Meditation is a lost art. "Amusement" has supplanted it. Meditation takes vigorous concentration. Shut out everything and meditate on the Word until you become like that tree "...that bringeth forth his fruit in his seasons..." (Ps. 1:3).

Visualize the scenes and events of the Word until you live it with them. Vicariously enter into the thrill and joy of all that is in the Bible. People watch TV and movies until they fantasize as though they were there. How much more should we enter into the Word of God.

Minister minute by minute. Paul says, "Be not overcome of evil, but overcome evil with good" (Rom. 12:21). That is the way to live. You must never be off duty. Get off the defense; get on the offense. Overcome evil with good. An idle mind is the devil's workshop, and idle hands are his tools. Look for ways to minister to every soul you contact. Big men do. Dr. Jack Hyles, Dr. Lee Roberson, Dr. Jerry Falwell constantly build up and boost those around them. Your people need that constant word of encouragement and exhortation. Brag on them, praise them, thank them, and they will treat you royally.

Seek the Lord. "...as long as he sought the LORD, God made him to prosper" (2 Chr. 26:5). He will you, too! Seek God, not His power. Seek Him! "Seek ye the LORD while he may be found, call ye upon him while he is near..." (Is. 55:6). Don't get cooled off. It's terrible. Don't get detoured. It's devastating. Don't be diluted. It's barren. Seek him while he is near. Respond! God said, "...when thou hearest the sound of a gong in the tops of the mulberry trees, that then thou shalt bestir thyself..." (2 Sam. 5:24). Seek him. Wise men still do.

The psalmist says, "...the Lord will give grace and glory: no good thing will he withhold from them that walk uprightly" (Ps. 84:11). What a staggering promise. "No good thing" is pretty inclusive. What good thing do you need, want, long for? It's yours if you walk uprightly. You won't have to beg or steal. No need to do without. God won't fail. Don't you fail God. No matter what others do, do right. Walk uprightly!

"For the eyes of the LORD run to and fro throughout the whole earth, to shew himself strong in the behalf of them whose heart is perfect toward him. . . ." (2 Chr. 16:9). This is stupendous. God is looking everywhere. There aren't many takers. They are few and far between. Will you be one who will keep your heart "perfect toward Him?" He will do great and mighty things! He'll show himself strong in your behalf. Others just won't understand your secret. You can't tell them. Oh, what a joy to live with this invisible means of support and power.

During the Civil War, Arthur MacArthur, General Douglas MacArthur's father, was the commander of a battalion from Wisconsin. Outside of Chattanooga, Tennessee, at Missionary Ridge, there was a strategic point MacArthur's commanding officer told him they must capture. He raised his sword, pointed to the hill, and cried to his men, "Charge, on Wisconsin!" They charged the hill. The fighting was fierce. Men fell all around him. They became stalled. He cried again, "On Wisconsin, charge!" They took heart and charged again. Men were being wounded and killed all around, but they finally won and captured the hill.

When they secured the hill, it was noticed MacArthur himself was wounded. A medic began to minister to him. MacArthur's commanding officer came by. He turned to the medic and said, "Take good care of that man. He just won the medal of honor."

Our Commander-in-Chief is coming one day. You will receive wounds and scars here but He too will say, "Take good care of him. He just won the medal of honor." May it be so of every minister of God.

APPENDIX

The Pastor's Wife

by
Celeste Wemp

Spiritual Qualifications

Assurance of salvation. Before one can serve Christ, of course, one must be genuinely saved. But beyond that, the pastor's wife needs to have *assurance* of her salvation. It is impossible for one to serve the Lord in an effective way if one is plagued by doubt. A good salesman, to successfully market his product, must be sold on it himself and be assured that it really works and is worth the cost.

The calling to serve God. Some people contend that "a woman is called to a man and a man is called to a ministry." This is not necessarily the order of the calls. I personally believe that the call to Christian service is as universal as the call to salvation. God will use anyone who is willing and available. If a woman falls in love with a man who is preparing for the ministry and she agrees to be his wife only because she loves him and not because she shares his desire to serve the Lord, she will not be able to withstand the stress of the ministry. She must have a confident assurance that she has yielded her life to the Lord and is available to serve Him wherever He leads. I was preparing to serve the Lord in Christian service even before I met my husband.

A godly example. Because a minister and his wife are looked up to by many and observed by many more, it is of utmost importance that the pastor's wife be a godly example of a Christian as outlined in 1 Timothy 4:12: "in word, in conversation [manner of life], in charity [love], in spirit [enthusiasm], in faith, in purity [of spirit, soul/mind, and body]."

Personal Devotions. Daily private communication with the Lord will provide the strength to be the example and to contribute to the spiritual life of her personal family and her church family. Family devotions, regular church attendance, prayer meeting, and studying the Sunday school lesson are all a part of her life, but they are not enough. She needs daily nourishment from the Word of God and a special time alone with the Lord.

Wifely Qualifications

Meeting her husband's needs. In many ways a pastor's wife has the same responsibilities as any loving Christian wife: to be what God created woman for, a helper "meet", or suited, for her husband. The needs of the pastor-husband may differ somewhat from men in other jobs, but in many areas they are the same. Men have spiritual needs, social needs, emotional needs, and physical needs. The word of Proverbs 31:12 should be her guide: "She will do him good and not evil all the days of her life."

Love and encouragement. It seems as though Satan's chief tool in the life of a minister is discouragement. The problems of the pastorate, the burdens of people, the opposition and criticism that are part of the minister's occupational hazards call for a wife to be especially supportive. With her encouragement and loving support none of these influences can conquer him. He needs her admiration, not only in private but in public, to bolster his confidence in himself and his ability.

A peaceful haven. Part of the job of a pastor's wife is to establish a peaceful haven to which her husband looks forward to retreating after a busy day. When he has listened to other people's problems all afternoon, he may not be very talkative when he returns home. A wise woman will allow him some time to unwind and rest a bit in a comfortable, clean home before sharing her joys, trials, and complaints of the day. Some ministers don't spend as much time at home as they would like to because they don't enjoy the clutter, constant confusion, and nagging complaints. If a woman makes her home a castle and treats her husband like a king, she will find herself being treated like a queen.

Guard his time and reputation. These two areas fall under the wife's responsibility to a large degree. There are many ways a pastor's wife can protect her husband, although sometimes they require inconvenience and self-sacrifice. As a good secretary screens her employ-

272

er's calls, so must a good pastor's wife tactfully screen her husband's calls.

It is amazing how many people will call the pastor's home instead of dialing directory assistance to get the telephone number of a church member. Or perhaps a member will call to find out the time or place of a service. Anyone in the pastor's family probably could give out the information, but the caller usually insists on speaking to the pastor. Much of his valuable time is stolen by these interruptions, which usually come at mealtimes when he is sure to be home. Often the pastor's wife can ask the caller if she may be of help, explaining that her husband is eating, out visiting, or whatever.

A good reputation is the pastor's most valuable possession. If it becomes tarnished in any way, his ministry suffers and sometimes dies. The admonition to "Abstain from all appearance of evil" (1 Thess. 5:22) should be heeded. A rumor does not have to be true to ruin a man's ministry. The wife can help prevent possible problems by accompanying her husband on visits to homes when women are alone, or by taking the baby-sitter home herself instead of sending her husband.

Can't you see how false rumors start? The pastor and his wife hire a teen-age girl to baby-sit for an evening. The pastor takes the girl home and the neighbor across the street just happens to see the pastor's car pull up and the girl get out. The neighbor casually mentions this to another neighbor, adding a few comments or questions leading to suspicion about what might have happened. By the time the story has gotten around, the pastor is having an affair. People are especially quick to believe the worst about a pastor. It might be impossible to prevent every rumor or misunderstanding; but many times, with a little forethought and caution, a wife can protect her husband from being falsely accused.

Counseling situations with women can be dangerous when held behind closed doors. An unscrupulous woman—and I am ashamed to say there are some—can make accusations against a pastor that may be false, but his innocence cannot be proved. There will always be a few people who choose to believe the worst. A pastor's wife needs to be enough of a student of the Word of God to counsel women herself.

273

I maintain a growing conviction that men should not counsel women except for general spiritual problems. Titus 2:2-5 very clearly teaches that the older women are to teach the younger women about their intimate, personal affairs.

Paul did not instruct young pastors to teach women how to love their husbands. He instructed the older women to do this job. We know many former pastors who are no longer in the ministry because of questionable involvement, of one type or another, with women other than their wives. Nine times out of ten, the involvement began in a counseling situation. So, pastor, train your wife and other qualified women in your church to teach and counsel in the areas of home and marriage.

Do your own work. During a Bible lecture at Moody Bible Institute, I recall Dr. Wilbur Simth's stopping and thundering a few gruff remarks to future pastors' wives: "Don't expect your husband to do your work. His time is more importantly spent in study." Needless to say, his statement made a vivid impression on me.

In these days of working wives, there may need to be some shared home responsibilities. If the wife is working to help her husband with his job of providing for the family, then it is only fair that he help her do her job of caring for the home. Some men like to cook once in a while; others may offer to help with cleaning or laundry. The point is, if the husband volunteers for or enjoys a particular task, fine, but a wife should not expect or demand him to do her work. She ought not feel resentful, for instance, when there is no offer of help when he comes in from a weary day of visitation.

Keep up spiritually and intellectually. Often a pastor will not even think of discussing a theological problem with his wife, because he has no confidence in her biblical knowledge. The same is true of her knowledge of politics or world affairs. It is sad but true that many women are unconcerned about anything that does not relate personally to them and their families. Their horizons are limited to their own homes and communities. By continued reading and studying, a pastor's wife can be well-informed and make interesting contributions to any conversation. Her husband should not have to be ashamed of her lack of knowledge. Mrs. Harlin J. Roper, a pastor's wife for many years, was addressing a class of future pastors' wives and admonishing them to study and read. "If you don't exercise your muscles, you get stiff, and if you don't exercise your mind, you get stupid," she exhorted. Professionals keep studying in order to be successful. The pastor's wife must do the same to be a helper fit for her pastor-husband.

Parental Qualifications

Love. The fact that Titus 2:4 instructs older women to teach younger women to love their children indicates that this knowledge and ability does not come naturally. God's way of love involves training, teaching, and discipline. Any Christian mother will be concerned about these areas of childrearing. Proverbs 22:6 speaks of spiritual training: "Train up a child in the way he should go: and when he is old, he will not depart from it." It is of utmost importance that the pastor's wife, together with her husband, train her child to know and obey the Lord. A personal relationship with Christ is not picked up by osmosis. Children may learn all about Christ, recite Bible stories and Christian doctrine without error, and be able to give the right answers to the right questions. Yet they may have no vital, personal relationship with Christ. Christian mothers must be realistic about this and be sensitive to the spiritual needs and crises of their children.

Children are taught by example when it comes to manners, thoughtfulness, responsibility, work, dependability, and similar social skills and attitudes. Never tell your children they must behave because of their father's position. It is difficult enough for pastors' children to be allowed to grow up normally without putting the burden of their father's reputation on them. Children need a sense of self-worth. Sometimes pastors' children get the idea that the church is more important to their parents than they are, and this causes resentment at the time and rebellion later on. Priorities for the pastor and his wife, as for other Christians, should be (1) Christ, (2) companion, (3) children, and (4) church/ministry/work.

A pastor and his wife often find it difficult to separate the church from Christ. Many times attending church activities becomes synonymous with obeying Christ—at the expense of the children. It might be more valuable for a pastor's wife to attend her son's Cub Scout program than to go to the Ladies Missionary Meeting. But often because of the pressure of what others might think or say, church activities come first, regardless of the needs of the family. Pastor's wives must graciously resist such pressure and maintain biblical priorities. Other women of the church will come to respect and follow the example of the pastor's wife who places proper importance on her family.

The Pastor's Wife and the Church

Faithfulness. "Even so must their wives be . . . faithful in all things" (1 Tim. 3:11). A pastor's wife sets the pace and is an example for the women of the congregation. One of the most obvious things to be faithful in is church attendance. How can the other women be expected to worship Sunday mornings if the pastor's wife rarely does so?

Serving in the church. The pastor's wife should not feel she must do every job that is forced upon her. Neither should she hold herself aloof and refuse to serve when needed. Just as other Christians, she needs to discern what her spiritual gifts are and endeavor to develop them by serving where those gifts are needed. Sometimes it takes experience in many areas of service to determine just where one's gifts lie. For the pastor's wife to be forced to serve in an area just because no one else will, especially when she is not gifted in that area, will result in ineffectiveness and resentment. Pastor's wives must learn to say no graciously and to trust the Lord to raise up the right person for the task.

Participation, not leadership. The pastor's wife must be willing to participate in church programs and activities; however, she should not assume the role of leader. She can encourage and help others to lead while she works behind the scene. This encourages leadership and confidence among the women.

Love the brethren. Nothing can take the place of a genuine, heartfelt love for the people of God whom you serve. Dr. Jack Mitchell once said to a group of ministerial students, "If you love your people and they know you love them, you can say anything to them and they will not be offended." How true this is. The secret is in their *knowing* that you love them. Tell them you love them. Show them you love them. Act like you love them, and tell others you love them. Don't speak critically to other people of your church members.

Be friendly. "A man [or woman] that hath friends must show himself friendly . . ." (Prov. 18:24). A warm smile, a handshake, a greeting to church members wherever they are seen, at church or on the street, goes a long way toward establishing friendly relationships. A pastor and his wife who have special close friends within the local church they serve usually, perhaps unknowingly, contribute to envy, jealousy, and criticism among the members. Naturally, it is easier to be friends with some people than with others. But as a word of caution, I would suggest you make close friends of other pastors' wives or Christians outside your local church.

Open your home. One of the requirements of a pastor is that he be "given to hospitality." His being hospitable will naturally affect his wife, and she, too, will need to have a hospitable attitude. There is a great difference between entertaining and hospitality. Being hospitable is allowing others to come into your home and enjoy its warmth and fellowship at any time, not just when invited for a particular occasion.

If the parsonage, especially the living room, is free from clutter, the pastor's wife will feel comfortable when someone drops by. If she is embarrassed or uncomfortable, her guest will be also. Not many people make visits before 9:00 or 10:00 A.M. If beds are made, dishes washed, and general clutter picked up each morning, the pastor's wife will find more freedom for herself and be more willing to welcome others into her home to minister to them.

Learn to receive. A pastor and his wife are often offered gifts or services free of charge. A servant of the Lord must learn to receive such gifts graciously, whether the item offered is desired or not. Take into account the heart and motivation of the giver.

In our first pastorate my husband was visiting one day in a rural area. At one house, the lady asked, "Brother Wemp, would you like a chicken?" "Oh, yes ma'am, I would be happy to have one," he answered, expecting her to go to her well-stocked freezer and hand him a dressed chicken. To his chagrin, she went outside, caught a chicken,

277

tied its legs, and handed it to him. He thanked her graciously and brought it home. Now, my husband and I are city-born and bred, and although we had seen our mothers kill and dress chickens, we had never done so ourselves. While my husband tried in vain to wring the chicken's neck, I was searching the cookbook for how to clean a chicken. Finally, resorting to a hatchet, my husband succeeded in chopping off the chicken's head only to get blood all over himself and all over the yard as the chicken flopped around. Meanwhile, I had boiled the water. We dunked the chicken in, but we left it in the steamy water too long—when we tried to pick the feathers, the skin came with them! After cutting the chicken up into unrecognizable pieces and frying it, we took one bite and decided we just weren't hungry after all. We really didn't want that live chicken, but we have learned to receive *anything* graciously.

The Pastor's Wife and the Community

Prestige. The pastor's wife, especially in a small town, has a position of prestige. Some people will want to grant her special favors and perhaps discounts or no-fee services. It is wonderful for the Lord to provide for the needs of His people in this way, and they should be humble and appreciative in return. However, when the pastor's family begins to *expect* special treatment or to request discounts, then the blessing of the Lord is lost.

Civic affairs. Since a pastor's wife is looked up to as a leader in the community, she will be prevailed upon to participate in various civic activities. Requests will come to collect for various charities, take an office in PTA, lead a Girl Scout troop, or join a women's club. All of these are fine and good, but again the question of priorities comes up. If the pastor's wife, after attending to the needs of her family, home, and church, has time and a desire to serve in the community, fine. If not, be assured there are other women in the community who will do these things who do not take part in church activities. However, if you have a real interest and the Lord leads you to participate, community service can provide opportunities of witness and outreach. For sure, the pastor's wife ought not to isolate herself from the community.

Summary

The life of the pastor's wife is one of the most rewarding areas of Christian service I know. The advantages and blessings far outweigh the disadvantages and burdens. Women who approach the pastorate with the fear of "living in a fishbowl" and having a hard life will probably have their fears confirmed. But pastors' wives who approach their role with a positive attitude and who look forward to the joy of serving Christ and his people through the ministry of a local church will find their life as rich, exciting, and rewarding as I have found mine.